3

כָּל יִשְׂרָאֵל

The Prayers of Our People

TEACHER'S EDITION

BY ELLEN J. RANK

Working effectively with students with special learning needs:
Lisa Friedman

Book and Cover Design: Itzhack Shelomi
Project Editor: Terry S. Kaye

Springfield, New Jersey
www.behrmanhouse.com
ISBN: 978-0-87441-824-1
Manufactured in the United States of America

CONTENTS

INTENT AND PURPOSE OF THE *KOL YISRAEL* SERIES

Welcome to *Kol Yisrael*—A Multimedia Jewish Educational Experience!

The *Kol Yisrael* series is the first Hebrew program to combine the best of Jewish education with the best of today's technology, integrating text-based lessons with digital learning. This approach helps you motivate your students as you guide them in an exploration of the rich traditions of Jewish life. And it works wherever they may be—in the classroom, at home, or in front of a computer! By sending students from the printed page to computer-based reinforcement activities and then back to the text again, *Kol Yisrael* helps you keep today's tech-savvy students engaged in the material and on track in their learning.

Kol Yisrael 3, the third in this three-volume series, introduces students to a selection of prayers that help the students feel comfortable participating in the Shabbat morning service, specifically the Torah service and concluding prayers. The seven lessons invite students to learn the meaning of each prayer, its background, and how it helps us live according to Jewish values. The text and digital application prepare students to mark becoming bar and bat mitzvah while it emphasizes our connection to the land and people of Israel. The final section of *Kol Yisrael 3* reviews all the blessings and prayers introduced in *Kol Yisrael 1, 2, and 3.*

Kol Yisrael 3 guides students in this world of Jewish learning and values with the help of Batya and Ben—twin characters around twelve or thirteen years old. Batya and Ben's everyday experiences and animated conversations help make the prayers relevant to the students' lives. With the twins' help and encouragement, students practice their Hebrew decoding skills, explore Torah teachings, link prayer words to modern Hebrew, and learn vocabulary they can use every day!

Batya and Ben grow alongside students as they make their way through Kol Yisrael 1, 2, and 3. Just like the students, the twins develop from beginning Jewish learners into young Jewish community members about to celebrate their bar or bat mitzvah. Like the students, Batya and Ben explore what it means to come of age as a Jewish adult. They learn what it means to connect with Israel, to play a role in the Jewish community, and, most importantly, to be a member of the Jewish family—to be a member of Kol Yisrael!

Why Use *Kol Yisrael*?

While the goals of *Kol Yisrael* are similar to the goals of other prayer series—fluent prayer reading with comprehension and familiarity with the worship service—the innovations of *Kol Yisrael*'s structure and methods set it apart.

The *Kol Yisrael* series:

- Uses kid-friendly language to explore the meanings of and reasons behind prayer—so students understand the words they are saying and why we pray.
- Draws life lessons from the prayers (we show loyalty to God when we pursue peace and justice; we are a unique people and it is our duty to contribute goodness to the world)—so students understand how prayers can help each of us act like a mensch.
- Places prayers in the context of a story about a boy and a girl just like your students—so students remain engaged with the text and see *kids just like themselves* praying.
- Uses the computer to add audio-visual components and a gaming approach to reading and comprehension exercises—so students work through the lessons in ways that entertain *and* educate.

The integrated learning model in *Kol Yisrael* draws on both traditional (*pencil-to-paper*) and new (*mouse-to-screen*) techniques. The *Kol Yisrael* digital application:

- Extends Jewish learning from the classroom into the home.
- Allows students of varying learning styles and capabilities to progress at their own pace.
- Challenges students to solve puzzles, play games, and complete activities that reinforce classroom learning.
- Includes assessment materials after lessons 3 and 7 that let you and your students check their progress.
- Recognizes the tech-savvy lifestyles and skills of today's students.
- Is based on the *Kol Yisrael* text! The text introduces the prayers, Hebrew words, and Jewish lessons that the digital application reviews and reinforces. Each chapter also includes the section "Clue to

Cyberspace," which presents an activity or puzzle that will help students succeed in the digital application, such as a clue to earn bonus points in a video game.

The *Kol Yisrael* text and computer software are partners. They complement each other, enrich each other, and work together to engage students in modern Jewish learning.

BIG IDEAS AND ESSENTIAL QUESTIONS

Kol Yisrael 1, 2, and *3* are centered around two Big Ideas:

- Prayers and rituals teach us about Jewish values and mitzvot.
- When we know how to recite prayers and what they mean, we feel like a participating member of our Jewish community.

An Essential Question, specific to the prayers in *Kol Yisrael 3*, is included in the introduction to each chapter.

USING THE TEACHER'S EDITION

This Teacher's Edition contains the entire text of *Kol Yisrael 3*, reproduced in reduced size. The pages are annotated with suggested activities, teaching methods, and other information to assist you in planning and executing your lessons. Every element in the textbook is covered, including the introduction of new vocabulary, the reading of each prayer, and the review and reinforcement of all material, as well as ways to integrate the computer software into classroom lessons.

Before assigning the computer activities, we urge you to play through the digital application in its entirety. This will help you feel comfortable using the software and confident assigning activities to your students. *It's important to assign digital activities consistently throughout the school year.*

Keep in mind that students learn in different ways, and any student's primary learning mode may be aural, visual, or tactile. Similarly, teachers teach in different ways. Don't feel obligated to use a method that does not match your teaching style. By the same token, remember that, since students learn in different ways, you should vary your teaching methods accordingly. Feel free to repeat an activity or method that works especially well for you and your students.

The information and suggestions in this Teacher's Edition are intended to assist you in developing your own teaching plan. You do not need to follow every suggestion on every page; rather, the guide provides you with many different options from which to choose. Only you know what works best for your class and your teaching style.

Remember that each congregation has its own traditions and preferred melodies. Be sure to check with your education director, rabbi, or cantor to determine which prayers and tunes are used in your congregation. You will find variations on prayers throughout *Kol Yisrael 3*. Plan ahead which of these variations your students will study.

Throughout this guide there are references to prayer books published by the Reform, Conservative, and Reconstructionist movements. All references are based on the following editions: Frishman, Elyse, ed. *Mishkan T'filah, A Reform Siddur, Shabbat*. New York: Central Conference of American Rabbis, 2007; Cahan, Leonard, ed. *Siddur Sim Shalom for Shabbat and Festivals*. New York: The Rabbinical Assembly, 1998; Teutsch, David, ed. *Kol Haneshamah: Shabbat Vehagim*. Jenkintown, PA: The Reconstructionist Press, 2009.

Structure of the Teacher's Edition

Each section of the Teacher's Edition indicates the corresponding page number in the student text. In addition, each chapter in the Teacher's Edition contains the following features:

ABOUT THE PRAYER A brief description of the prayer or blessings presented in the chapter. The history or source of the liturgy is often included.

LEARNING OBJECTIVES Specific learning goals for each chapter.

ESSENTIAL QUESTION: A thoughtful, important question that one can revisit throughout one's life.

NEW WORDS AND PHRASES A comprehensive list of new Prayer Words.

INSTRUCTIONAL MATERIALS A listing of text pages, relevant word cards, and the level in the computer program.

WHERE WE ARE A brief synopsis of what the characters Batya and Ben are doing, and how their experience relates to the prayer(s) your students are about to study.

INTRODUCING THE LESSON A set induction to introduce students to the central ideas of the chapter's prayer(s) or blessings.

INTO THE TEXT A discussion or activity connected to the first page of each chapter in the student edition. This first page serves to introduce one key theme of the prayer(s) or blessings before students see the actual text.

DIGITAL APPLICATION A prompt for students to use the computer software—either at home or in school—as well as ideas for introducing digital activities or reinforcing their lessons during class.

ASSESSMENT Techniques for assessing reading fluency and knowledge of prayer content. Includes online assessment at www.behrmanhouse.com.

WHAT'S NEXT? A discussion introducing students to the prayer(s) or blessings of the upcoming chapter.

Each chapter in this Teacher's Edition also contains many of the following kinds of enrichment ideas, supplementary information, and activities:

Reading and Reciting—Ideas and techniques to help students improve their reading fluency.

Prayer Vocabulary—Ideas and activities to help students learn and retain new vocabulary.

Digital Application—Directions about when students should reinforce activities in the book on their computers.

Understanding Prayer—Enrichment activities and discussions to help your students understand the core meaning of prayers and blessings.

Game Box—Review exercises and activities to enhance the lesson's learning experience.

Repeating Roots—Discussions and exercises to illustrate the relationship between words that share the same root letters.

Photo Op—Ideas for using the book's photos and captions as teaching tools.

Our Tradition—Stories and excerpts from classical Jewish texts that reflect core Jewish values.

Middot* and *Mitzvot—Activities and discussions that focus on Jewish values.

Torah Travel—Study of a biblical text related to a core idea of the chapter.

Parashah Reading—Indicates that a biblical verse in the student edition is a selection from the Torah or haftarah reading of a weekly parashah.

Pacing

Students differ in ability. Teachers differ in style. Schools differ in the number of class sessions scheduled each week. Ultimately, you must decide how to pace your class through the text.

The seven chapters in *Kol Yisrael 3* vary in length from eight to fourteen pages. Some may take three class sessions to cover, while others may take four or more. Remember that the digital application is an ideal way to extend classroom instruction time into the home. Individual digital activities are addressed separately in the Teacher's Edition. You can also assign students the entire chapter's digital activities for *one* at-home learning session. For more information about pacing and timing, see "Time Management" on page 15.

Family Education

A partnership between home and school can help your students reach their greatest potential, and every effort should be made to facilitate this partnership. The digital application for *Kol Yisrael 3* is the perfect way to encourage home review and practice. Students will enjoy the interactive games while reviewing and practicing the prayers and blessings they studied in class. The digital application can provide students with additional contact, repetition, and reinforcement of material they have already learned in class. It extends your classroom time and is a terrific way to involve parents in their children's studies.

You may wish to e-mail or send home a letter after the first day of class telling parents about *Kol Yisrael 3*. Explain that you will be able to assess students' progress online (see Using the Digital Application, page 6, and Assessment, page 16). You can find a sample letter online among the *Kol Yisrael* resources at www.behrmanhouse.com. The letter contains steps for using the digital application, including sign-on instructions, and a link to a demo site for parents to try out the online activities themselves.

Reinforcing Prayer Awareness

At the start of the year, ask your education director for a list of prayers your students have learned to date. Begin each class with a short (two- to seven-minute) recap of these prayers. Ask individual students to take turns as leaders. You may choose to end the prayer recitation by having the class recite the blessing for engaging in study: לַעֲסוֹק בְּדִבְרֵי תוֹרָה, which students learned on page 24 in *Kol Yisrael 1*.

Using the Chalkboard, Whiteboard, or Interactive Whiteboard

Use the chalkboard or whiteboard to introduce new words and prayers, answer questions, play games, and present assignments. Vary the ways you use the board. You might, for example, draw, or have students draw, illustrations related to prayer vocabulary and to rituals. Invite students to come to the board to practice vocabulary.

If you have a computer projector or an interactive whiteboard in your school, use it to introduce students to the *Kol Yisrael* digital application. Demonstrate the sign-on procedure and the contents page (set on a map of Israel). Allow students to practice their reading interactively and to play a few digital games in front of their classmates. Remember that with an interactive whiteboard students act as a live, digital "mouse."

Alef-Bet and Prayer Word Review

Consider beginning the year with a thorough review of the letters and vowels in the Hebrew alphabet. Use an *alef-bet* poster or *alef-bet* flashcards. Consider using the *Back-to-School Hebrew Reading Refresher* (Behrman House). You might also use the word cards from *Kol Yisrael 1* and *2* to review and drill Hebrew decoding before students begin *Kol Yisrael 3*.

Group Work

As students study prayers, there will be opportunities for them to work together in groups. Consider creating index cards that describe the jobs of group members. Jobs will vary depending on the type of group work. Some possible jobs include: Reader—reads information aloud to the group; Recorder—records the group's suggestions or findings that will be reported to the class; Reporter—reports the group's work to the rest of the class; Illustrator—illustrates an idea to be presented to the class; Motivator—encourages group members to stay on task. Laminate the cards and distribute them each time your students work in groups.

Ongoing Anchor Activities

Consider setting up a year-long project about places in Israel. Have students, individually or with a partner, choose one of the seven sites labeled on the map on page 3. You may wish to add additional places, such as Eilat, Beit She'an, and Modi'in. Direct students to create a travel guide for their site. The guide might include, for example, the history of the place, special sites to visit, how to get to the city, photographs, or recommended restaurants. The guide can be in any format you and the students choose: poster, brochure, booklet, web page, or PowerPoint presentation.

Look for different opportunities for students to work on their travel guides. Individual students might, for example, have time for the project when they finish a classroom activity early or if they arrive early to class. Several students might work on their projects when you are busy with another group of students. Or, you may decide to allow all students to work on their travel guides at the end of a day.

If students will be using the Internet, be sure to locate and recommend websites ahead of time. Encourage students to research places that appear in the photographs in the digital application.

At the end of the year, invite all students to present their projects to the class. A perfect time to do this would be when, on page 82 of the student edition, students select the city they think Ben and Batya should choose for their bar and bat mitzvah celebration.

USING THE DIGITAL APPLICATION

Your students will delight in playing the online games and activities in *Kol Yisrael 3*. These exercises reinforce the prayer concepts and vocabulary introduced in the textbook.

Introducing the Digital Application

When introducing students to the *Kol Yisrael 3* text, point to one of the computer mouse icons that appear throughout the chapters. The mouse icon indicates that there is a corresponding activity, such as a reading exercise or a matching game, in the digital application. (The Teacher's Edition also will remind you when to prompt students to use the digital application.) Your students may recognize the icon from *Kol Yisrael 1* and *2*.

Students are also motivated to solve riddles and puzzles in the text ("Clue to Cyberspace") that provide clues to score bonus points in the digital application.

Before assigning activities for the first time in the *Kol Yisrael 3* digital application, make sure students note the class serial number. Every student in the class uses the same serial number to become a member of the *Kol Yisrael 3* digital database. You can use the serial number to assess your class's progress online. After entering the class's serial number in their computer, students will be asked to register with a unique user name and password. The students will then be members, and the database will begin to track and store their results on the activities.

You may wish to record students' user names so you have a master list in case students forget. You may also wish to send the class's serial number and the student's user name home to his or her parents. Students can keep their passwords private.

Tracking Students' Digital Activities

There are three ways to assess students' progress in the digital application:

1. Log on to www.behrmanhouse.com and click the blue "Assessment" button at the bottom left of the screen. Click on *Kol Yisrael* and select the picture of *Kol Yisrael 3*. Enter your class's serial number. Review your students' results.
2. Students can print out a lesson summary and bring it in to class.
3. Students can e-mail the lesson summary directly to you. You may wish to set up a separate e-mail account to receive this information.

Inform your students how often you intend to assess their progress online. You may wish to check their progress each time you assign an activity, or you may prefer to do so after they complete a chapter in the book.

The following chart outlines the games and activities included in the digital application for *Kol Yisrael 3*:

Indicates that students should use the clue from the textbook.

CONTENTS OF DIGITAL APPLICATION

Prayer	Game/Activity	Purpose
Chapter 1 אֵין כָּמוֹךָ/אַב הָרַחֲמִים	Photos of Jerusalem	Virtual visit to Jerusalem.
	Reading אֵין כָּמוֹךָ	Practice reading and chanting the prayer.
	Matching	Review new vocabulary from אֵין כָּמוֹךָ.
	Reading אַב הָרַחֲמִים	Practice reading and chanting the prayer.
	Crossword	Review prayer words from אַב הָרַחֲמִים.
	Reading הַתִּקְוָה	Practice reading and singing Israel's national anthem.
	Lion's Bird House	Play game and review new vocabulary from אֵין כָּמוֹךָ and אַב הָרַחֲמִים.
Chapter 2 כִּי מִצִּיּוֹן/בָּרוּךְ שֶׁנָּתַן/ שְׁמַע/גַּדְּלוּ לַייָ/לְךָ יְיָ	Photos of the Negev	Virtual visit to the Negev Desert.
	Reading כִּי מִצִּיּוֹן and וַיְהִי בִּנְסֹעַ	Practice reading the prayers.
	Reading בָּרוּךְ שֶׁנָּתַן	Practice reading the prayer.
	Reading גַּדְּלוּ לַייָ	Practice reading שְׁמַע/גַּדְּלוּ לַייָ.
	Reading לְךָ יְיָ	Practice reading and chanting the prayer.
	Matching	Review Hebrew words related to בַּשָּׁמַיִם וּבָאָרֶץ.
	Word Search	Review new vocabulary from לְךָ יְיָ
	Carnival Duck	Play game and practice reading new prayer words.
Chapter 3 בִּרְכוֹת הַתּוֹרָה/ וְזֹאת הַתּוֹרָה	Photos of Tel Aviv-Yafo	Virtual visit to Tel Aviv-Yafo (Jaffa).
	Before reading בִּרְכוֹת הַתּוֹרָה	Practice reading and chanting the prayer.
	After reading בִּרְכוֹת הַתּוֹרָה	Practice reading and chanting the prayer.
	Matching	Review new vocabulary.

Prayer	Game/Activity	Purpose
	Reading וְזֹאת הַתּוֹרָה	Practice reading and chanting the prayer.
	Tic-Tac-Toe	Review new vocabulary.
	Stampede	Play game and practice reading prayer words.
Chapter 4 בִּרְכוֹת הַהַפְטָרָה/ עֵץ חַיִּים הִיא	Photos of Haifa	Virtual visit to Haifa.
	Before הַהַפְטָרָה	Practice reading and chanting the prayer.
	After הַהַפְטָרָה	Practice reading and chanting the prayer.
	Expanded בִּרְכוֹת הַהַפְטָרָה	Practice reading and chanting the prayer.
	Matching	Review new vocabulary.
	Reading יְהַלְלוּ and הוֹדוֹ	Practice reading and chanting the prayer.
	Crossword	Review new vocabulary and names of places in Israel.
	Lion's Bird House	Play game and review new vocabulary.
Chapter 5 עָלֵינוּ	Photos of Masada	Virtual visit to Masada.
	Reading עָלֵינוּ	Practice reading and chanting the prayer.
	Matching	Review the Hebrew names of the days of the week.
	Word Search	Review new vocabulary.
	Carnival Duck	Play game and practice reading prayer words.
Chapter 6 קַדִּישׁ	Photos of Be'er Sheva	Virtual visit to Be'er Sheva.
	Reading קַדִּישׁ	Practice reading the קַדִּישׁ.
	Matching	Review the Hebrew names of places with בֵּית־.
	Tic-Tac-Toe	Review vocabulary.
	Stampede	Play game and review related Hebrew and Aramaic words.

Prayer	Game/Activity	Purpose
Chapter 7 אֵין כֵּאלֹהֵינוּ/אֲדוֹן עוֹלָם	Photos of Tiberias	Virtual visit to Tiberias.
	Reading אֵין כֵּאלֹהֵינוּ	Practice reading and chanting אֵין כֵּאלֹהֵינוּ.
	Matching	Review Hebrew pronouns.
	Reading אֲדוֹן עוֹלָם	Practice reading and chanting אֲדוֹן עוֹלָם.
	Text Twist	Review new and previously learned vocabulary.
	Stampede	Play game and review new vocabulary.
	Reading the שֶׁהֶחֱיָנוּ	Practice reading and chanting the שֶׁהֶחֱיָנוּ.
Review 1		Review vocabulary and prayer concepts in Lessons 1–3.
Review 2		Review vocabulary and prayer concepts in Lessons 4–7.

WORD CARDS: MASTER LIST

The following is a list of Prayer Words included in *Kol Yisrael 3*.

1.	אֵין	(there is) none
2.	כָּמוֹךָ	like You
3.	מַלְכוּתְךָ	Your sovereignty
4.	בְּכָל־דֹּר וָדֹר	from generation to generation
5.	עֹז	strength
6.	אַב, אָב	parent, father
7.	הָרַחֲמִים	merciful, the mercy
8.	חוֹמוֹת	walls
9.	וְנִשָּׂא	and exalted
10.	עוֹלָמִים	eternal
11.	מִצִּיּוֹן	out of Zion, from Zion
12.	תֵּצֵא	shall go forth
13.	מִירוּשָׁלָיִם	from Jerusalem
14.	שֶׁנָּתַן	who gave, that gave
15.	לְעַמּוֹ	to God's people
16.	בִּקְדֻשָּׁתוֹ	in (God's) holiness
17.	אֶחָד	one
18.	שְׁמוֹ	(God's) name, his name
19.	גַּדְּלוּ	glorify
20.	הַגְּדֻלָּה	the greatness
21.	וְהַגְּבוּרָה	and the power
22.	בַּשָּׁמַיִם	in heaven
23.	וּבָאָרֶץ	and on earth
24.	בָּחַר	chose (choosing)
25.	בָּנוּ	us
26.	מִכָּל	from all
27.	הָעַמִּים	the nations
28.	וְנָתַן	and gave (and giving)
29.	לָנוּ	to us
30.	תּוֹרָתוֹ	God's Torah
31.	נוֹתֵן	gives
32.	תּוֹרַת	Torah of
33.	אֱמֶת	truth
34.	וְחַיֵּי	and life (of)
35.	עוֹלָם	eternal, world
36.	וְזֹאת	and this is
37.	אֲשֶׁר	that, which
38.	שָׂם	set, put
39.	מֹשֶׁה	Moses
40.	לִפְנֵי	before
41.	בְּיַד	by the hand of
42.	נְבִיאִים	prophets
43.	טוֹבִים	good
44.	בְּדִבְרֵיהֶם	with their words
45.	הַנֶּאֱמָרִים	spoken
46.	בֶּאֱמֶת	in truth
47.	עַבְדּוֹ	his (God's) servant
48.	וָצֶדֶק	and righteousness (justice)
49.	צוּר	rock
50.	הַנֶּאֱמָן	the One who is faithful
51.	הָאוֹמֵר	the One who says
52.	לְכָבוֹד	for honor
53.	מוֹדִים	thank (plural)
54.	תָּמִיד	forever
55.	יְהַלְלוּ	(let us) praise
56.	שֵׁם	name

57.	תְּהִלָּה	praise
58.	עֵץ חַיִּים	tree of life
59.	מְאֻשָּׁר	happy
60.	דְּרָכֶיהָ	its ways, its paths
61.	נֹעַם	pleasantness
62.	חַדֵּשׁ	renew
63.	יָמֵינוּ	our days
64.	עָלֵינוּ	it is upon us (our duty)
65.	לְשַׁבֵּחַ	to praise
66.	לַאֲדוֹן	to God
67.	הַכֹּל	of all
68.	וַאֲנַחְנוּ	and we
69.	כּוֹרְעִים	bend the knee
70.	מֶלֶךְ מַלְכֵי הַמְּלָכִים	Ruler of the rulers of rulers
71.	וְנֶאֱמַר	and it is said
72.	יִתְגַּדַּל	will be great
73.	וְיִתְקַדַּשׁ	and will be holy
74.	שְׁמֵהּ	God's name
75.	בְּעָלְמָא	in the world
76.	מַלְכוּתֵהּ	God's kingdom
77.	בִּרְכָתָא	the blessings
78.	שְׁלָמָא	peace
79.	אֵין כּ־	there is none like
80.	מִי כּ־	who is like
81.	נוֹדֶה ל־	we will give thanks to
82.	אַתָּה הוּא	You (God) are
83.	אֱלֹהֵינוּ	our God
84.	אֲדוֹנֵינוּ	our Sovereign
85.	מַלְכֵּנוּ	our Ruler
86.	מוֹשִׁיעֵנוּ	our Savior
87.	אֲדוֹן	Sovereign
88.	הָיָה	(God) was
89.	הֹוֶה	(God) is
90.	יִהְיֶה	(God) will be
91.	בְּלִי רֵאשִׁית	without a beginning
92.	בְּלִי תַכְלִית	without an end
93.	גֹּאֲלִי	my Redeemer

WORD CARD TECHNIQUES AND GAMES

There are 93 word cards for *Kol Yisrael 3*. They include the words listed in the section called "Prayer Words" in each chapter. The Teacher's Edition offers specific suggestions for presenting the Prayer Words. The word cards may be used for games and review activities, such as the following:

1. Display a number of word cards on the board. Provide a clue about one of the words and ask students to find and read the correct word. For example: Which word has the same root letters as מַלְכוּתְךָ? (מַלְכוּתֵהּ)
2. Distribute several word cards to the class. Have students look only at the Hebrew words or phrases on the cards. Call out, one at a time, the English meanings of the Hebrew words or phrases. Ask the student with the corresponding Hebrew card to stand up, display the card, and read the word or phrase. For a variation, call out the Hebrew words and have students identify the English meaning for each one.
3. Post at least six words in a column on the board. Ask individuals or teams to take turns "climbing up the ladder" by reading and/or translating the words in ascending order. Score one point for each word translated correctly. Then play again by having students read the words in descending order to climb down the ladder.
4. Display several word cards on the board. Have students take turns choosing a word card, naming a prayer in which the word is found, and, for an extra challenge, saying the phrase that includes that word.

CLASSROOM GAMES

Games can add variety and energy to your classroom. They reinforce learning and capture students' attention through a fun, lively medium. As you plan to use the games below, or others you may develop or choose to use, keep the following considerations in mind:

1. Choose games that contribute to improving specific skills and reading fluency—games that have pedagogic value.
2. Use games that move quickly. Don't spend more time on a game than it deserves.
3. Stop when students' interest begins to wane.
4. Choose games appropriate to the age group.
5. Use games that are easy to follow and organize. Explain rules clearly. Avoid complicated directions. You want students' attention focused on the skills being reinforced, not on rules.
6. Maintain control of the class.
7. When playing a game with the entire class, make sure that all students are actively involved and can experience success.

The Secret Word

Invite two students to the front of the room to be the "contestants." Show everyone but the two contestants a word card (the secret word). Students raise their hands to volunteer one-word clues to help the contestants guess the word. Contestants take turns calling on other students until one of the contestants correctly guesses the secret word. The contestant who identifies the secret word remains at the front of the class; the student who gave the final clue takes the place of the other contestant.

שֶׁקֶט, בְּבַקָּשָׁה!

Distribute word cards for words contained in a single prayer or blessing (you need not have all of the prayer or blessing words to do this activity). Students must arrange themselves in order of the appearance of the words in the prayer or blessing. without making any sound. How fast can they complete this task with no mistakes? Once students are standing in the correct sequence, invite the class to recite the prayer or blessing.

אוֹי!

Materials: Small pieces of paper; shoe box or coffee can

Neatly write 10 to 15 prayer words or related words on pieces of paper. Write אוֹי! on three pieces of paper. Fold all pieces of paper in half and place them in the box or can. Divide the class into three or four teams. Teams take turns picking words. If they read and translate the word correctly they get to keep the word. If not, they must return the word to the box/can. If a team draws an אוֹי!, they yell אוֹי! and then return all their words (except the "אוֹי!") to the box or can.

When no more words remain in the box or can, or you have reached a pre-set time limit, the team with the most words wins.

Odd Word Out

Write four words on the board. Three should be related, and one should be unrelated. Challenge students to circle the "Odd Word Out." (example: בְּרִיךְ — שְׁלָמָא — קָדוֹשׁ — שְׁמַיָּא)

Mishpaḥah Madness

Divide the class into two teams (two families—*mishpaḥot*). Assign, or have teams choose, a Hebrew family name, such as Ben-David, for their team. Invite the first student player from each team to come to the front of the room. Show the two students a word card. The students raise their hands if they know how to read and translate the word. Call on the first student who raises his or her hand. If that student correctly reads and translates the word, the team earns two points. If not, the other player tries to read and translate the same word card. If neither player gives the correct answer, their teammates can raise their hands and, after being called on, read and translate. One point is earned when a teammate, rather than a player, answers correctly. For variety, you may wish to challenge students to name a prayer or blessing in which the word appears or an occasion on which a phrase is said. The team with the most points after all word cards have been presented is the winning team.

מָצָאתִי—I Found It!

Have students locate a word or phrase on a given page, based on clues that you provide.

Sample clues may include:

- Find the word in עָלֵינוּ with the root letters גדל. *(גְּדֻלָּה)*
- Find the word in עָלֵינוּ that is a number. *(אֶחָד)*
- Find the word that has "Torah" as part of its meaning. *(בְּתוֹרָתוֹ)*

Have students call !מָצָאתִי ("I found it!") when they locate the word or phrase. The first student who calls !מָצָאתִי should read the word or phrase correctly. If successful, he or she receives a point. If not, the other students have an opportunity to call !מָצָאתִי, read the word or phrase, and score.

Hebrew Baseball

Using four chairs (one for each base), create a mock baseball diamond in your classroom. Divide the class into two teams and have them sit on opposite sides of the room. Choose a team to be at bat. That team will send one student "batter" at a time to home plate. The batter chooses the difficulty level of the question that he or she will answer: a single, double, triple, or home run. You may wish to prepare questions for each level in advance.

Sample questions:

- For a single: What is the English translation of the word כָּמוֹךָ? *(like You)*
- For a double: During which part of the Shabbat morning service do we recite אֵין כָּמוֹךָ? *(at the beginning of the Torah service)*
- For a triple: Which words in אֵין כָּמוֹךָ are built on the root מלכ? *(מָלָךְ, מַלְכוּתְךָ, מַלְכוּת, מֶלֶךְ, יִמְלֹךְ)*
- For a home run: Why did Ezra read from the Torah on Mondays and Thursdays? *(because that was when many people gathered in the marketplace to do business)*

If the answer is correct, the student advances that number of bases (and anyone already on base advances the same number as well). If the student answers incorrectly, he or she is out. After three outs the next team comes to bat. Play as many innings as you'd like, but make sure the teams get an equal number of turns at bat.

Concentration

Create one set of 3″ x 5″ index cards with Hebrew words, and one set of cards with the English translations (or illustrations). You may wish to use the same words reviewed in the digital application's Prayer Word Concentration game. All cards should be blank on one side. Combine both sets and shuffle together.

Place all cards, word-side up, on the floor or a large table. Then turn the cards over so the blank sides face up. Ask students individually (or in teams) to try to match the Hebrew and English (or picture) pairs by turning any two cards over.

If they match, award the player the matched pair of cards. If they do not match, return the cards to their original position and ask another student (or team) to go. Continue the game until all cards have been removed. The player or team with the most matches wins.

Tic-Tac-Toe

Draw a Tic-Tac-Toe board on the board. Divide students into two teams, א and ב. Show a word card or a word reviewed in that lesson's digital version of Tic-Tac-Toe. Then, call on a student from Team א to read the Hebrew word. If the student reads correctly, ask him or her to place an א in one of the squares. Then it is Team ב's turn to read another word card.

Variations:

- Students must read the word on the word card and the line in which the word appears in the prayer passage before placing a mark in a square. (You can facilitate the game by telling the student which line contains the word.)
- Students must read the Hebrew and give the English meaning before placing an א or a ב in a square.
- Students must answer questions about the prayer passage(s) in order to place an א or a ב in a square.

מַה הַמִּילָה?—What's the Word?

Have a student choose a word from the chapter. The other students must guess what the word is, based on questions they ask.

Suggested questions:

- Can one draw the word?
- Is the word a person, place, or thing?
- How many letters are there in the word?

The class may ask an unlimited number of questions, but each student may guess only once. The student who guesses correctly receives a point and chooses the next word. The student with the most points at the end of ten rounds is the winner.

Siddur Squares

This game can be played using the questions from one of the lessons, or as a review of several lessons. Before the game, prepare א and ב signs by writing a large א on six sheets of construction paper and a large ב on another six sheets.

Select nine students to serve as the "siddur squares." You might place three chairs in a row. Direct three students to sit in the chairs, three to stand behind the chairs, and three to sit on the floor in front of the seated students. Divide the remaining students into two teams, א and ב.

When the first player on Team א selects one of the nine siddur squares, ask a question from the lesson being reviewed. The selected siddur square student should give an answer, and the Team א player must agree or disagree. If the Team א player is correct (that is, agrees with a correct answer or disagrees with an incorrect answer), then Team א should receive that square, and the siddur square student who answered the question should hold up an א sign.

Continue in the same fashion with Team ב. Continue, alternating teams, until one team has three squares in a row diagonally, vertically, or horizontally.

TIME MANAGEMENT

Deciding how to spend valuable class time is crucial when planning your lessons. Ideally, each class session should be divided into at least four distinct components:

1. An opening activity to review previous material or set the tone for the new lesson
2. Introduction of new material
3. Reinforcement of new material
4. A closing activity to summarize and reinforce the lesson's content and prepare students for the next lesson

The amount of time spent on each component will depend on the overall amount of time available for Hebrew instruction and on what you wish to accomplish. Preparing a lesson plan in advance of every class session will help you manage your time and meet your goals. Keep in mind that the computer program allows you to extend your class time with at-home learning sessions.

Your lesson plan should include (1) lesson goals, (2) instructional materials needed, (3) planned activities and time estimates, (4) homework, and (5) notes.

If You Meet Once a Week for Hebrew Instruction...

If your school meets once a week for thirty weeks (1–1½ hours per week), allow approximately three classroom sessions for each chapter and for the *Kol Yisrael* Wrap-Up. Keep in mind that the number of new Hebrew words and phrases introduced in a single chapter ranges from seven to twenty-two. In addition, some chapters focus on blessings and prayers comprising almost twice as many lines as other chapters. Therefore, some chapters will require more than three classroom sessions.

If You Meet Twice a Week for Hebrew Instruction...

If your school meets twice a week for thirty weeks (2 hours or more per week), allow four to six classroom sessions per chapter. Use as many of the techniques described in this Teacher's Edition as possible to enrich the content of the text and digital application.

ASSESSMENT

Assessment enables you to gain a clear understanding of where each student is in the learning process and what the next steps should be. It also allows students to personally assess their own progress. Assessment is primarily a process for helping students grow and learn. It can also help you plan future lessons and check how well you yourself are doing.

A variety of assessment tools are available for *Kol Yisrael 3*:

- **PRAYER MASTERY ASSESSMENT CHART**—Toward the end of each chapter, check each student's reading fluency and comprehension of the prayer meaning and its key words and phrases. Photocopy the chart on the next page for each student. Keep a record of the student's progress by writing a comment and dating the chart after each assessment is complete. Keep the charts in a dedicated folder or binder.
- **REVIEW SHEETS**—You will find worksheets with answer keys online at www.behrmanhouse.com. Use the worksheets to review key prayer concepts and vocabulary at the end of each chapter.
- **DIGITAL APPLICATION**—Assess students' progress in the computer program at www.behrmanhouse.com. The digital application also includes reviews after Lessons 3 and 7. (Refer to page 7 for information about how to assess progress online.)

PRAYER MASTERY ASSESSMENT CHART

Student Name: ______________________________

Understands key words and phrases	Explains meaning of prayer	Reads prayer fluently	
			1. אֵין כָּמוֹךָ
			2. אַב הָרַחֲמִים
			3. הַתִּקְוָה
			4. כִּי מִצִּיּוֹן/בָּרוּךְ שֶׁנָּתַן
			5. שְׁמַע/גַּדְּלוּ לַייָ
			6. לְךָ יְיָ
			7. בִּרְכוֹת הַתּוֹרָה Blessing Before the Torah Reading
			8. בִּרְכוֹת הַתּוֹרָה Blessing After the Torah Reading
			9. וְזֹאת הַתּוֹרָה
			10. בִּרְכוֹת הַהַפְטָרָה Blessing Before the Haftarah Reading
			11. בִּרְכוֹת הַהַפְטָרָה Blessing After the Haftarah Reading
			12. יְהַלְלוּ, הוֹדוֹ
			13. עָלֵינוּ
			14. קַדִּישׁ
			15. אֵין כֵּאלֹהֵינוּ
			16. אֲדוֹן עוֹלָם
			17. שֶׁהֶחֱיָנוּ

WORKING EFFECTIVELY WITH STUDENTS WITH SPECIAL LEARNING NEEDS

All children learn and develop differently, and no two students will acquire Hebrew skills in exactly the same way. Students with special learning needs may bring additional challenges to the classroom, and teachers can serve their students best by recognizing each child's individual strengths. *Kol Yisrael 3* provides a broad variety of activities, including both traditional pencil-to-paper exercises and mouse-to-screen reinforcement activities, that can be modified for all types of learners. Consult with your religious school director to learn about each student's specific learning needs.

While these strategies are geared toward students with special learning needs, all students can benefit from the techniques and modifications listed below:

- **Form a bond with your students.** Reach out before school starts by sending home a letter or e-mail or by calling to introduce yourself to your students. Begin the year with a "get-to-know-you" game. Throughout the year, show a personal interest in your students to help them feel safe, valued, and respected. Students who believe that their teacher takes a genuine interest in their lives outside of Hebrew school are more likely to stretch academically.
- **Start with an assessment.** Give students the opportunity to review their basic decoding skills. Reteach letters and vowels as necessary. It is more effective to move gradually into the content than to remediate once a student has fallen behind. This will also help to prevent students from feeling as if they are failing at a task.
- **Create a partnership with parents.** Short periods of daily practice at home will help students retain what they have learned in class and build toward fluency and accuracy. Parents can "sign off" on a record-keeping sheet even if they themselves do not feel that they are competent Hebrew readers. Encourage parents to take adult Hebrew courses to build their own skills and serve as effective models for their children.

For a student with:

- **Attention problems:** Seat the student close to you and minimize distractions, such as students tapping their pencils on their desks or noise in the hallway. Repeat directions. Privately establish a refocusing system with the student, such as a gentle tap on the shoulder or approaching his or her desk. Help the student organize his or her papers and supplies. Provide an extra copy of texts for use at home. Ensure homework assignments are written down.
- **Auditory processing issues:** Minimize noise and distractions. Have the student repeat directions back to you to ensure understanding. Provide students with a written copy of verbal instructions. Provide extra time to complete assignments. Review new concepts more than once. Do not assume that students will retain new information later during that class or the next session.
- **Visual processing difficulty:** Read written directions aloud. For individual seatwork, allow the student to work with a *madrich* or *madrichah* or a buddy to read the information aloud. Have the student use an index card to track the line being read or cover the portion of the page not being worked on. Provide an alternative activity such as highlighting instead of circling key vocabulary, or shorten the assignment where appropriate.
- **Emotional concerns, such as shyness or lack of self-esteem:** Allow students to participate in choral reading, if they prefer, rather than reading out loud individually. Assess students one-on-one until they feel more confident. Provide positive reinforcement regularly to boost self-esteem.
- **Behavioral problems:** Set firm but reasonable expectations. Minimize transitions such as changing activities abruptly, and inform students of schedule changes. Maintain a positive relationship with parents—for example, by returning messages promptly. Find out what works for the student at home and in secular school to mirror in your own classroom where possible.

Remember, students may fall into more than one category and will benefit from a combination of strategies. Above all, embrace your students, knowing that each is created *b'tzelem Elohim* (in God's image).

1 אֵין כָּמוֹךָ/אַב הָרַחֲמִים

ABOUT THE PRAYER

The אֵין כָּמוֹךָ and אַב הָרַחֲמִים prayers open the Torah service and help prepare us to receive the words of Torah. אֵין כָּמוֹךָ declares that there is none like our God and that God is the eternal Ruler of the Jews. As we recite אַב הָרַחֲמִים, we describe God as a merciful parent and trustworthy ruler. As we prepare to hear the words of the Torah, it is God, not the Torah, that we praise.

LEARNING OBJECTIVES

Students will be able to:

- Identify אֵין כָּמוֹךָ and אַב הָרַחֲמִים as the opening prayers of the Torah service.
- Recite אֵין כָּמוֹךָ and אַב הָרַחֲמִים fluently.
- Define key words and the roots מלכ and רחמ.
- Locate Jerusalem on a map of Israel.
- Name the days on which we read Torah and explain why we read it year after year.
- Join in singing הַתִּקְוָה.

ESSENTIAL QUESTION

How and why do we prepare our hearts and minds to receive the words of Torah?

NEW WORDS AND PHRASES

Prayer Words:

(there is) none	אֵין
like You	כָּמוֹךָ
Your sovereignty	מַלְכוּתְךָ
from generation to generation	בְּכָל-דּוֹר וָדוֹר
strength	עֹז
parent, father	אַב, אָב
merciful, the mercy	הָרַחֲמִים
walls	חוֹמוֹת
and exalted	וְנִשָּׂא
eternal	עוֹלָמִים

INSTRUCTIONAL MATERIALS

Text pages 4–13

Word cards 1–10

Digital Application: Level 1—אֵין כָּמוֹךָ and אַב הָרַחֲמִים (see page 8 for a list of games and activities)

TITLE OF THE SERIES

Draw students' attention to the title of the book, כָּל יִשְׂרָאֵל.

Explain, or if your students have studied *Kol Yisrael 1 and 2*, review: One of the names for the Jewish people is Israel, יִשְׂרָאֵל. The Torah describes how God gave Abraham's grandson, Jacob, a new name: Israel, יִשְׂרָאֵל. The Torah tells us that יִשְׂרָאֵל had twelve sons from whom the Jewish people are descended. Since יִשְׂרָאֵל is considered to be the ancestor of all the Jewish people, we call ourselves בְּנֵי יִשְׂרָאֵל, Children of Israel, or simply יִשְׂרָאֵל. (Note: It may be helpful to draw a diagram of the above information on the board as you present it to your students.)

Tell students that כָּל means "all." Challenge students to translate the phrase כָּל יִשְׂרָאֵל. *("All of Israel" or "All of the Jewish people")* Ask: Who is included in כָּל יִשְׂרָאֵל? *(Responses may include: everyone in our synagogue, all the Jews in Israel, all the Jews in the world)*

INTRODUCING THE TEXT

Review the general themes of *Kol Yisrael 1 (Celebrating at Home and Sh'lom Bayit)* and *2 (Worshiping Together and the Community)*, in which students learned key blessings and prayers to use at home, the opening prayers of the Shabbat morning service, and the Amidah. Inform students that the main theme of *Kol Yisrael 3* is Our People and Becoming a Bar and Bat Mitzvah. As students learn the Shabbat morning Torah service and the concluding prayers of the Shabbat morning service in *Kol Yisrael 3*, they will prepare to become bar and bat mitzvah and will reflect on their personal role as an adult member of the Jewish people.

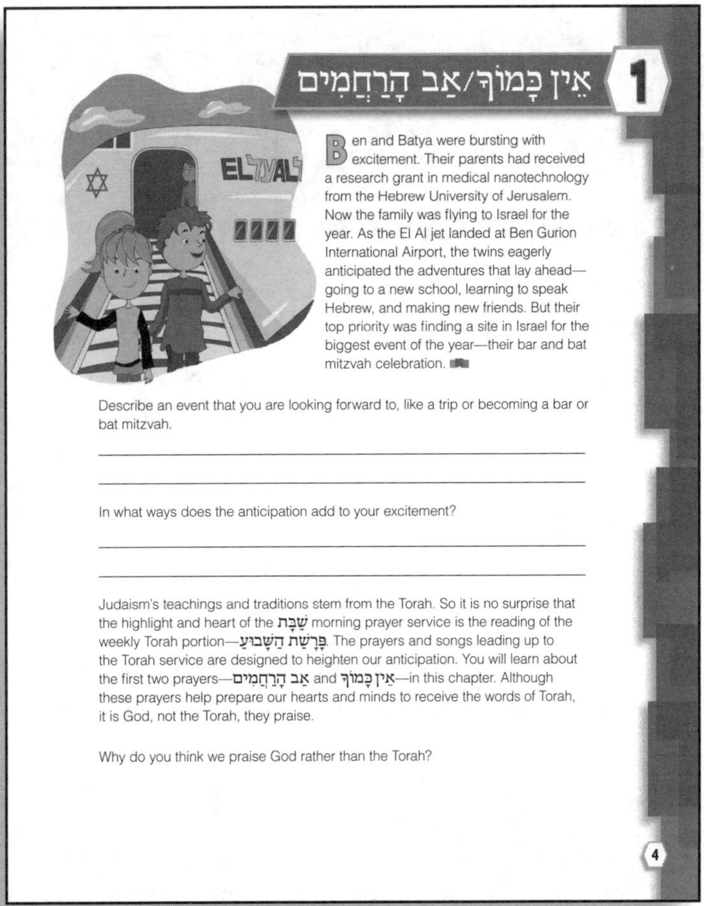

1 אֵין כָּמוֹךָ/אַב הָרַחֲמִים

Ben and Batya were bursting with excitement. Their parents had received a research grant in medical nanotechnology from the Hebrew University of Jerusalem. Now the family was flying to Israel for the year. As the El Al jet landed at Ben Gurion International Airport, the twins eagerly anticipated the adventures that lay ahead—going to a new school, learning to speak Hebrew, and making new friends. But their top priority was finding a site in Israel for the biggest event of the year—their bar and bat mitzvah celebration.

Describe an event that you are looking forward to, like a trip or becoming a bar or bat mitzvah.

____

____

In what ways does the anticipation add to your excitement?

____

____

Judaism's teachings and traditions stem from the Torah. So it is no surprise that the highlight and heart of the שַׁבָּת morning prayer service is the reading of the weekly Torah portion—פָּרָשַׁת הַשָּׁבוּעַ. The prayers and songs leading up to the Torah service are designed to heighten our anticipation. You will learn about the first two prayers—אַב הָרַחֲמִים and אֵין כָּמוֹךָ—in this chapter. Although these prayers help prepare our hearts and minds to receive the words of Torah, it is God, not the Torah, they praise.

Why do you think we praise God rather than the Torah?

4

Record students' responses on the board. Ask: What questions do you have about the Torah service and its prayers? *(Possible questions include: How is a Torah written? What blessing is said before the Torah is read?)* Record students' questions on chart paper. Display these questions on a board for reference. Inform students that some of these questions are answered in *Kol Yisrael 3*, and that you will do your best to answer the others. During the year, put a check next to each question once it has been addressed.

Invite students to open to page 4 and to read chorally the name of the chapter, אֵין כָּמוֹךָ/אַב הָרַחֲמִים. Write on the board: אֵין כָּמוֹךָ–מִי כָמֹכָה. Challenge students to identify the words that are similar in these two phrases (כָּמֹכָה־כָּמוֹךָ) and, if your students have studied *Kol Yisrael 2*, to say their meaning. *(like You)* Tell students that אֵין כָּמוֹךָ means "There is none like You," and invite the students to guess what the prayer will be about. As a class, read aloud the name of the second prayer, אַב הָרַחֲמִים. If your students have studied *Kol Yisrael 2*, write on the board: וְרַחֲמִים —אָבוֹת. Have students work with a partner to derive the meaning of אַב הָרַחֲמִים *(Merciful Parent)*. Note: If students have not studied *Kol Yisrael 2*, write the meaning of the words on the board for the students.

QUICK LOOK

Invite students to page through *Kol Yisrael 3*. If students have studied *Kol Yisrael 1* and *2*, they will be familiar with many of book's features. Introduce, or review, the repeating features, such as "At the Root," "Language Link," and "Putting It in ConTEXT."

Explain that students will be able to practice Hebrew on their computer at home. For every chapter in the book, there is a corresponding chapter in the digital application. They'll be able to play fun games online such as "Stampede," "Carnival Duck," and "Lion's Bird House."

WHERE WE ARE

We meet Batya and Ben as they are landing in Israel and are about to begin a year of preparing to become b'nai mitzvah. Just as the students prepare themselves to become bat and bar mitzvah, when we recite אֵין כָּמוֹךָ and אַב הָרַחֲמִים we prepare our hearts and minds to receive the words of Torah.

INTRODUCING THE LESSON

Stretch or do a few jumping jacks to get your students' attention. Ask: How do these kinds of exercises help us to warm up and prepare for more intense exercise? *(get our minds to focus on the activity and get our bodies ready)* Explain that two prayers in our service, אֵין כָּמוֹךָ and אַב הָרַחֲמִים, help get our hearts and minds ready for the Torah reading.

INTO THE TEXT

Ask: If you could celebrate your bar or bat mitzvah in Israel, how would you go about deciding how and where you would celebrate? *(ask other people; research on the Internet; tour Israel and visit sites)* Inform students that in *Kol Yisrael 3*, they will follow Ben and Batya as the twins travel around Israel and look for a site for their bar and bat mitzvah celebration. Like Batya and Ben, your students will study the prayers that are recited during the Torah service.

As a class, have students brainstorm what they know about the Torah service and its prayers.

Call on volunteers to describe the illustration of Batya and Ben disembarking. Ask: How might Batya and Ben be feeling? What might they be thinking? What might they be hoping for?

Direct students to read and complete page 4. Explain that nanotechnology is the science of designing, producing, and using structures and devices, like microscopic robots, that are measured by a nanometer, which is one billionth of a meter.

Ask: What is the highlight of the Shabbat morning prayer service? *(reading the weekly Torah portion—פָּרָשַׁת הַשָּׁבוּעַ)* Which two prayers prepare us to receive the words of Torah? *(אֵין כָּמוֹךָ and אַב הָרַחֲמִים)*

Invite students to suggest why, as we prepare to read the Torah, we praise God rather than the Torah. *(Answers may include: Because God gave us the Torah; because we pray to God and not the Torah)*

The Torah Service

Before beginning this conversation, ascertain when the Torah is read in your congregation. In class, ask: When do we read from the Torah in our congregation? Which day of the week and what time of day will the Torah be read when you become a bar or bat mitzvah?

Torah Travel

Direct students to read "The Torah Service" with a partner. Ask: When is the Torah read? *(Shabbat morning and afternoon, Monday and Thursday mornings, certain holidays)* What is the origin of reading Torah at these times? *(2,500 years ago, Ezra read from the Torah at public gatherings. People gathered on Shabbat, on holidays, and on Mondays and Thursday, the market days.)* Lead students in a choral reading of Nehemiah 8:2–3. Have students underline the Hebrew for Ezra (עֶזְרָא) and Torah (תּוֹרָה). Ask students to turn to the map on page 3 and circle יְרוּשָׁלַיִם.

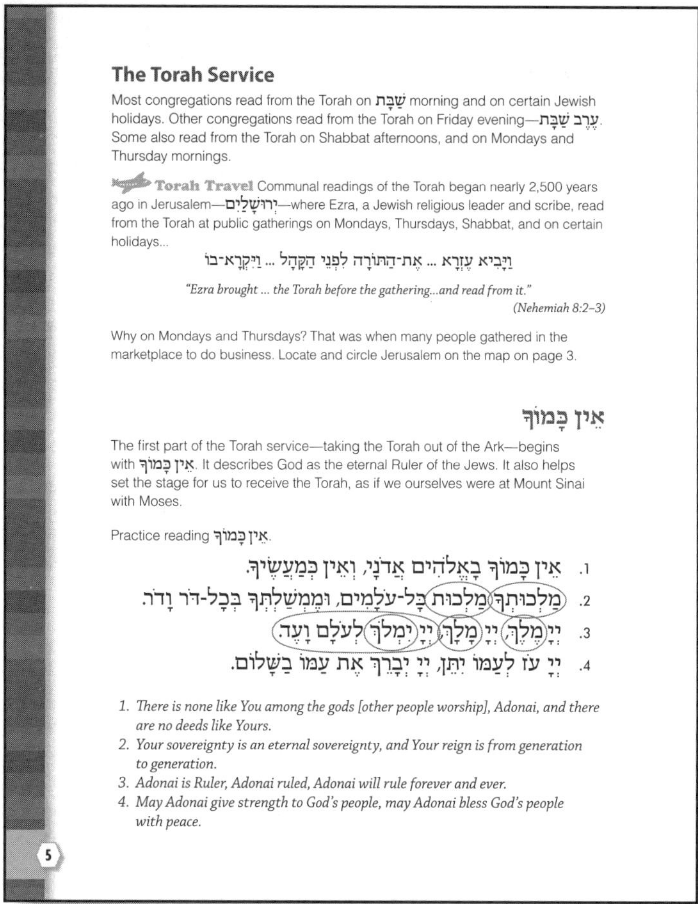

The Torah Service

Most congregations read from the Torah on שַׁבָּת morning and on certain Jewish holidays. Other congregations read from the Torah on Friday evening—עֶרֶב שַׁבָּת. Some also read from the Torah on Shabbat afternoons, and on Mondays and Thursday mornings.

Torah Travel Communal readings of the Torah began nearly 2,500 years ago in Jerusalem—יְרוּשָׁלַיִם—where Ezra, a Jewish religious leader and scribe, read from the Torah at public gatherings on Mondays, Thursdays, Shabbat, and on certain holidays...

וַיָּבִיא עֶזְרָא ... אֶת־הַתּוֹרָה לִפְנֵי הַקָּהָל ... וַיִּקְרָא־בוֹ

"Ezra brought ... the Torah before the gathering...and read from it."

(Nehemiah 8:2–3)

Why on Mondays and Thursdays? That was when many people gathered in the marketplace to do business. Locate and circle Jerusalem on the map on page 3.

אֵין כָּמוֹךָ

The first part of the Torah service—taking the Torah out of the Ark—begins with אֵין כָּמוֹךָ. It describes God as the eternal Ruler of the Jews. It also helps set the stage for us to receive the Torah, as if we ourselves were at Mount Sinai with Moses.

Practice reading אֵין כָּמוֹךָ.

1. אֵין כָּמוֹךָ בָאֱלֹהִים אֲדֹנָי, וְאֵין כְּמַעֲשֶׂיךָ.
2. מַלְכוּתְךָ מַלְכוּת כָּל-עֹלָמִים, וּמֶמְשַׁלְתְּךָ בְּכָל-דֹּר וָדֹר.
3. יְיָ מֶלֶךְ, יְיָ מָלָךְ, יְיָ יִמְלֹךְ לְעֹלָם וָעֶד.
4. יְיָ עֹז לְעַמּוֹ יִתֵּן, יְיָ יְבָרֵךְ אֶת עַמּוֹ בַשָּׁלוֹם.

1. *There is none like You among the gods [other people worship], Adonai, and there are no deeds like Yours.*
2. *Your sovereignty is an eternal sovereignty, and Your reign is from generation to generation.*
3. *Adonai is Ruler, Adonai ruled, Adonai will rule forever and ever.*
4. *May Adonai give strength to God's people, may Adonai bless God's people with peace.*

5

אֵין כָּמוֹךָ

Have students read silently the paragraph describing אֵין כָּמוֹךָ. Read line 1 in Hebrew aloud to the students, and have students respond by chorally reading its English meaning. Repeat this with lines 2, 3, and 4. Check that students understand the meaning of *sovereignty* (supreme power, free from external control) and *reign* (to rule as a supreme power).

Read lines 1–4 of אֵין כָּמוֹךָ, one Hebrew phrase at a time, having students chorally repeat each phrase, and then each line. Have partners practice reading these lines. Challenge students to identify words from this passage by asking them questions such as: Which words have the root letters מלכ? (מַלְכוּתְךָ, מַלְכוּת, מֶלֶךְ, מָלָךְ, יִמְלֹךְ) Which word in line 4 has bless or praise as part of its meaning? (יְבָרֵךְ) Which word is spelled two different ways? (אֲדֹנָי, יְיָ)

Digital Application

Tell students that at home, before the next class, they should sign onto the software, then click on Jerusalem on the Contents map or אֵין כָּמוֹךָ/אַב הָרַחֲמִים to enter Level 1—and then click on the Torah scroll to practice reading

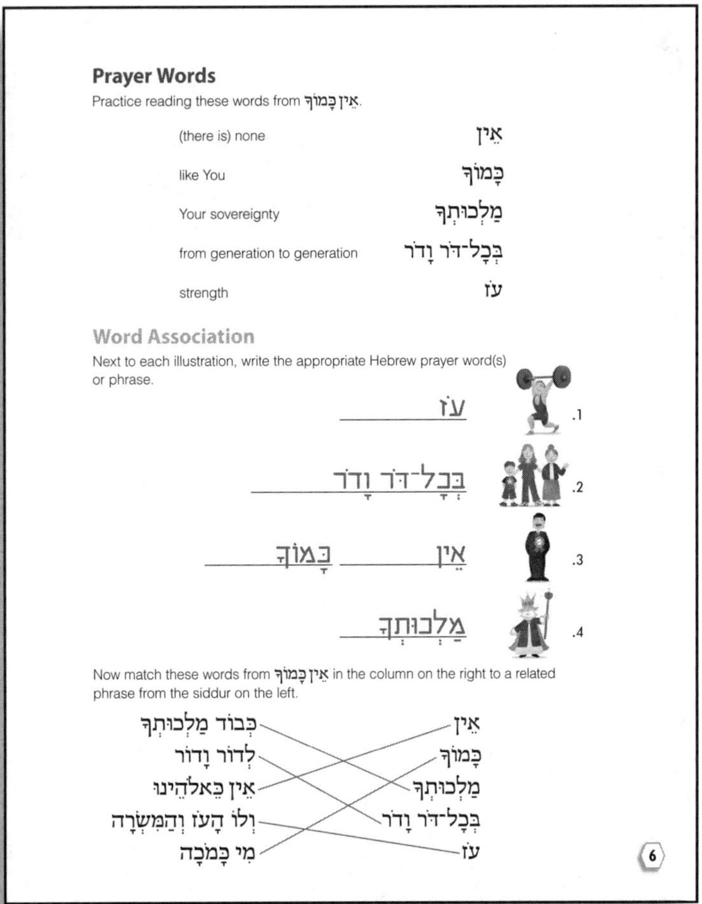

Prayer Words

Practice reading these words from אֵין כָּמוֹךָ.

(there is) none	אֵין
like You	כָּמוֹךָ
Your sovereignty	מַלְכוּתְךָ
from generation to generation	בְּכָל־דֹּר וָדֹר
strength	עֹז

Word Association

Next to each illustration, write the appropriate Hebrew prayer word(s) or phrase.

1. עֹז
2. בְּכָל־דֹּר וָדֹר
3. אֵין כָּמוֹךָ
4. מַלְכוּתְךָ

Now match these words from אֵין כָּמוֹךָ in the column on the right to a related phrase from the siddur on the left.

כְּבוֹד מַלְכוּתְךָ	אֵין
לְדוֹר וָדוֹר	כָּמוֹךָ
אֵין כֵּאלֹהֵינוּ	מַלְכוּתְךָ
וְלוֹ הָעֹז וְהַמִּשְׂרָה	בְּכָל־דֹּר וָדֹר
מִי כָּמֹכָה	עֹז

6

word is related to "rule." Have each group present its clue to the class.

Have students individually complete the first part of "Word Association" by writing the appropriate Hebrew word or phrase next to each illustration. Students then check their work with a partner.

Direct partners to take turns reading the Hebrew words in columns as follows: Student א reads the first word in the right-hand column (אֵין); student ב responds by reading its related phrase (אֵין כֵּאלֹהֵינוּ). Student ב then reads the next word in the right hand column, and student א reads the matching phrase. Students draw lines to match the words to the related phrases.

Consider challenging students to name prayer(s) that include the related phrases. *(From top to bottom:* אַשְׁרֵי*; Shabbat Amidah* קְדוּשָּׁה*;* אֵין כֵּאלֹהֵינוּ*;* אֲדוֹן עוֹלָם*;* מִי כָמֹכָה*)*

Digital Application

In Level 1 of the digital application, have students click on the activities light bulb and then "Matching." Here, אֵין כָּמוֹךָ. In the next session, divide the class into two groups: א and ב. Have א students practice reading lines 1 and 2 with a partner, and ב students practice reading lines 3 and 4 with a partner. After group members are comfortable reading their section, direct each א student to partner with a ב student. Partners practice reading the entire prayer; students coach one another to gain fluency.

Teach, or invite the cantor or music specialist to teach, students to chant אֵין כָּמוֹךָ. Consider teaching lines 1 and 2 during one class session, and lines 3 and 4 during the next session.

Adonai and *Elohim*

Focus students on the two spellings of *Adonai*: יְיָ and אֲדֹנָי. Remind students that יְהוָה is also pronounced *Adonai*. However, when יְהוָה immediately follows אֲדֹנָי, the vocalization of יְהוָה is similar to that of אֱלֹהִים and the phrase is read as *Adonai Elohim*. Consider having your students use a humash to find and read aloud אֲדֹנָי יְהוָה in Genesis 15:2, Genesis 15:8, or Deuteronomy 9:26.

Prayer Words

Display word cards 1–5 on the ledge of the chalkboard or whiteboard. Ask: Which two words have the same suffix? (מַלְכוּתְךָ, כָּמוֹךָ) What is the basic meaning of this suffix? *(you or your)* If students have studied *Kol Yisrael 2*, challenge them to identify the phrases that mean "from generation to generation" (בְּכָל־דֹּר וָדֹר), like You (כָּמוֹךָ), and Your sovereignty (מַלְכוּתְךָ). Invite volunteers to act out the meanings of עֹז and אֵין. Classmates guess which word is acted out.

Word Association

Divide the class into five groups. Assign each group one key prayer word, and direct groups to create a clue to remember the meaning of their word. For example, the ךָ ending in מַלְכוּתְךָ tells us that "you" or "your" are part of the word's meaning, and the root letters מלכ tell us the students will review new vocabulary by matching illustrations to מַלְכוּתְךָ, אֵין כָּמוֹךָ, יִשְׂרָאֵל, עֹז, and בְּכָל־דּוֹר וָדוֹר. In the next class session, use word cards 1–5 (a set of both Hebrew and English words) to play a matching game in class.

You and Yours

To give your students extra practice in decoding, direct students to turn back to page 5 and to identify the four words that end in ךָ. (וּמֶמְשַׁלְתְּךָ, מַלְכוּתְךָ, כְּמַעֲשֶׂיךָ, כָּמוֹךָ) Write these words on the board. For fun, invite a student to come to the board and point to one word at a time, in any order. Ask students, or small groups of students, to chorally read the word as the student points to it. Challenge students to read the four words fluently in under fifteen, and then in under ten, seconds.

At the Root

Direct students to read the first three sentences of "At the Root" silently. Ask: What is the basic meaning of the root מלכ? *(ruler, king, or sovereign)* What does מֶלֶךְ mean? *(ruler, king)* Write the letters כּ, כ, and ךְ on the board. Remind students that these three letters are the same letter in different forms. Direct students to work with a partner and complete "At the Root."

Challenge students to circle all the words on page 5 that have the root מלכ. *(line 2—*מַלְכוּת, מַלְכוּתְךָ*; line 3—*מֶלֶךְ, מָלָךְ, יִמְלֹךְ*)* Have partners read aloud phrases 1–6 at the bottom of page 7. Students should mark a crown above the words that have "ruler" or "king" as part of their meaning *(1—*מֶלֶךְ*; 2—*מַלְכוּתֶךָ*; 3—*מַלְכוּתוֹ*; 4—*מֶלֶךְ*; 5—*בְּמַלְכוּתְךָ*; 6—*לְמֶלֶךְ*)* and put a check next to the phrases in which God is called יְיָ מֶלֶךְ *(1 and 4)*.

At the Root

אֵין כָּמוֹךָ speaks of God as a מֶלֶךְ, which means ruler or king (sometimes translated as **sovereign**).

The root of מֶלֶךְ is מלכ.

The root מלכ tells us that **ruler** or **king** is part of a word's meaning.

God is sometimes called יְיָ מֶלֶךְ. Fill in the missing English translation:

Adonai (is) Ruler

Reread אֵין כָּמוֹךָ on page 5 and circle the words that are built on the root מלכ.

How many words did you circle? 5

The suffix ךָ means **you** or **your**. Write the word in line 2 of אֵין כָּמוֹךָ that is built on the root מלכ and ends with the suffix meaning **your**. מַלְכוּתְךָ

How many other words in line 2 end with the suffix meaning **you** or **your**? 1

Practice reading the following prayer phrases. Draw a crown above each word that has **ruler** or **king** as part of its meaning. Put a check next to the phrases in which God is called יְיָ מֶלֶךְ.

✔ 1. וַיֵּשֶׁב יְיָ מֶלֶךְ לְעוֹלָם

2. וְעֵינֵינוּ תִּרְאֶינָה מַלְכוּתֶךָ

3. בָּרוּךְ שֵׁם כְּבוֹד מַלְכוּתוֹ לְעוֹלָם וָעֶד

✔ 4. יְיָ מֶלֶךְ לְעוֹלָם וָעֶד

5. יִשְׂמְחוּ בְמַלְכוּתְךָ שׁוֹמְרֵי שַׁבָּת

6. וְהָיָה יְיָ לְמֶלֶךְ עַל כָּל הָאָרֶץ

7

Word Tree

To reinforce the concept of Hebrew roots:

- On a sheet of construction paper, draw a tree with three roots, eight branches, and one or two large leaves on each branch.
- Write מלכ on the roots—one letter on each root.
- Write מַלְכוּתְךָ on one leaf. Invite students to fill in the other leaves with the words circled on page 5 (מַלְכוּתְךָ, מַלְכוּת, מֶלֶךְ, מָלָךְ, יִמְלֹךְ) and the words marked with a crown on page 7 (מֶלֶךְ, מַלְכוּתְךָ, מַלְכוּתוֹ, מֶלֶךְ, בְּמַלְכוּתְךָ, לְמֶלֶךְ). Inform students that they will add additional leaves as they study new prayers.

Ruler Readings

As a class, practice reading the prayer phrases at the bottom of page 7. Divide the class into two groups, א and ב. Explain that Group א will read all the words in a phrase, except for words that have the root letters מלכ. Those words will be read by Group ב. For example, when reading line 1, א reads וַיֵּשֶׁב יְיָ, Group ב reads מֶלֶךְ, and Group א reads לְעוֹלָם. After groups have read all six lines, have the groups reverse their roles. Group ב reads all the words except for those that have the root letters מלכ. Those words are read by Group א.

אַב הָרַחֲמִים

The first part of the Torah service continues with אַב הָרַחֲמִים. This prayer describes God as a merciful parent and trustworthy ruler. It also asks for God's protection over Jerusalem. Practice reading אַב הָרַחֲמִים.

1. אַב הָרַחֲמִים, הֵיטִיבָה בִרְצוֹנְךָ אֶת צִיּוֹן;
2. תִּבְנֶה חוֹמוֹת יְרוּשָׁלָיִם.
3. כִּי בְךָ לְבַד בָּטָחְנוּ, מֶלֶךְ אֵל רָם וְנִשָּׂא,
4. אֲדוֹן עוֹלָמִים.

1. Merciful Parent, favor Zion with Your goodness;
2. rebuild the walls of Jerusalem.
3. For in You alone do we trust, sovereign God, high and exalted,
4. eternal Ruler.

At the Root

The root of הָרַחֲמִים is רחמ.

The root רחמ tells us that **mercy** or **compassion** is part of a word's meaning.

God is sometimes called אַב הָרַחֲמִים. Fill in the missing English translation:

Merciful Parent

Here are three other names by which God is known. Circle the root letters רחמ in each phrase.

אֵל מָלֵא רַחֲמִים	אֵל רַחוּם וְחַנּוּן	הָרַחֲמָן
God Full of Mercy	Compassionate and Gracious God	The Merciful One

Why do you think Judaism emphasizes that God is merciful? ______________

____

8

As a class, discuss why it is important for us to act with mercy. Together, define mercy. (*treating someone who is in a bad situation with kindness and compassion*)

Word Tree

Create a tree based on the root רחמ, as you did for מלכ (see page 23). Include the four words found in "At the Root." (הָרַחֲמָן, הָרַחֲמִים, רַחֲמִים, רַחוּם)

אַב הָרַחֲמִים

Have students read silently the paragraph introducing אַב הָרַחֲמִים. Read aloud the first Hebrew phrase of line 1. Have the class chorally read this phrase after you. Call on pairs of students to read the phrase. Repeat this with the second phrase of line 1, and then with all of line 1. Have the class chorally read the English meaning for this line. Repeat this for each of the remaining lines of אַב הָרַחֲמִים.

Call on volunteers to read in Hebrew and in English the line which: describes God as the eternal Ruler *(line 4)*; speaks of God as a merciful parent *(line 1)*; states that God is our trustworthy Ruler *(line 3)*; asks that God protect Jerusalem *(line 2)*.

Digital Application

Tell students that at home, before the next class, they should enter Level 1—and then click on the Torah scroll to practice reading אַב הָרַחֲמִים. In the next class, divide the class into two groups: א and ב. Have א students practice reading lines 1 and 2 with a partner, and ב students practice reading lines 3 and 4 with a partner. After group members are comfortable reading their section, direct each א student to partner with a ב student. Partners practice reading the entire prayer while students coach one another to gain fluency.

Teach, or invite the cantor or music specialist to teach, students to chant אַב הָרַחֲמִים. Then lead students in singing אֵין כָּמוֹךָ (page 5) followed by אַב הָרַחֲמִים.

At the Root

Call on a volunteer to read aloud the English words of "At the Root." Have students complete all but the final question of the activity with a partner. Individually, students write why they believe Judaism emphasizes that God is merciful. Students share their response with their partner. *(Responses may include: to give us hope, to encourage us to be merciful, to stress the importance of mercy.)*

Prayer Words

Present word cards 6–10. As you display each card, call on students to read the word in Hebrew and to say its English meaning.

Invite a student to the front of the room. Direct the student to stand in front of you, facing the class. As you stand behind the student, show the rest of the class one of the words. Challenge the student standing in front of you to guess which word is being displayed. The student may ask the class "yes" and "no" (or כֵּן and לֹא) questions about the word. For example, a student might ask, "Does the word end in ם?" Once the student has guessed the word and said its meaning, invite another student to guess a second word.

Call on a student to name the word that has the root letters רחמ. (הָרַחֲמִים)

It's Our Motto

Have students work with a partner to complete "It's Our Motto."

Distribute, or ask students to take out, a few coins and/or dollar bills. Challenge students to find the phrase on the coin or bill that mentions God. *(IN GOD WE TRUST)* Inform students that this phrase, which first appeared on coins in the 1860s, has appeared on almost every coin in the United States since 1938 and on every bill since the mid-1960s. Discuss, What is your opinion about having this phrase on our money?

Digital Application

Tell students to click on the activities light bulb in Level 1 and play "Crossword" to review new vocabulary, which includes the five new prayer words as well as: צִיּוֹן (Zion), תּוֹרָה (Torah), and שַׁבָּת (Shabbat). At the next class, display word cards 6–10. Ask: Which of these words describes something that surrounds Jerusalem? (חוֹמוֹת)

Prayer Words

Practice reading these words from אַב הָרַחֲמִים.

parent, father	אַב, אָב
merciful, the mercy	הָרַחֲמִים
walls	חוֹמוֹת
and exalted	וְנִשָּׂא
eternal	עוֹלָמִים

It's Our Motto

Write the English meaning next to each Hebrew word. Then copy the boxed letters to find the missing word below.

1. אַב — p a r e n [t]
2. עוֹלָמִים — e t e [r] n a l
3. הָרַחֲמִים — m e r c i f [u] l
4. חוֹמוֹת — w a l l [s]
5. וְנִשָּׂא — a n d e x a l [t] e d

The motto of the United States is: In God we t r u s t (1 2 3 4 5)

Bonus Points: Write the word in line 3 of אַב הָרַחֲמִים on page 8 that means **we trust**.

Hint: The root letters are בטח.

בָּטַחְנוּ

9

Prayer Chart

Inform students that this year they will learn about the Torah service and the concluding Shabbat morning prayers. Explain that as they study *Kol Yisrael 3* they will create a display that outlines its prayers. Your students may have created a similar chart of the Shabbat morning prayers while studying *Kol Yisrael 2*.

Write אֵין כָּמוֹךָ on a 4″ x 6″ index card and affix it to a bulletin board. Write אַב הָרַחֲמִים on a second card and affix it below the אֵין כָּמוֹךָ card. Tell students that each time they learn a new prayer in *Kol Yisrael 3*, they will add the name of the prayer to the display.

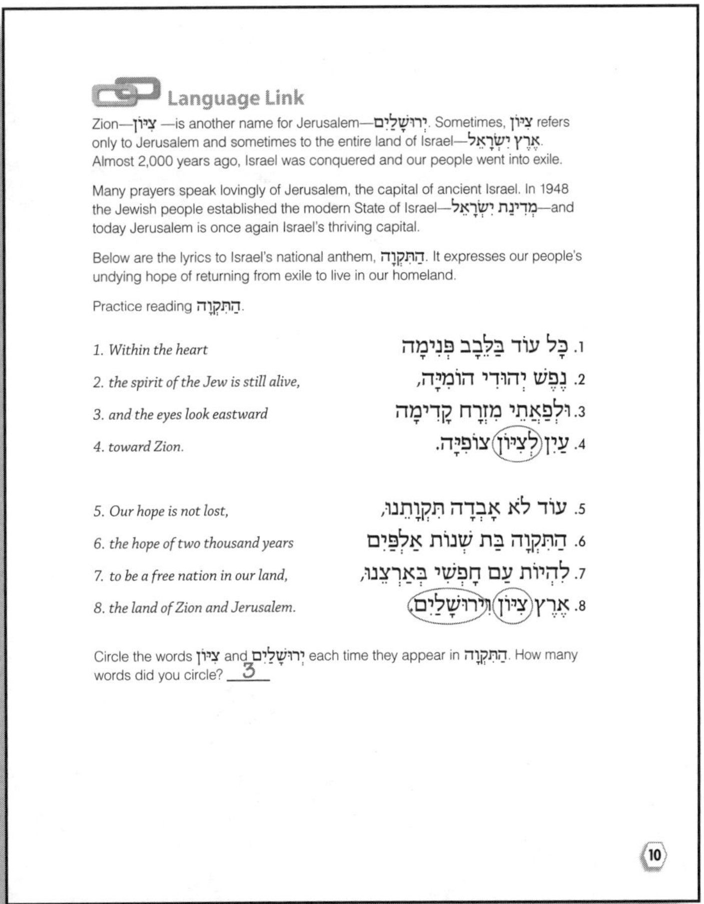

Language Link

Zion—צִיּוֹן —is another name for Jerusalem—יְרוּשָׁלַיִם. Sometimes, צִיּוֹן refers only to Jerusalem and sometimes to the entire land of Israel—אֶרֶץ יִשְׂרָאֵל. Almost 2,000 years ago, Israel was conquered and our people went into exile.

Many prayers speak lovingly of Jerusalem, the capital of ancient Israel. In 1948 the Jewish people established the modern State of Israel—מְדִינַת יִשְׂרָאֵל—and today Jerusalem is once again Israel's thriving capital.

Below are the lyrics to Israel's national anthem, הַתִּקְוָה. It expresses our people's undying hope of returning from exile to live in our homeland.

Practice reading הַתִּקְוָה.

1. Within the heart	1. כָּל עוֹד בַּלֵּבָב פְּנִימָה
2. the spirit of the Jew is still alive,	2. נֶפֶשׁ יְהוּדִי הוֹמִיָּה,
3. and the eyes look eastward	3. וּלְפַאֲתֵי מִזְרָח קָדִימָה
4. toward Zion.	4. עַיִן לְצִיּוֹן צוֹפִיָּה.
5. Our hope is not lost,	5. עוֹד לֹא אָבְדָה תִּקְוָתֵנוּ,
6. the hope of two thousand years	6. הַתִּקְוָה בַּת שְׁנוֹת אַלְפַּיִם
7. to be a free nation in our land,	7. לִהְיוֹת עַם חָפְשִׁי בְּאַרְצֵנוּ,
8. the land of Zion and Jerusalem.	8. אֶרֶץ צִיּוֹן וִירוּשָׁלַיִם.

Circle the words צִיּוֹן and יְרוּשָׁלַיִם each time they appear in הַתִּקְוָה. How many words did you circle? 3

10

teach, the national anthem to your class. Alternatively, show students a variety of YouTube videos of הַתִּקְוָה being sung. If students already know how to chant הַתִּקְוָה, call on a volunteer to hold up an Israeli flag and invite the class to stand and join in singing הַתִּקְוָה.

Digital Application

Tell students that at home, before the next class, they should click on אֵין כָּמוֹךָ/אָב הָרַחֲמִים to enter Level 1—and then click on the Torah scroll to practice reading הַתִּקְוָה. Consider establishing the singing of הַתִּקְוָה as a regular opening or closing ritual for your classes.

Have students click on the camera in Level 1 to view photographs of Jerusalem. Included are photos of (1) the welcome sign at Ben Gurion airport; (2) the Dome of the Rock in the Old City; (3) the Western Wall and its plaza; (4) a playful sculpture, called *Musi and Musa,* from the Ruth Youth Wing of the Israel Museum; and (5) the bronze monument, located across the street from the Knesset, of the Menorah from the Holy Temple.

Language Link

Have students read "Language Link" silently. Ask recall and open-ended questions, such as: What does צִיּוֹן refer to? *(Jerusalem and/or the entire land of Israel)* Approximately how many years ago did Israel become a state? *(current year - 1948 = x)* Why do you think someone would write a poem about the hope of returning to the land of Israel? *(Responses may include: Israel has been our homeland for thousands of years, they may not be able to live freely as Jews in their own country, they want a homeland where all Jewish people are welcome.)*

If you have access to a computer in class, have students research the origins of הַתִּקְוָה. *(written in the 1870s, decades before Israel became a state; many years later in November, 2004, became the official national anthem of the State of Israel.)*

Read aloud line 1 in Hebrew. Have students respond by reading its English translation. Read all of הַתִּקְוָה, alternating Hebrew and English. Have students work in small groups and reflect on the meaning of הַתִּקְוָה. Give groups a set of guiding questions. For example: Which lines tell you that this poem was written before Israel became a state? What makes הַתִּקְוָה a Jewish poem? How do you know הַתִּקְוָה is about our connection with the Land of Israel? What image do you like best in הַתִּקְוָה? Why? Call on a representative from each group to share its responses.

Direct students to complete the activity at the bottom of the page. Challenge students to circle these same words in the prayer אָב הָרַחֲמִים (page 8). *(last word in lines 1 and 2)*

Have students practice reading הַתִּקְוָה with a partner. Suggest that partners begin by reading line 1 together, then each partner reads it alone, and finally the partners read the line together again.

Have partners repeat this process—reading together, reading individually, reading together—for each of the lines of הַתִּקְוָה.

If your students are not familiar with הַתִּקְוָה, teach, or invite the cantor or music specialist to

The Israel Connection

Write אַהֲבַת צִיּוֹן on the board and have the entire class, and then groups of students, read this phrase aloud. Tell students that אַהֲבַת צִיּוֹן, love of Israel, is a key Jewish value.

Divide the class into groups of 3–4 students. Direct each group to read the opening paragraph on page 11 together. Group members should then discuss other ways to show אַהֲבַת צִיּוֹן and suggest how these activities strengthen one's Jewish identity. *(Answers might include: Listening to Israeli music connects me to musicians and teens in Israel today; I feel connected to Israel and proud of being Jewish when I follow Israeli sports.)* Call on a representative from each group to share its suggestions. After the class has heard from each group, students independently complete "The Israel Connection."

Pick the Pix

Invite the class to chorally read the caption below the two photographs. Ask: What is the English meaning of the caption? *(The land of Zion and Jerusalem)* What do we learn about Israel from these photos? *(Responses may include: Israel is both ancient and modern; Israelis go shopping just like us)* Inform students that throughout Israel one sees constant reminders, such as remnants of an ancient wall near a modern building, that Israel is both ancient and modern.

Have students individually complete "Pick the Pix." Ask all students who chose the photo of the Western Wall to go to one side of the classroom and ask those who chose the photo of the store to go to the other side of the room. Direct each group to list five reasons why they think the photo they chose best illustrates Israel. Invite a representative from each group to read its list.

Direct students to now choose which of the two places they would rather visit. Ask all students who want to visit the wall to go to one side of the classroom and all those who would rather shop in the store to go to the other side of the room. Call on volunteers to explain their choice.

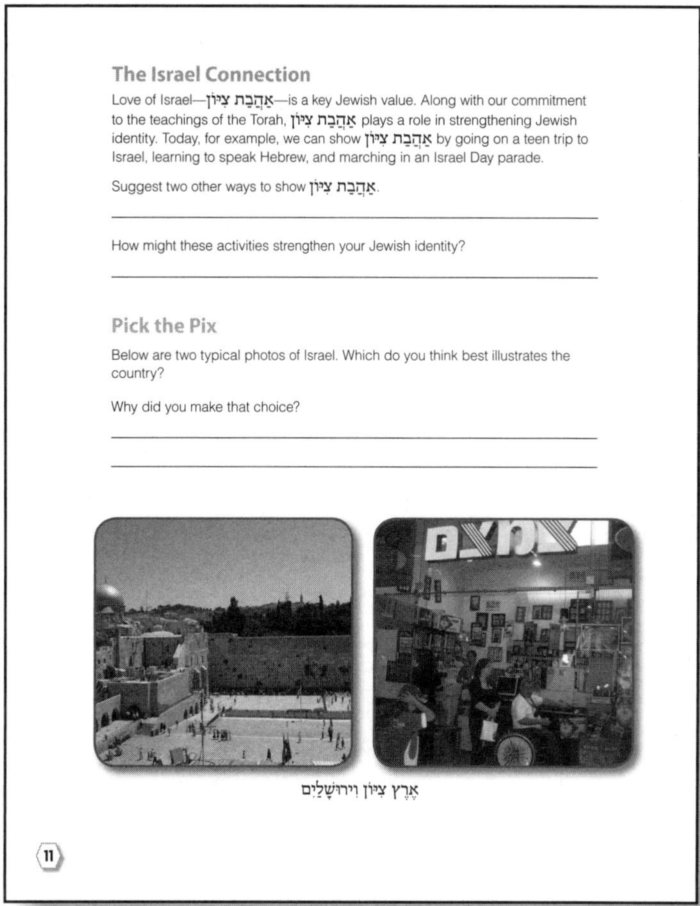

The Israel Connection

Love of Israel—אַהֲבַת צִיּוֹן—is a key Jewish value. Along with our commitment to the teachings of the Torah, אַהֲבַת צִיּוֹן plays a role in strengthening Jewish identity. Today, for example, we can show אַהֲבַת צִיּוֹן by going on a teen trip to Israel, learning to speak Hebrew, and marching in an Israel Day parade.

Suggest two other ways to show אַהֲבַת צִיּוֹן.

How might these activities strengthen your Jewish identity?

Pick the Pix

Below are two typical photos of Israel. Which do you think best illustrates the country?

Why did you make that choice?

אֶרֶץ צִיּוֹן וִירוּשָׁלַיִם

11

Reroll the Scroll

The תּוֹרָה is divided into 54 portions—פָּרָשׁוֹת. Each Shabbat we read a portion—פָּרָשָׁה—in synagogue. It takes one full year to complete our reading of the תּוֹרָה. And, as soon as we finish, on the holiday of שִׂמְחַת תּוֹרָה, we roll the scroll back to the beginning and start over again.

The ancient sage Ben Bag-Bag (yes, that's his name!) taught:

הֲפֹךְ בָּהּ וַהֲפֵךְ בָּהּ...

Turn it [the Torah] again and again, for everything is in it; think about it... (Pirke Avot 5:25)

Explain what you think Ben Bag-Bag meant.

____

____

Why do *you* think we read the Torah, year after year, from our youth through old age?

____

____

Parashah Quiz

Read aloud the names of the first six פָּרָשׁוֹת in the Torah. Circle the פָּרָשָׁה that tells the story of Noah and the ark. Underline the פָּרָשָׁה that refers to our matriarch Sarah.

בְּרֵאשִׁית (נֹחַ) לֶךְ־לְךָ וַיֵּרָא <u>חַיֵּי שָׂרָה</u> תּוֹלְדֹת

Challenge: Copy the name of the פָּרָשָׁה that includes the story of creation AND is the name of the first book of the Torah. בְּרֵאשִׁית

12

Reroll the Scroll

Ask volunteers to name the Torah portion they will read the day that they become bar or bat mitzvah and to tell something they know about their Torah or haftarah reading.

Have students silently read the opening paragraph on page 12. Ask both recall and open-ended questions about the paragraph. Questions may include: How many Torah portions are there? *(54)* How long does it take to complete the reading of the Torah? *(one year; three years for congregations that follow the triennial cycle. Those congregations read approximately the first third of a parashah one year, the second third the following year, and the third part in the third year.)* Why do you think there is a holiday to celebrate the completion and beginning of reading the Torah? *(Answers may include: because it is such an important occasion; to remind us of the continuous cycle of Torah reading.)*

As a class, chorally read the Hebrew and English quote from Ben Bag-Bag. (Your students may be amused to know that the next teaching in Pirkei Avot [5:26] is a quote from Ben Hei-Hei.) Divide the class into groups of 3–4 students. Direct groups to discuss and then write what they think Ben Bag-Bag meant and why they think we read the Torah every year. Ask a representative from each group to share its responses with the class.

Call on volunteers to identify stories in the Torah they have studied more than once. *(Responses may include: the Creation story; the story of Noah; the story of Jonah)* Ask students to describe differences between the first and second times they studied the story. *(Answers may include: When I first learned the story of Creation, I only thought about the creations for each day. Later I thought about the belief that we are created in God's image and that it is our responsibility to care for others and for the world. When I first heard the story of Jonah, I thought it was a great adventure story; now I understand that it teaches us to change our ways to do better.)*

Parashah Quiz

Read aloud the names of the six פָּרָשׁוֹת, one פָּרָשָׁה at a time, pausing for students to chorally read each name after you. Lead the students in a choral reading of all six names. Have students practice reading the names with a partner. Direct partners to complete the activity and check their work with another pair of students.

Ask students to identify the פָּרָשָׁה that will be read when they become a bat or bar mitzvah. If possible, obtain a list of your students' פָּרָשׁוֹת from your education director. Create a chart that includes the name of the student, his or her פָּרָשָׁה, and when it will be read. List the פָּרָשׁוֹת according to the order in which students will become bar or bat mitzvah. Display the list.

Throughout this Teacher's Edition, you will see a פָּרָשָׁה icon indicating that a verse quoted in the student edition is read in a particular פָּרָשָׁה. For example, there is a note and a on page 32 of this Teacher's Edition indicating that Genesis 12:9—which appears on page 14 of the student edition—is found in פָּרָשַׁת לֶךְ־לְךָ. Be sure to alert students when the student edition includes a verse that appears in their Torah or haftarah reading.

My Reflections on the Prayer

As a year-long project, consider having each student create a folder of reflections on the prayers. Note that your students may have done a similar folder or booklet when studying *Kol Yisrael 2*. Prepare a page of prompts for each student to complete for every prayer. Prompts can include: The name of this prayer is.... Some important words in this prayer are.... Root letters that repeat in this prayer are.... In this prayer we.... This prayer is important because.... I carry out a Jewish value or mitzvah related to this prayer when I.... Your students may add a new page to their personal reflections as they study each new prayer. Keep each student's sheets in a folder. Students will compile the pages and create a cover at the end of the year.

Clue to Cyberspace

Have students work with a partner to answer the questions and fill in the missing words in Clue to Cyberspace. After filling in the words, students read the sentences aloud with a partner. Direct one partner to read the even-numbered sentences and the other to read the odd-numbered sentences. Students should then switch so that they each read all of the sentences. As a class, chant all of אֵין כָּמוֹךָ and אַב הָרַחֲמִים.

Place word cards 1–10 plus any five word cards from later chapters on the ledge of the chalkboard or whiteboard. Invite a student to pick out the words that are part of אֵין כָּמוֹךָ and אַב הָרַחֲמִים. Tell students that at home, before the next class, they should click on the joystick to play the Lion's Bird House game. In the first two boards, they must smash the eggs containing words that are not part of אֵין כָּמוֹךָ or אַב הָרַחֲמִים, and then smash the word from the prayer.

Remind students to use the clue—מֶלֶךְ—to score bonus points on the third board of this online game in Level 1—אֵין כָּמוֹךָ and אַב הָרַחֲמִים.

Clue to Cyberspace

מַלְכוּתְךָ מַלְכוּת מֶלֶךְ מָלָךְ יִמְלֹךְ

Write the root on which these words are built. מ ל כ

Write the general meaning of these words. ruler, king

Now choose the correct words from the list above to fill in the blanks. *Hint 1:* You will use one of the words twice. *Hint 2:* If you need help, turn to pages 5 and 8.

1. אֵין כָּמוֹךָ בָאֱלֹהִים אֲדֹנָי, וְאֵין כְּמַעֲשֶׂיךָ.
2. מַלְכוּתְךָ מַלְכוּת כָּל־עֹלָמִים, וּמֶמְשַׁלְתְּךָ בְּכָל־דּוֹר וָדֹר.
3. יְיָ מֶלֶךְ, יְיָ מָלָךְ, יְיָ יִמְלֹךְ לְעֹלָם וָעֶד.
4. יְיָ עֹז לְעַמּוֹ יִתֵּן, יְיָ יְבָרֵךְ אֶת עַמּוֹ בַשָּׁלוֹם.
5. אַב הָרַחֲמִים, הֵיטִיבָה בִרְצוֹנְךָ אֶת צִיּוֹן;
6. תִּבְנֶה חוֹמוֹת יְרוּשָׁלָיִם.
7. כִּי בְךָ לְבַד בָּטָחְנוּ, מֶלֶךְ אֵל רָם וְנִשָּׂא,
8. אֲדוֹן עוֹלָמִים.

Which word did you use twice? מֶלֶךְ

Use this clue to complete the last board in the "Lion's Bird House" game in Level 1 on your computer.

13

Assessment

As students are working on any of the above activities, meet individually with students to assess reading fluency and knowledge of prayer content. Use the Prayer Mastery Assessment Chart on page 17 of the Teacher's Edition to keep track of student progress. You can also assess students' progress online at www.behrmanhouse.com. Click on the blue "Assessment" button at the bottom of the screen, select *Kol Yisrael 3*, and type in your class's serial number to see how students are doing in the software. Students can also e-mail their lesson summary to you directly or print out a lesson summary and bring it in to class.

What's Next?

Draw two columns on a large sheet of paper. Label one column: We expect; label the second column: We find. Ask: What might you expect to be expressed in the prayers recited as we open the Ark and take the Torah out of the Ark? *(Possible answers include: the Torah is holy; we thank God for giving us the Torah; we care about the Torah.)* List students' suggestions in the "We expect" column. Inform students that in the next chapter they will learn the meaning of the prayers that are recited as we open the Ark and remove the Torah from the Ark. They will then compare their expectations of the prayers to the actual prayers.

2 כִּי מִצִּיּוֹן/בָּרוּךְ שֶׁנָּתַן/שְׁמַע/גַּדְּלוּ לַייָ/לְךָ יְיָ

ABOUT THE PRAYER

We recite גַּדְּלוּ לַייָ, שְׁמַע, בָּרוּךְ שֶׁנָּתַן, כִּי מִצִּיּוֹן and לְךָ יְיָ as we open the Ark and remove the Torah. The words of these prayers link our past to our present and future, honor the Land of Israel and the Torah, and praise God for giving us the Torah,

LEARNING OBJECTIVES

Students will be able to:

- Recite גַּדְּלוּ לַייָ, שְׁמַע, בָּרוּךְ שֶׁנָּתַן, כִּי מִצִּיּוֹן and לְךָ יְיָ fluently.
- Explain that these prayers affirm our loyalty to God and praise God's greatness.
- Describe the choreography associated with removing the Torah from the Ark, according to the customs of your congregation.
- Define key words and the roots שלמ and קדש.
- Locate the Negev on a map of Israel.

ESSENTIAL QUESTION

How are the Land of Israel and the Torah continuing sources of strength to the Jewish people?

NEW WORDS AND PHRASES

Prayer Words:

(God's) name, his name	שְׁמוֹ
glorify	גַּדְּלוּ
the greatness	הַגְּדֻלָּה
and the power	וְהַגְּבוּרָה
in heaven	בַּשָּׁמַיִם
and on earth	וּבָאָרֶץ
out of Zion, from Zion	מִצִּיּוֹן
shall go forth	תֵּצֵא
from Jerusalem	מִירוּשָׁלַיִם
who gave, that gave	שֶׁנָּתַן
to God's people	לְעַמּוֹ
in (God's) holiness	בִּקְדֻשָּׁתוֹ
one	אֶחָד

INSTRUCTIONAL MATERIALS

Text pages 14–25

Word cards 11–23

Digital application: Level 2— גַּדְּלוּ לַייָ/לְךָ יְיָ/ כִּי מִצִּיּוֹן/בָּרוּךְ שֶׁנָּתַן (see page 8 for a list of games and activities)

WHERE WE ARE

Walking in the Negev Desert with Ben and Batya, we connect to our past as we recall Abraham, who journeyed in the same desert thousand of years ago. Similarly, the prayers we recite as we take the Torah from the Ark connect us with our past, and our future, as we give honor to the Land of Israel, to the Torah, and to God.

INTRODUCING THE LESSON

Take your students to your congregation's sanctuary or chapel. Direct students to stand as you open the Ark for them to see the Torahs. Call on volunteers to describe the Torahs and their ornaments. Ask students to sit as you close the Ark. Have students brainstorm a list of items they will want to know to prepare them to properly take a Torah out of the Ark. Record the students' suggestions. Tell the students that they will learn all about taking a Torah out of the Ark as they study Chapter 2 of *Kol Yisrael 3*.

2 כִּי מִצִּיּוֹן/בָּרוּךְ שֶׁנָּתַן/שְׁמַע/גַּדְּלוּ לַייָ/לְךָ יְיָ

"Israel is awesome." Batya said to Ben, several weeks after their arrival. "One moment we're in the Negev Desert walking the same paths as Abraham. The next we're seeing signs of the future—like the Negev's drip irrigation system. Did you know Israel is called the Silicon Valley of water technology?"

Torah Travel Genesis 12:9 says: וַיִּסַּע אַבְרָם הָלוֹךְ וְנָסוֹעַ הַנֶּגְבָּה "Abram continued on his way toward the Negev." Locate and circle the Negev—נֶגֶב—on the map on page 3.

Which do you think would be more interesting, meeting Abraham in the Negev or meeting someone who lives in the future? Why? ______________________

____

כִּי מִצִּיּוֹן, the prayer we recite as we remove the Torah from the Ark, provides yet another link in the age-old chain connecting our past and future. It honors the Land of Israel and the Torah as continuing sources of strength.

Why do you think the study of Torah—תַּלְמוּד תּוֹרָה—is an essential part of Jewish tradition?

____

____

14

INTO THE TEXT

As a class, read aloud the title of the chapter: כִּי מִצִּיּוֹן/בָּרוּךְ שֶׁנָּתַן/שְׁמַע/גַּדְּלוּ לַייָ/לְךָ יְיָ. Explain that these five prayers are recited as we take the Torah from the Ark. Challenge students to identify and to say the English meaning of Hebrew words or roots they recognize in the names of these prayers. *(*צִיּוֹן*—Zion;* בָּרוּךְ*—blessed, praised;* גדל*—great, big;* יְיָ*—Adonai)* Invite students to guess, based on these words, what they expect the prayers to be about.

Invite students to tell about a historical place they have visited and to describe how it felt being at the exact location that a famous event took place or a famous person once stood. A student might say, for example, that it was awesome visiting Independence Hall in Philadelphia, where Benjamin Franklin signed the Constitution. Explain that Ben and Batya experienced this sense of amazement when they visited the Negev Desert and walked the same paths as Abraham.

Ask questions about the Negev based on the illustration on page 14. Suggested questions include: How can you tell it is very hot in the Negev? *(People are wearing shorts and hats.)* Why is there little vegetation? *(There is little rain in the desert; people plant the vegetation and then have to irrigate the land.)* What do you think it is like to live in the desert? *(open-ended)* Assign students a web search of photos or information about the Negev.

Digital Application

At home, or in class, have students click on the Negev on the Contents map or on the prayers listed for Level 2 and then click on the camera to view photographs of the Negev. Included are photos of (1) camels and horses in the desert, (2) an irrigation hose on a giant spool, (3) irrigated fields, (4) hills, (5) desert plants and trees, and (6) rock formations.

Direct students to read silently the first paragraph on page 14. Explain that a drip irrigation system is different from a sprinkler system. Drip irrigation applies water slowly and directly to the soil, only where the water is needed. Check that your students understand that "the Silicon Valley of" means that Israel is *the* high-tech place for water technology.

Torah Travel

As a class, chorally read the verse from Genesis 12:9.

Inform students that this verse is read as part of פָּרָשַׁת לֶךְ־לְךָ. Explain that according to Genesis 17:5, when God tells אַבְרָם that God will make him the father of a great nation, God changes אַבְרָם's name to אַבְרָהָם. Write on the board: מִצְרָיְמָה = to מִצְרַיִם; אַרְצָה = to the אֶרֶץ. Challenge students to derive the meaning of this ָה ending *(to)* and of הַנֶּגְבָּה *(to the Negev)*. Have students locate and circle the נֶגֶב on the map on page 3.

Direct students to read and discuss the rest of page 14 with a partner. Allow students time to write their responses. Invite volunteers to share what they have written. Have students suggest questions they would like to ask Abraham. *(Possible questions include: How did you get water in the desert? What were your neighbors like? What was your greatest challenge?)*

Call on volunteers to explain why, in their opinion, תַּלְמוּד תּוֹרָה is an essential part of Jewish tradition. *(Responses may include: because the Torah teaches us the story of our people, because the Torah teaches us mitzvot, because the Torah teaches us about important Jewish values.)*

כִּי מִצִּיּוֹן

Direct students to read silently the first sentence on page 15. Have students underline what the כִּי מִצִּיּוֹן prayer expresses. *(our connection to Torah; our hope that the Torah's lessons of justice and peace will spread throughout the world)*

Read aloud the first Hebrew quote from Leviticus. Challenge students to identify and say the English of familiar words. *(וְאָהַבְתָּ—you shall love; כָּמוֹךָ—like you)* Lead the class in reading all three quotes in both Hebrew and English. Pause after each quote and call on students to explain their understanding of the quote and how it applies to us today. *(Line 1—We should care about other people as much as we care about ourselves, we should put ourselves in the other person's shoes; Line 2—Don't take advantage of someone who has a handicap, don't mislead someone by purposely giving bad advice; Line 3—Donate food to or help feed the hungry)*

Have students choose the quote they find most important. Direct students who chose the first quote to walk to one corner of the room, students who chose the second quote to walk to another corner, and those who chose the third quote to walk to a third corner. Allow the groups a few minutes to discuss why they feel their quote is the most important. Call on a representative from each group to describe the importance of their quote.

Inform students that all of these quotes are read as part of פָּרָשַׁת קְדֹשִׁים, in which we read that, since we are a holy people, we must behave according to certain rules. All of these quotes teach important laws that help us to make the world a better place.

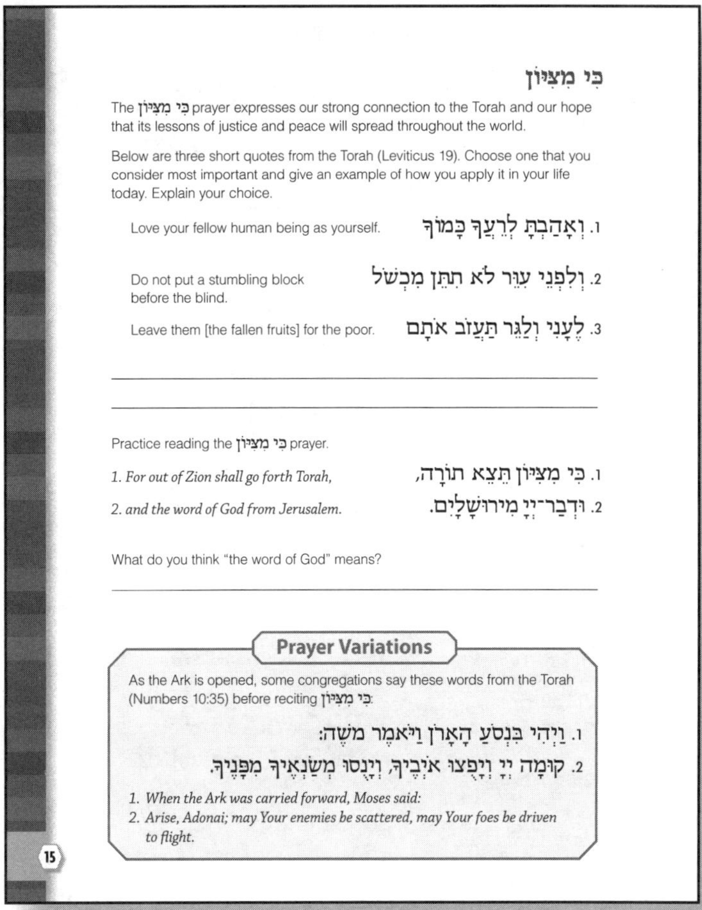

כִּי מִצִּיּוֹן

The כִּי מִצִּיּוֹן prayer expresses our strong connection to the Torah and our hope that its lessons of justice and peace will spread throughout the world.

Below are three short quotes from the Torah (Leviticus 19). Choose one that you consider most important and give an example of how you apply it in your life today. Explain your choice.

Love your fellow human being as yourself.	1. וְאָהַבְתָּ לְרֵעֲךָ כָּמוֹךָ
Do not put a stumbling block before the blind.	2. וְלִפְנֵי עִוֵּר לֹא תִתֵּן מִכְשֹׁל
Leave them [the fallen fruits] for the poor.	3. לֶעָנִי וְלַגֵּר תַּעֲזֹב אֹתָם

Practice reading the כִּי מִצִּיּוֹן prayer.

1. For out of Zion shall go forth Torah,	1. כִּי מִצִּיּוֹן תֵּצֵא תוֹרָה,
2. and the word of God from Jerusalem.	2. וּדְבַר־יְיָ מִירוּשָׁלָיִם.

What do you think "the word of God" means?

Prayer Variations

As the Ark is opened, some congregations say these words from the Torah (Numbers 10:35) before reciting כִּי מִצִּיּוֹן:

1. וַיְהִי בִּנְסֹעַ הָאָרֹן וַיֹּאמֶר מֹשֶׁה:
2. קוּמָה יְיָ וְיָפֻצוּ אֹיְבֶיךָ, וְיָנֻסוּ מְשַׂנְאֶיךָ מִפָּנֶיךָ.

1. When the Ark was carried forward, Moses said:
2. Arise, Adonai; may Your enemies be scattered, may Your foes be driven to flight.

15

Reading כִּי מִצִּיּוֹן

Read aloud line 1 in Hebrew. Have the class chorally repeat. Call on pairs of students to read the line. Repeat with line 2. Challenge students to identify and give the English meaning of familiar words. *(צִיּוֹן—Zion, תּוֹרָה—Torah, יְרוּשָׁלַיִם—Jerusalem)* Have the class chorally read the English translation of lines 1 and 2. Call on volunteers to explain their understanding of "the word of God." Inform students that lines 1 and 2, which have similar meanings, are an example of ancient Hebrew poetry, which often has parallel ideas in different lines.

Prayer Variations וַיְהִי בִּנְסֹעַ

Introduce the Hebrew of וַיְהִי בִּנְסֹעַ as you have done with previous prayers: Read a Hebrew phrase, have the students chorally read the phrase; introduce a new phrase, have students repeat that phrase; string the two phrases together, have students chorally read the two phrases.

Continue introducing the remainder of the prayer phrase by phrase.

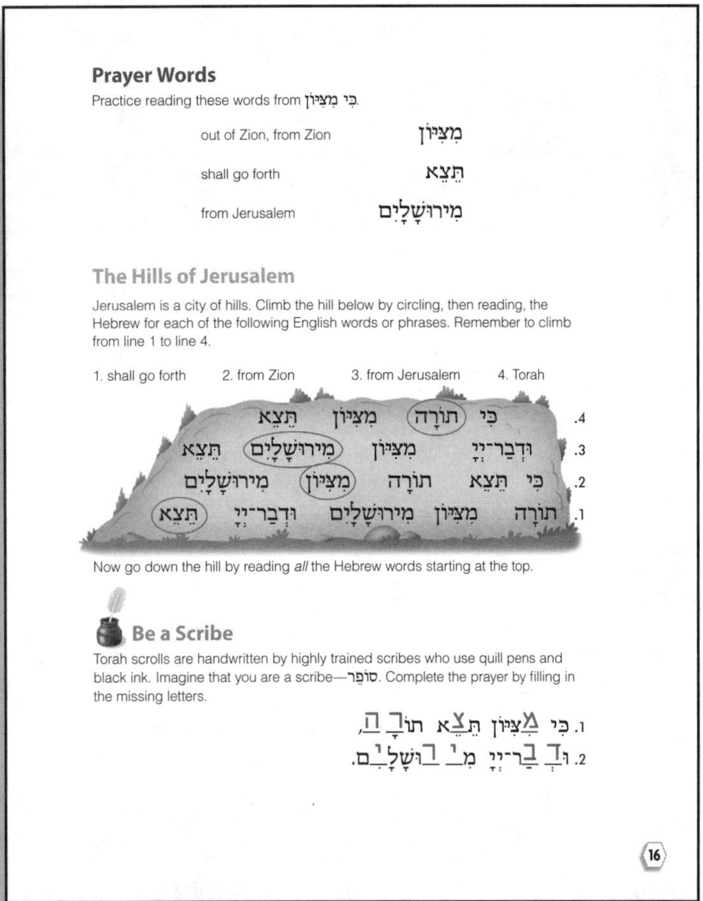

Prayer Words

Practice reading these words from כִּי מִצִּיּוֹן.

out of Zion, from Zion	מִצִּיּוֹן
shall go forth	תֵּצֵא
from Jerusalem	מִירוּשָׁלָיִם

The Hills of Jerusalem

Jerusalem is a city of hills. Climb the hill below by circling, then reading, the Hebrew for each of the following English words or phrases. Remember to climb from line 1 to line 4.

1. shall go forth 2. from Zion 3. from Jerusalem 4. Torah

Now go down the hill by reading *all* the Hebrew words starting at the top.

Be a Scribe

Torah scrolls are handwritten by highly trained scribes who use quill pens and black ink. Imagine that you are a scribe—סוֹפֵר. Complete the prayer by filling in the missing letters.

1. כִּי _צִיּוֹן תֵּצֵא תוֹ_ _,
2. וּ_ _ר־יְיָ מִ_ _וּשָׁלָ_ם.

16

volunteer to open the Ark, and motion for all students to stand as the Ark is opened and they chant כִּי מִצִּיּוֹן and וַיְהִי בִּנְסֹעַ.

Alternatively, take your class to the congregation's chapel to practice singing these prayers, opening the Ark, and standing while the Ark is open.

Prayer Words

Present word cards 11–13. As you display each card, call on students to read the word in Hebrew and to say its English meaning. Ask: Which two words have similar meanings? *(מִצִּיּוֹן and מִירוּשָׁלָיִם)* Which part of these words mean "from"? *(מִ)*

The Hills of Jerusalem

Have students work with a partner. Partners begin by reading aloud line 1, the bottom line, and then circling the word that means "shall go forth." (תֵּצֵא) Partners continue reading line by line and circling the Hebrew for the English words or phrases. Direct partners to chorally read all the words starting at the top, and to then take turns reading alternate lines.

Call on a volunteer to read line 1 as a narrator, and another volunteer to do a dramatic reading of line 2 as Moses. Note that וַיְהִי בִּנְסֹעַ is a verse found in פָּרָשַׁת בְּהַעֲלֹתְךָ. Inform students that the Ark mentioned in this verse is the Ark of the Covenant, not an Ark in which we place a Torah. According to tradition, the Ark of the Covenant was built during the time of Moses as a portable wooden box, covered in gold, to house the tablets of the Ten Commandments. Ask: Why do you think the Ark of the Covenant was connected with defeating enemies? *(Responses may include: God's laws helped the Israelites be strong and fight enemies; God's word gave them courage.)*

Digital Application

Tell students that at home, before the next class, they should click on the Negev on the Contents map or on the prayers listed for Level 2, and then click on the Torah scroll to practice reading כִּי מִצִּיּוֹן. In the next session, divide the class into two groups: א and ב. Have א students practice reading lines 1 and 2 with a partner, and ב students practice reading lines 3 and 4 with a partner.

After group members are comfortable reading their section, direct each א student to partner with a ב student. Partners practice reading the entire prayer; students coach one another to gain fluency.

Teach, or invite the cantor or music specialist to teach, students to chant כִּי מִצִּיּוֹן and וַיְהִי בִּנְסֹעַ.

Experiencing Torah

Ask your education director or rabbi if there is a miniature Ark and Torah (printed on paper, not a kosher Torah) for use in the classroom. If so, set the Ark up by the eastern wall of the class.

Once students have learned to chant כִּי מִצִּיּוֹן and וַיְהִי בִּנְסֹעַ, use the Ark as you practice reciting the prayers along with the choreography of the Torah service.

Lead students in singing אֵין כָּמוֹךָ (page 5) followed by אַב הָרַחֲמִים (page 8). Call on a

Challenge students to identify words from this activity. For example, ask students to read the word or phrase: whose meaning is similar to the meaning of מִירוּשָׁלָיִם *(מִצִּיּוֹן)*; that includes God's name *(וּדְבַר־יְיָ)*; that means "shall go forth." *(תֵּצֵא)*

Be a Scribe

Direct students to individually complete the prayer by filling in the missing letters. Walk around the room to do an informal assessment of students' familiarity with these words. As a class, read these two lines chorally.

Putting It in ConTEXT

Inform your students that the prophet Isaiah was born in Jerusalem in the eighth century BCE. Remind students that BCE indicates "before the common era," meaning before the year 0, or before the birth of Jesus. Challenge your students to calculate approximately how many years ago Isaiah was born. *(765 + current year = x)* Explain that Isaiah prophesied during the time that the Assyrians conquered the northern kingdom of Israel and threatened to destroy the southern kingdom, Judah.

Have students read silently the introductory paragraph. Read aloud the first Hebrew line of Isaiah 2:4, direct students to chorally read its English meaning. Continue alternating reading each Hebrew line and having students chorally read the corresponding English.

If your class has access to the Internet, divide the class into four groups. Assign each group one of the following tasks: find and print one or two images of a plowshare; find and print one or two images of a pruning hook; prepare a definition of a plowshare; prepare a definition of a pruning hook. Have each group share its image or definition with the class.

If your class does not have access to the Internet, prepare and present these images and definitions to help students gain a greater understanding of this quote from Isaiah.

Putting It in ConTEXT

The words of כִּי מִצִּיּוֹן come from Isaiah 2:3. The next verse, Isaiah 2:4, introduces the prophet's vision of how there will be peace throughout the world when all nations follow ethical laws:

...וְכִתְּתוּ חַרְבוֹתָם לְאִתִּים
וַחֲנִיתוֹתֵיהֶם לְמַזְמֵרוֹת.
לֹא־יִשָּׂא גוֹי אֶל־גּוֹי חֶרֶב
וְלֹא־יִלְמְדוּ עוֹד מִלְחָמָה.

...They shall beat their swords into plowshares
and their spears into pruning hooks.
Nation shall not raise sword against nation
and never again will they know war.

Describe what peace means to you. How does your vision compare to Isaiah's?

____

____

____

At the Root

Part of the name יְרוּשָׁלַיִם is built on the root שׁלמ. Words that are built on שׁלמ have **wholeness** or **peace** as part of their meaning. In fact, Jerusalem is often called the "City of Peace."

Write the root letters of יְרוּשָׁלַיִם: מ ל שׁ *Reminder:* ם is a final מ.

17

Call on volunteers to act out the first two lines of Isaiah 2:4. Ask: What kind of work do people do with plowshares and pruning hooks? *(agricultural)* What do people do with swords and spears? *(fight)* What kind of world was Isaiah envisioning? *(Responses may include: a world in which people no longer needed weapons; Isaiah hoped for peace; he wanted people to be able to farm and not have to go to war.)* Guide students to understand that Isaiah was envisioning a world in which people could be productive and not destructive, and the Jewish people could live freely.

Direct students to complete individually "Putting It in ConTEXT" and to share their responses with a partner.

Teach, or invite the cantor or music specialist to teach, students to sing "Lo Yisa Goy."

At the Root

Write יְרוּשָׁלַיִם and שׁלמ on the board. Call on a volunteer to circle the root letters found in יְרוּשָׁלַיִם.

Direct students to complete the activity and write the root letters of the second part of יְרוּשָׁלַיִם.

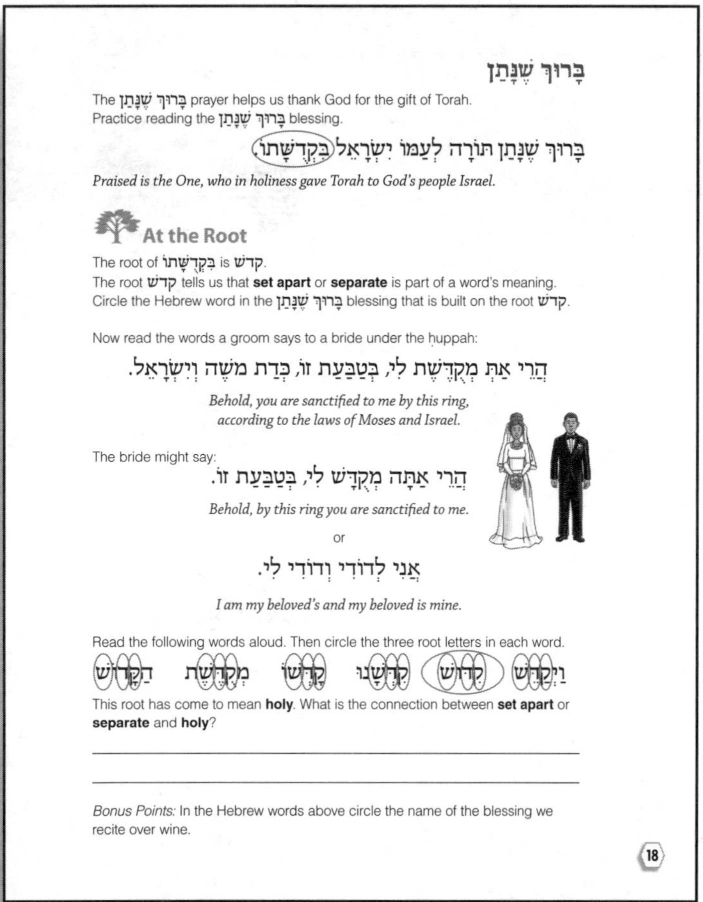

בָּרוּךְ שֶׁנָּתַן

The בָּרוּךְ שֶׁנָּתַן prayer helps us thank God for the gift of Torah.
Practice reading the בָּרוּךְ שֶׁנָּתַן blessing.

בָּרוּךְ שֶׁנָּתַן תּוֹרָה לְעַמּוֹ יִשְׂרָאֵל בִּקְדֻשָּׁתוֹ.

Praised is the One, who in holiness gave Torah to God's people Israel.

At the Root

The root of בִּקְדֻשָּׁתוֹ is קדשׁ.
The root קדשׁ tells us that **set apart** or **separate** is part of a word's meaning.
Circle the Hebrew word in the בָּרוּךְ שֶׁנָּתַן blessing that is built on the root קדשׁ.

Now read the words a groom says to a bride under the ḥuppah:

הֲרֵי אַתְּ מְקֻדֶּשֶׁת לִי, בְּטַבַּעַת זוֹ, כְּדַת מֹשֶׁה וְיִשְׂרָאֵל.

Behold, you are sanctified to me by this ring, according to the laws of Moses and Israel.

The bride might say:

הֲרֵי אַתָּה מְקֻדָּשׁ לִי, בְּטַבַּעַת זוֹ.

Behold, by this ring you are sanctified to me.

or

אֲנִי לְדוֹדִי וְדוֹדִי לִי.

I am my beloved's and my beloved is mine.

Read the following words aloud. Then circle the three root letters in each word.

וַיְקַדֵּשׁ קָדוֹשׁ קִדְּשָׁנוּ קָדְשׁוֹ מְקֻדֶּשֶׁת הַקָּדוֹשׁ

This root has come to mean **holy**. What is the connection between **set apart** or **separate** and **holy**?

____

____

Bonus Points: In the Hebrew words above circle the name of the blessing we recite over wine.

18

Word Tree

Consider creating a tree based on the root שלם, as you did for מלכ (see page 23). Include, for example, שָׁלוֹם, בִּשְׁלוֹמֶךָ, and יְרוּשָׁלַיִם.

בָּרוּךְ שֶׁנָּתַן

Read the first three Hebrew words of בָּרוּךְ שֶׁנָּתַן aloud. Direct the class to read these same words chorally. Read and then have the class repeat the next two words. Read aloud בִּקְדֻשָּׁתוֹ; have students practice reading this word. Have partners practice reading the full line.

Direct students to work with a partner to write four questions based on this verse. The questions should start as follows: Who...? How...? Why...? What...? Partners might write, for example: *Who gave Israel the Torah? How did Israel get the Torah? Why do we praise God? What was given to the people Israel?* Invite volunteers to ask one of their questions and to call on classmates to answer the question.

Teach, or invite the cantor or music specialist to teach, students to chant בָּרוּךְ שֶׁנָּתַן.

Digital Application

Tell students that at home, before the next class, they should click on the Negev or on the prayers listed for Level 2 and then click on the Torah scroll to practice reading בָּרוּךְ שֶׁנָּתַן.

At the Root

Write בִּקְדֻשָּׁתוֹ on the board. Invite a volunteer to circle its root letters (קדשׁ). If your students have studied *Kol Yisrael 2*, challenge them to define the meaning of קדשׁ *(holy, set apart, separate)*. As a class, brainstorm places and things that are holy. *(Answers might include: Jerusalem, a synagogue; Torah, prayer book.)* Inform students that in the Bible and siddur, the Jewish people are often described as an עַם קָדוֹשׁ, a holy nation. According to Leviticus 19:1–2, God instructs Moses to speak to all of the Israelite community and say to them: "You shall be holy, because I, Adonai your God, am holy." Ask: What does it mean to be a holy people? *(Possible answers include: to act ethically; to have a special relationship with God.)* What are the responsibilities of a holy people? *(Suggestions may include: to treat others with respect; to take care of the needy; to give thanks to God.)* Explain that just as our relationship with God is holy, the relationship of a married couple is holy.

Have students read silently the first three sentences of "At the Root" and circle the Hebrew word built on קדשׁ in בָּרוּךְ שֶׁנָּתַן. *(בִּקְדֻשָּׁתוֹ)*

Read aloud the Hebrew words recited by a groom under the ḥuppah. Have students chorally read the English. Ask: Which English word indicates that the relationship being established is holy? *(sanctified)* Which phrase tells us that this is according to Jewish law? *(according to the laws of Moses and Israel.)* Explain that this statement legally binds two people in marriage. Read the Hebrew sentences a bride might recite, and have the students chorally read the English.

Have students work with a partner to complete the activities at the bottom of the page.

Word Tree

Create a tree based on the root קדשׁ, as you did for מלכ (see page 23). Include the words בִּקְדֻשָּׁתוֹ, קִדְּשָׁנוּ, קָדוֹשׁ, וַיְקַדֵּשׁ, מְקֻדָּשׁ, מִקְדֶּשֶׁת, קָדְשׁוֹ, and הַקָּדוֹשׁ, found in "At the Root" on page 18.

Prayer Words

Present the Hebrew and English of word cards 14–16. Ask questions about the new vocabulary, such as: Which word is built on the root letters קדשׁ? (בִּקְדֻשָּׁתוֹ) What is the Hebrew word for "to God's people"? (לְעַמּוֹ) Challenge students to find and underline each of the new prayer words in בָּרוּךְ שֶׁנָּתַן on page 18. *(second, fourth, and sixth words)*

To review prayer words from this chapter: Display word cards 11–16 on the board. Provide clues for each of the words, one word at a time, and ask students to find and read the correct word. For example: Which word includes the name of a city in Israel? (מִירוּשָׁלַיִם)

To God's People

Direct students to follow along silently as you read the English in "To God's People" and to join with you in chorally reading the Hebrew. For example, in the first line, you will read, "Look at the word." Students then join with you in reading "לְעַמּוֹ."

Have students individually circle the word part that means "his" *(*וֹ*)* in the five Hebrew words listed on the page and then check their work with a partner.

If your students have studied *Kol Yisrael 2*, challenge them to name and translate words that are related to the words listed in "To God's People." *(Words may include:* עַמְּךָ*—Your people;* קְדוּשָּׁה*—holiness;* אוֹר*—light;* שִׁמְךָ*—your name.)*

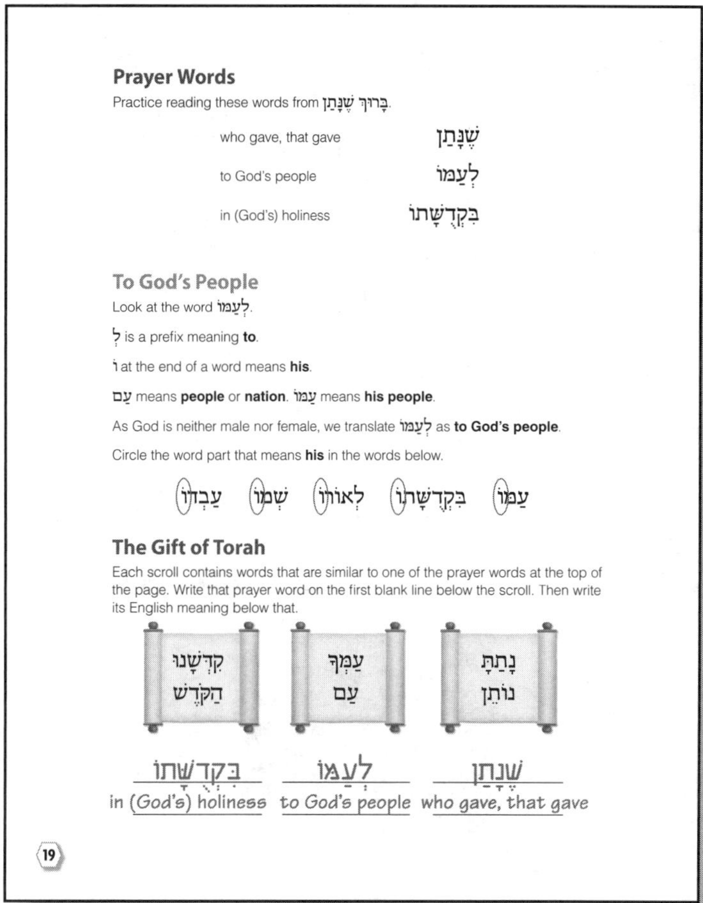

Prayer Words

Practice reading these words from בָּרוּךְ שֶׁנָּתַן.

who gave, that gave	שֶׁנָּתַן
to God's people	לְעַמּוֹ
in (God's) holiness	בִּקְדֻשָּׁתוֹ

To God's People

Look at the word לְעַמּוֹ.

לְ is a prefix meaning **to**.

וֹ at the end of a word means **his**.

עַם means **people** or **nation**. עַמּוֹ means **his people**.

As God is neither male nor female, we translate לְעַמּוֹ as **to God's people**.

Circle the word part that means **his** in the words below.

עַמּוֹ בִּקְדֻשָּׁתוֹ לְאוֹרוֹ שְׁמוֹ עַבְדּוֹ

The Gift of Torah

Each scroll contains words that are similar to one of the prayer words at the top of the page. Write that prayer word on the first blank line below the scroll. Then write its English meaning below that.

קִדְּשָׁנוּ הַקֹּדֶשׁ	עַמְּךָ עַם	נָתַתָּ נוֹתֵן
בִּקְדֻשָּׁתוֹ	לְעַמּוֹ	שֶׁנָּתַן
in (God's) holiness	to God's people	who gave, that gave

19

The Gift of Torah

Direct students to read the words in the Torah scrolls with a partner. Challenge students to circle two or three letters that the words in each scroll have in common. *(From right to left:* נת *[the final* נ *of the root has dropped out of the word* נָתַתָּ*];* עמ *[*ם *is the final form of* מ*];* קדשׁ*)* Have students individually complete the activity. Walk around the room to informally assess how well students can identify related words.

Pledging Our Allegiance

In many congregations, after the Torah scroll—סֵפֶר תּוֹרָה—is taken out of the Ark, the person who holds it recites the two statements below—one at a time—first alone, then with the congregation. In other synagogues, everyone recites the lines in unison. These statements are like a pledge of allegiance to God.

Practice reading these lines.

1. שְׁמַע יִשְׂרָאֵל, יְיָ אֱלֹהֵינוּ, יְיָ אֶחָד.

1. Hear O Israel: Adonai is our God, Adonai is One.

2. אֶחָד אֱלֹהֵינוּ, גָּדוֹל אֲדוֹנֵנוּ, קָדוֹשׁ שְׁמוֹ.

2. Our God is One and is great; God's name is holy.

What is the name of the prayer on the first line above? Why do you think we recite it when we take the Torah out of the Ark?

Prayer Variations

Some congregations add a third line. The person holding the Torah scroll turns to face the Ark and bows while reciting this line.

גַּדְּלוּ לַייָ אִתִּי, וּנְרוֹמְמָה שְׁמוֹ יַחְדָּו.

Glorify Adonai with me, and together let us exalt God's name.

סֵפֶר תּוֹרָה

20

then have students chorally read this phrase. Repeat this with the second phrase.

Teach, or invite your cantor or music specialist to teach, your students to chant גַּדְּלוּ לַייָ.

Remember to follow the tradition of your congregation. In some congregations, the leader recites each line alone and then with the congregation. In others, everyone recites the lines in unison.

Demonstrate, either in the chapel or in the classroom, singing שְׁמַע and אֶחָד אֱלֹהֵינוּ as you hold the Torah, then turn to face the Ark and bow as you chant גַּדְּלוּ לַייָ. Have all the students stand and chorally chant these three lines, bowing as they recite גַּדְּלוּ לַייָ. Invite individual volunteers to hold a Torah and lead the class in reciting these lines.

Photo Op

As a class, chorally read the photo's caption. Explain that a Torah scroll is called a סֵפֶר תּוֹרָה, literally, a book of Torah. Ask: How do you think the boy might be feeling? *(Answers may include: excited, nervous, proud.)*

Pledging Our Allegiance

Call on volunteers to define the term "pledge of allegiance." *(an oath or a promise of loyalty)* Have students read silently the opening paragraph on page 20. Ask recall and open-ended questions such as, Who recites these two declarations? *(the person holding the Torah)* Why do you think the whole congregation recites these lines? *(Answers may include: so each person promises to be loyal to God; to show we are a united community.)*

Read line 1 aloud in Hebrew, and have students chorally read the line after you. Have students join with you in reading the English meaning. Repeat this with line 2. Direct students to practice reading both lines with a partner. Ask students to reread the English and to jot down why, in their opinion, these statements are considered to be a "pledge of allegiance." Call on volunteers to share their ideas. *(Suggestions may include: because we are saying that Adonai is our God; because we declare our loyalty when we say that Adonai is our only God.)*

Have partners discuss why they think we recite the שְׁמַע as we take the Torah out of the Ark. Invite volunteers to share their ideas with the class. *(Possible responses include: "Hear O Israel" reminds us to listen to the words of the Torah; reciting these words reminds us that while we are all focusing our attention on the Torah, God alone is to be worshiped.)* Inform students that we do not cover our eyes when reciting this line of the שְׁמַע during the Torah service.

Teach, or invite your cantor or music specialist to teach, your students to chant these two lines.

Demonstrate, either in your congregation's chapel or in the classroom using a miniature Torah, taking the Torah out of the Ark and holding the Torah as you chant these lines. Invite volunteers to practice.

Prayer Variations

If your congregation recites גַּדְּלוּ לַייָ, introduce this prayer to your students. Read the first three words, and

Digital Application

Tell students that at home, before the next class, they should click on the Negev or on the prayers listed for Level 2 and then click on the Torah scroll to practice reading גַּדְּלוּ לַייָ. In the next class, have partners practice reading the entire prayer; encourage students to coach one another to gain fluency.

Prayer Words

Present the Hebrew and English of word cards 17–19. Invite a student to act out one of the words. Have others guess the word. The student who guesses correctly acts out another word.

If your students have studied *Kol Yisrael 2*, they will already be familiar with the word אֶחָד and related words, such as שִׁמְךָ *(Your name)* and גָּדְלֶךָ *(Your greatness)*.

Odd Word Out

Have partners read each of the lines aloud, circle the word that is not related, and write its English meaning. Challenge students to identify the three root letters, and their basic meaning, on which the related words of each line are built. *(1—מלכ—ruler, king; 2—קדש—set apart, separate, holy; 3—אהב—love)*

Consider having students cover page 20 as they individually complete the prayer at the bottom of page 21. Walk around the room to assess students' knowledge of the verses in the prayer.

Reading Review

Divide the class into two teams: א and ב. Provide clues for teams to identify and read a word in "Odd Word Out." For example, ask a team to read the word that: tells us to glorify God *(גַּדְּלוּ)*; is part of the blessing formula for a בְּרָכָה שֶׁל מִצְוָה *(קִדְּשָׁנוּ)*; is a number *(אֶחָד)*. Teams take turns identifying the words. If a team does not identify a word correctly, the other team is given the same clue. Award a team one point for each word it correctly identifies. The team with the most points wins.

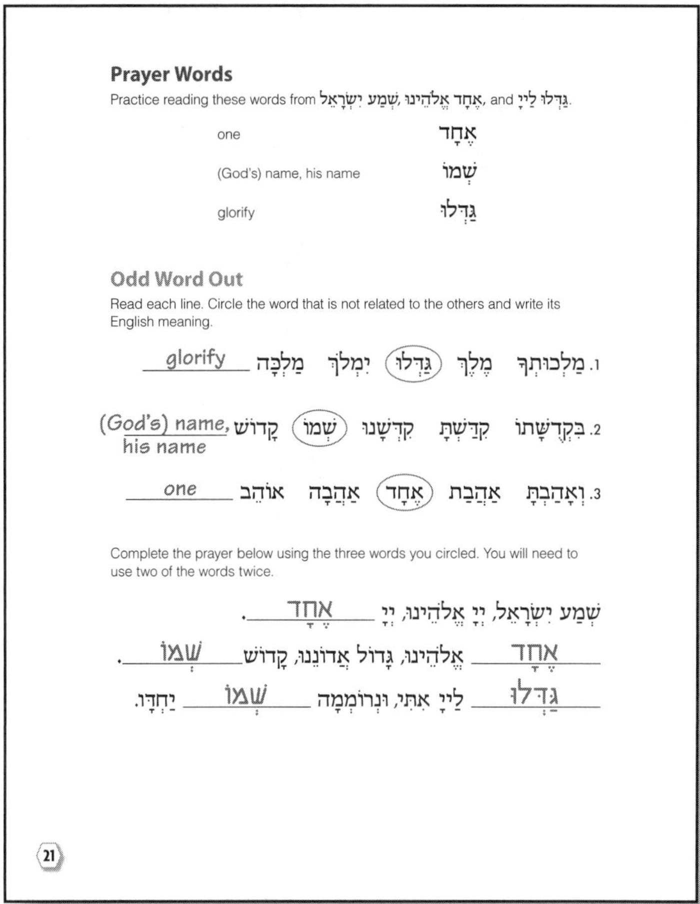

Prayer Words

Practice reading these words from שְׁמַע יִשְׂרָאֵל, אֶחָד אֱלֹהֵינוּ, and גַּדְּלוּ לַייָ.

one	אֶחָד
(God's) name, his name	שְׁמוֹ
glorify	גַּדְּלוּ

Odd Word Out

Read each line. Circle the word that is not related to the others and write its English meaning.

1. מַלְכוּתְךָ מֶלֶךְ גַּדְּלוּ יִמְלֹךְ מַלְכָּה ___glorify___
2. בִּקְדֻשָּׁתוֹ קִדַּשְׁתָּ קִדְּשָׁנוּ שְׁמוֹ קָדוֹשׁ ___(God's) name, his name___
3. וְאָהַבְתָּ אַהֲבַת אֶחָד אַהֲבָה אוֹהֵב ___one___

Complete the prayer below using the three words you circled. You will need to use two of the words twice.

שְׁמַע יִשְׂרָאֵל, יְיָ אֱלֹהֵינוּ, יְיָ ___אֶחָד___.

___אֶחָד___ אֱלֹהֵינוּ, גָּדוֹל אֲדוֹנֵנוּ, קָדוֹשׁ ___שְׁמוֹ___.

___גַּדְּלוּ___ לַייָ אִתִּי, וּנְרוֹמְמָה ___שְׁמוֹ___ יַחְדָּו.

21

Focus on גַּדְּלוּ לַייָ

If your congregation includes this verse, direct students to turn back to page 20 and to chorally read its English meaning. Ask: What does it mean to exalt? *(praise, give honor to)* What does it mean to glorify? *(praise, honor, give glory)* What are the parallels between the first three and last three words of this verse? *(They are both about honoring or praising God; they are both phrases made up of three words.)* In what other prayer did we see parallel, similar phrases? *(כִּי מִצִּיּוֹן, on page 15)* What is the leader inviting the congregation to do when the leader says גַּדְּלוּ לַייָ אִתִּי? *(to join the leader in praising God)* What would you expect to be included in the prayer that follows this verse? *(Answers may include: words that praise God, words that tell of God's greatness)*

לְךָ יְיָ

Have you ever held a Torah scroll? If so, you know how heavy it is! When you celebrate your bat or bar mitzvah, just before the Torah reading begins, you (or perhaps one of your family members) are likely to have the honor of carrying the Torah, fully dressed in its mantle and ornaments, up and down the rows of congregants.

Everyone will turn to keep the Torah—and you!—in sight. Some people touch the Torah with the fringes of their טַלִּיתוֹת or with their סִדּוּרִים, which they then kiss. During the procession we sing לְךָ יְיָ, a prayer that praises God. It reminds us that although we *honor* the Torah, we *worship* God.

Describe how you think it will feel to carry the Torah scroll through the sanctuary.

____

____

Practice reading לְךָ יְיָ.

1. לְךָ יְיָ הַגְּדֻלָּה וְהַגְּבוּרָה וְהַתִּפְאֶרֶת וְהַנֵּצַח וְהַהוֹד,
2. כִּי כֹל בַּשָּׁמַיִם וּבָאָרֶץ, לְךָ יְיָ הַמַּמְלָכָה
3. וְהַמִּתְנַשֵּׂא לְכֹל לְרֹאשׁ.

1. *Yours, God, is the greatness, and the power, and the glory, and the eternity, and the majesty,*
2. *for all that is in heaven and on earth is Yours. Yours is the sovereignty, God,*
3. *You are supreme over all.*

22

Demonstrate, either in the chapel or in the classroom, how the leader walks around the sanctuary with the Torah while chanting לְךָ יְיָ. Encourage your students to practice touching their prayer books to the Torah, and then kissing the prayer books, as the leader passes by with the Torah.

Digital Application

Tell students that at home, before the next class, they should click on the Negev or on the prayers listed for Level 2 and then click on the Torah scroll to practice reading לְךָ יְיָ. In the next class, divide the class into two groups: א and ב. Have א students practice reading line 1 with a partner, and ב students practice reading lines 2 and 3 with a partner. After group members are comfortable reading their section, direct each א student to partner with a ב student. Partners practice reading the entire prayer, students coach one another to gain fluency.

Word Tree

If you have created a word tree for the root מלכ (see page 23), add the word הַמַּמְלָכָה.

לְךָ יְיָ

Ask students to raise their hands if they have ever carried a Torah scroll. Call on volunteers to describe the experience.

Direct students to read the opening paragraphs about לְךָ יְיָ. Ask recall and open-ended questions.

Suggested questions include: When do we carry the Torah around the sanctuary? *(before the Torah reading)* How is the Torah dressed when we march with it? *(The Torah is dressed in its mantle and ornaments.)* Why do you think we praise God as we carry around the Torah? *(Answers may include: to declare our loyalty to God; because we worship God, not the Torah.)*

Demonstrate, in the sanctuary or in your classroom, how people touch the Torah with a tallit fringe (*tzitzit*) or siddur, and then kiss the spot that touched the Torah. Explain that we are not kissing the Torah; rather we are symbolically bringing the words of Torah to our lips.

Have students write how they think it will feel to carry the Torah through the sanctuary. Invite students to share their responses with a partner.

Read aloud the first three words of line 1. Have the class chorally read this phrase after you. Call on pairs of students to read the phrase. Repeat this with the next two words of line 1, and then with these two phrases combined. Next present the last two words of line 1, as you did the two previous phrases. Finally, have the class chorally read the full Hebrew line and its English meaning. Introduce the remaining lines of לְךָ יְיָ phrase by phrase.

Challenge students to identify various words and phrases. For example, have students read: the phrase that declares that all that is in heaven and on earth is God's *(line 2, first phrase)*; the word that is built on the root letters מלכ (*הַמַּמְלָכָה*); the two words that appear together twice (*לְךָ יְיָ*).

Teach, or invite your cantor or music specialist to teach, your students to chant לְךָ יְיָ.

Prayer Words

Present the Hebrew and English of word cards 20–23. As you display each card, call on students to read the word in Hebrew and to say its English meaning.

Invite a student to the front of the room. Direct the student to stand in front of you, facing the class. As you stand behind the student, show the rest of the class one of the words. Challenge the student standing in front of you to guess which word is being displayed. The student may ask the class "yes" and "no" (or כֵּן and לֹא) questions about the word. For example, a student might ask, Does the word end in ה? Once the student has guessed the word and said its meaning, invite another student to guess a second word.

The Secret Word

To review prayer words from this chapter play "The Secret Word" (see page 13) using word cards 11–23. For an added challenge, include word cards 1–10.

Digital Application

Tell students to click on the activities light bulb in Level 2 and play "Word Search" to review new vocabulary, which includes these Hebrew words: הַגְּדֻלָּה (the greatness), וְהַגְּבוּרָה (and the power), בַּשָּׁמַיִם (in heaven), and וּבָאָרֶץ (and on earth). At the next class, display word cards 18 and 20–23. Ask: Which of these words is related to the word גַּדְּלוּ? *(הַגְּדֻלָּה)*

Search and Circle

Have students work with a partner as they write the Hebrew words and circle them in the word search grid. Call on volunteers to read aloud the Hebrew words.

Have students find and underline the prayer words in לְךָ יְיָ on page 22. *(lines 1 and 2, third and fourth words)* Direct students to follow along as you read לְךָ יְיָ and to join with you in chorally reading the prayer words as you read those words. Next read the prayer by having half of the class, Group א, read all but the prayer words, and the other half of the class, Group ב, read only the prayer words. Finally, have the students switch so that Group ב reads all but the prayer words, and Group א reads only the prayer words.

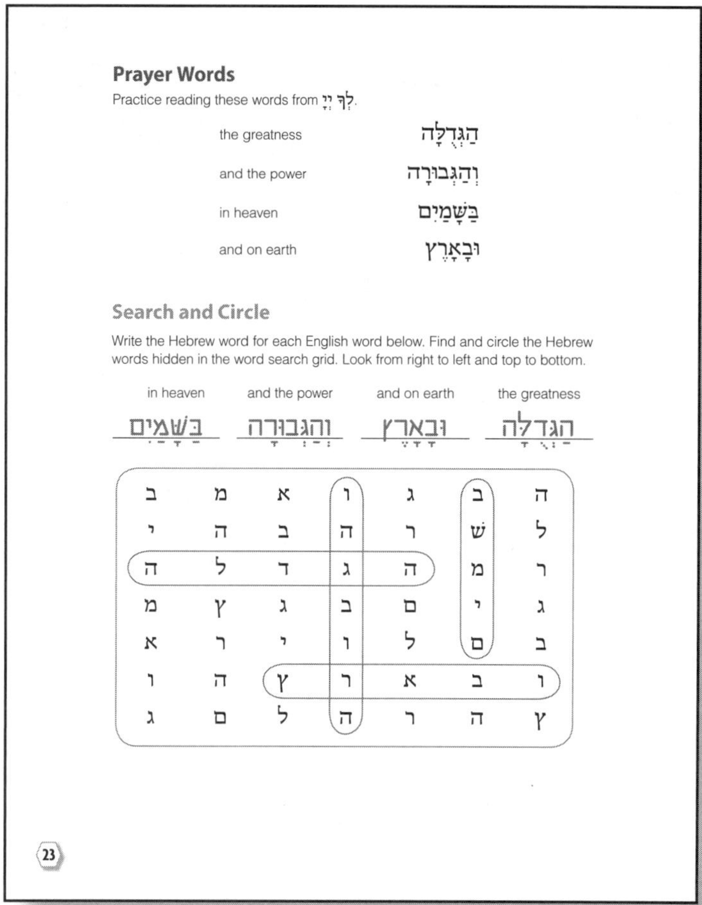

Prayer Words

Practice reading these words from לְךָ יְיָ.

the greatness	הַגְּדֻלָּה
and the power	וְהַגְּבוּרָה
in heaven	בַּשָּׁמַיִם
and on earth	וּבָאָרֶץ

Search and Circle

Write the Hebrew word for each English word below. Find and circle the Hebrew words hidden in the word search grid. Look from right to left and top to bottom.

in heaven	and the power	and on earth	the greatness
בַּשָּׁמַיִם	וְהַגְּבוּרָה	וּבָאָרֶץ	הַגְּדֻלָּה

ב	מ	א	ו	ג	ב	ה
י	ה	ב	ה	ר	שׁ	ל
ה	ל	ד	ג	ה	מ	ר
מ	ץ	ג	ב	ם	י	ג
א	ר	י	ו	ל	ם	ב
ו	ה	ץ	ר	א	ב	ו
ג	ם	ל	ה	ר	ה	ץ

23

What's It All About?

Review the list of expectations the class created during the "What's Next" activity at the end of Chapter 1 (see page 30). Draw an arrow from each correct prediction to the "We find" column. Ask students to name and list in the "We find" column elements that are found in the prayers from the Torah service that they did not predict. For example, students may not have predicted that these prayers would include the belief that "everything on earth belongs to God."

Prayer Chart

If you have begun a chart of the Shabbat morning service (see page 25), write each of the following on a 4" x 6" index card: כִּי מִצִּיּוֹן, בָּרוּךְ שֶׁנָּתַן, שְׁמַע, גַּדְּלוּ לַייָ, and לְךָ יְיָ, and add these new prayers to the chart.

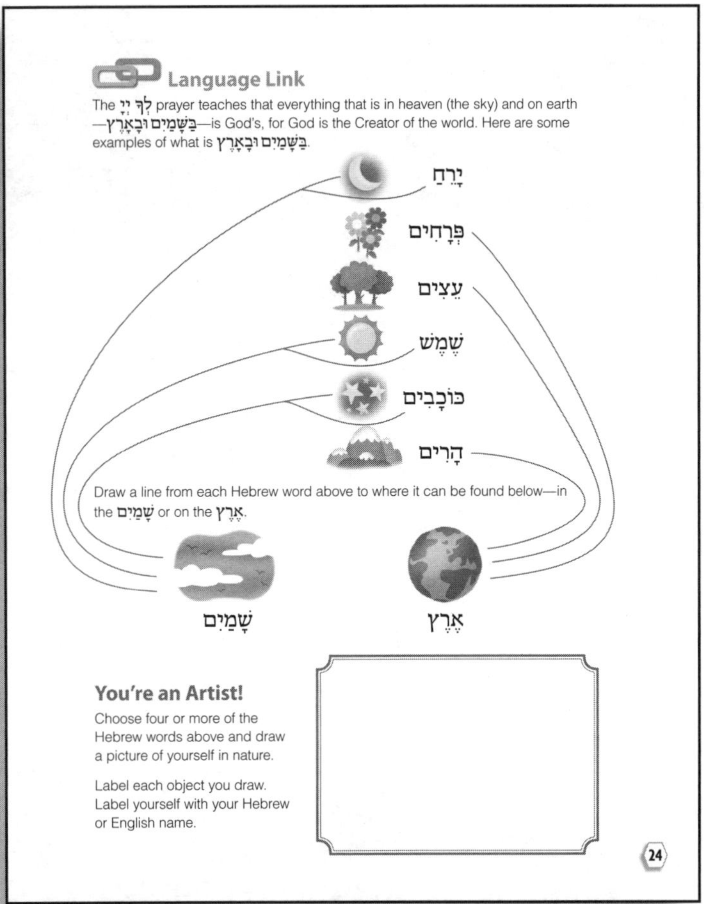

Language Link

The לְךָ יְיָ prayer teaches that everything that is in heaven (the sky) and on earth—בַּשָּׁמַיִם וּבָאָרֶץ—is God's, for God is the Creator of the world. Here are some examples of what is בַּשָּׁמַיִם וּבָאָרֶץ.

Draw a line from each Hebrew word above to where it can be found below—in the שָׁמַיִם or on the אֶרֶץ.

You're an Artist!

Choose four or more of the Hebrew words above and draw a picture of yourself in nature.

Label each object you draw. Label yourself with your Hebrew or English name.

24

My Reflections on the Prayer

If your students are creating a booklet of reflections on the prayers, give each student two pages of prompts to complete (see page 29). The first page should be devoted to בָּרוּךְ שֶׁנָּתַן, כִּי מִצִּיּוֹן, and שְׁמַע, and the second to גַּדְּלוּ לַייָ and לְךָ יְיָ. In addition, remember to have students draw an illustration or symbol to represent each prayer. Add these new pages to their folder or binder of personal reflections.

Language Link

Remind students that the לְךָ יְיָ prayer teaches that everything in heaven and the sky and on earth is God's. Display word cards 22 and 23, בַּשָּׁמַיִם and וּבָאָרֶץ. As a class, brainstorm a list of things that are found בַּשָּׁמַיִם *(stars, sun, moon, clouds)* and a list of things found בָּאָרֶץ *(trees, animals, rocks, flowers)*. Use this as an opportunity to practice the Hebrew words בַּשָּׁמַיִם and וּבָאָרֶץ.

Direct students to read Language Link with a partner. Partners read the list of Hebrew words aloud and then draw a line from each Hebrew word to either the illustration of the שָׁמַיִם or of the אֶרֶץ.

Digital Application

In Level 2 of the digital application, have students click on the activities light bulb and then "Matching." Here, students will review Hebrew terms by matching illustrations to פְּרָחִים, עֵצִים, שֶׁמֶשׁ, כּוֹכָבִים, and הָרִים. In the next class session, challenge students to name the Language Link word that was not included in the "Matching" activity. *(יָרֵחַ)*

You're an Artist!

Direct students to draw a picture of themselves in nature that includes images of four or more of the Hebrew words from the list. Invite volunteers to describe their pictures using the new Hebrew words. A student might say, for example, "I am standing under tall עֵצִים because the שֶׁמֶשׁ is very bright and hot. I am looking at the הָרִים that are covered with פְּרָחִים."

Dress Rehearsal

Lead, or invite volunteers to lead, the class in chanting all the prayers that were presented in this chapter. (שְׁמַע, בָּרוּךְ שֶׁנָּתַן, כִּי מִצִּיּוֹן, גַּדְּלוּ לַייָ, and לְךָ יְיָ) Be sure to incorporate all of the movements, such as bowing as you recite גַּדְּלוּ לַייָ, that accompany these prayers in your congregation.

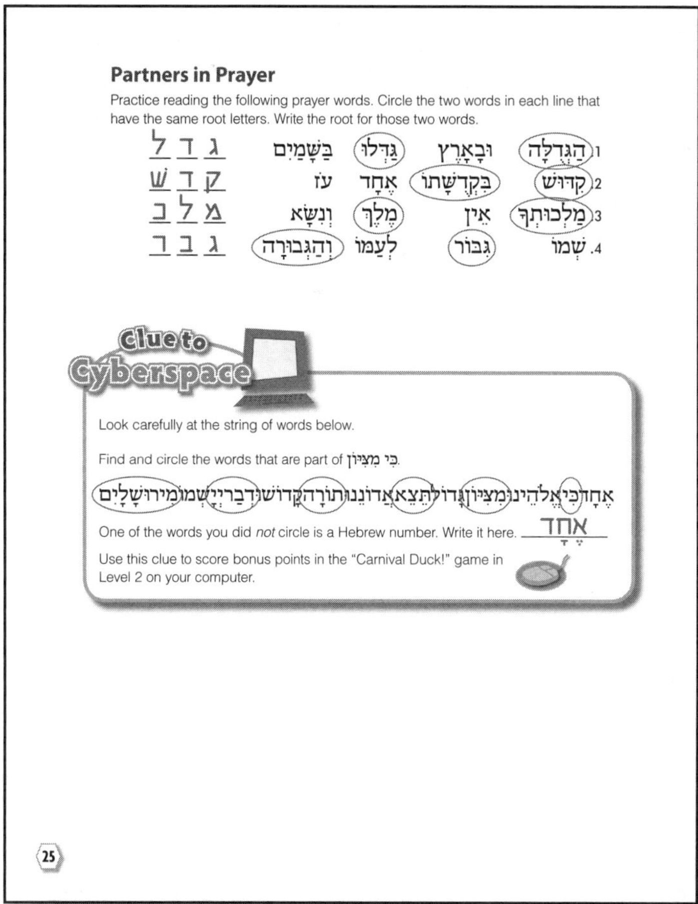

Partners in Prayer

Practice reading the following prayer words. Circle the two words in each line that have the same root letters. Write the root for those two words.

1	הַגְדֻלָּה	וּבָאָרֶץ	גַּדְּלוּ	בַּשָּׁמַיִם	ג ד ל
2	קָדוֹשׁ	בִּקְדֻשָּׁתוֹ	אֶחָד	עֹז	ק ד שׁ
3	מַלְכוּתְךָ	אֵין	מֶלֶךְ	וְנִשָּׂא	מ ל כ
4.	שְׁמוֹ	גִּבּוֹר	לְעַמּוֹ	וְהַגְּבוּרָה	ג ב ר

Clue to Cyberspace

Look carefully at the string of words below.

Find and circle the words that are part of כִּי מִצִּיּוֹן.

אֶחָדכִּיאֱלֹהֵינוּמִצִּיּוֹןגָּדוֹלתֵּצֵאאֲדוֹנֵנוּתוֹרָהקָדוֹשׁוּדְבַריְיָשְׁמוֹמִירוּשָׁלָיִם

One of the words you did *not* circle is a Hebrew number. Write it here. אֶחָד

Use this clue to score bonus points in the "Carnival Duck!" game in Level 2 on your computer.

25

Partners in Prayer

Use index cards to make word cards for קָדוֹשׁ—holiness, Kiddush; גִּבּוֹר—mighty, powerful; and מֶלֶךְ—ruler, king. If your students have studied *Kol Yisrael 2*, they will be familiar with these words. Display the Hebrew of these three cards along with word cards 1, 3, 5, 9, and 15–23. As a class, review each word and its meaning.

Divide the class into two teams: א and ב. Teams take turns picking and reading a word card (1 point) and saying its meaning (1 point) or picking and reading two word cards that are built on the same root letters (2 points) and saying their meanings (2 points). Remove a word from the display once it has been correctly read and translated. For example, a team that reads and translates לְעַמּוֹ earns 2 points. If the team reads it correctly but does not know the meaning, the team earns 1 point. A team that reads and translates גַּדְּלוּ and הַגְּדֻלָּה earns 4 points. Play until all words have been removed from the display. The team with the most points wins.

Have partners practice reading the prayer words from this activity. Suggest, for example, that partners first read the lines aloud together and then take turns reading each line individually.

Direct students to complete the activity independently. Walk around the room to informally assess how well your students recognize shared root letters. For enrichment, challenge students to write, and perhaps deduce, the general English meaning of each root. *(*גדל*—great, big;* קדשׁ*—holiness;* מלכ*—rule;* גבר*—power)*

Clue to Cyberspace

Have students work with a partner to find and circle the words that are part of כִּי מִצִּיּוֹן.

Challenge students to identify the remaining words. (אֱלֹהֵינוּ, גָּדוֹל, אֲדוֹנֵנוּ, קָדוֹשׁ, שְׁמוֹ, אֶחָד)

Tell students that at home, before the next class, they should click on the joystick to play the Carnival Duck game. In the game they will review prayer words by targeting words from כִּי מִצִּיּוֹן. Remind students to use the clue—אֶחָד—to score bonus points in Level 2 in this game.

Assessment

As students are working on any of the above activities, meet individually with students to assess reading fluency and knowledge of prayer content. Use the Prayer Mastery Assessment Chart on page 17 of the Teacher's Edition to keep track of student progress. You can also assess students' progress online at www.behrmanhouse.com. Click on the blue "Assessment" button at the bottom of the screen, select *Kol Yisrael 3*, and type in your class's serial number to see how students are doing in the software. Students can also e-mail their lesson summary to you directly or print out a lesson summary and bring it in to class.

What's Next?

Have students brainstorm what they know about how the Torah is read. *(Answers may include: The reading is divided into several aliyot; different people are called up to recite blessings.)* Tell students that they will learn the blessings and customs for reading the Torah in the next chapter.

3 בְּרְכוֹת הַתּוֹרָה

ABOUT THE PRAYER

We recite blessings before and after each section of the Torah portion is read. In these blessings, we praise God for choosing us and giving us the Torah of truth. After we finish reading from the Torah scroll, an honoree raises the open Torah so that we can all see its words. As we look at the words of the Torah, we recite וְזֹאת הַתּוֹרָה, declaring that the words of Torah that we just read are the same ones that Moses shared with the Israelites thousands of years ago.

LEARNING OBJECTIVES

Students will be able to:

- Recite בְּרְכוֹת הַתּוֹרָה and וְזֹאת הַתּוֹרָה fluently.
- Define key words and the root עלה.
- Locate Tel Aviv-Jaffa on a map of Israel.
- Identify the role of a תִּקּוּן and demonstrate how it is used.
- Explain that these blessings praise God for giving us the Torah.
- Describe the physical movements associated with reciting the Torah blessings and lifting the Torah, according to the customs of your congregation.
- Use synagogue terms, such as הַגְבָּהָה and גְּלִילָה.

ESSENTIAL QUESTION

What do we learn about the Torah from the honors, blessings, and traditions of the Torah service?

NEW WORDS AND PHRASES

Prayer Words:

chose (choosing)	בָּחַר
us	בָּנוּ
from all	מִכָּל
the nations	הָעַמִּים
and gave (and giving)	וְנָתַן
to us	לָנוּ
God's Torah	תּוֹרָתוֹ
gives	נוֹתֵן
Torah of	תּוֹרַת
truth	אֱמֶת
and life (of)	וְחַיֵּי
eternal, world	עוֹלָם
and this is	וְזֹאת
that, which	אֲשֶׁר
set, put	שָׂם
Moses	מֹשֶׁה
before	לִפְנֵי
by the hand of	בְּיַד

INSTRUCTIONAL MATERIALS

Text pages 26–37

word cards 24–41

Digital Application: Level 3—בְּרְכוֹת הַתּוֹרָה (see page 8 for a list of games and activities)

WHERE WE ARE

Batya and Ben are in Tel Aviv, thinking about going up to the top of the city's tallest building.

When they celebrate their bat and bar mitzvah, they will also be thinking about going up. At that time, they will be going up on the *bimah* for an עֲלִיָּה—literally, "going up"—to recite the Torah blessings.

INTRODUCING THE LESSON

Ask: What are some ways we honor others? *(Suggestions may include: praise a person—either in writing or verbally; give someone a gift; have them sit in a special place, a seat of honor.)* Explain that, according to Jewish tradition, one of the ways we honor people is by calling them up to recite the Torah blessings. In this chapter, students will learn to recite the blessings before and after the Torah reading, as well as the prayer that is recited when we hold the Torah high for all to see.

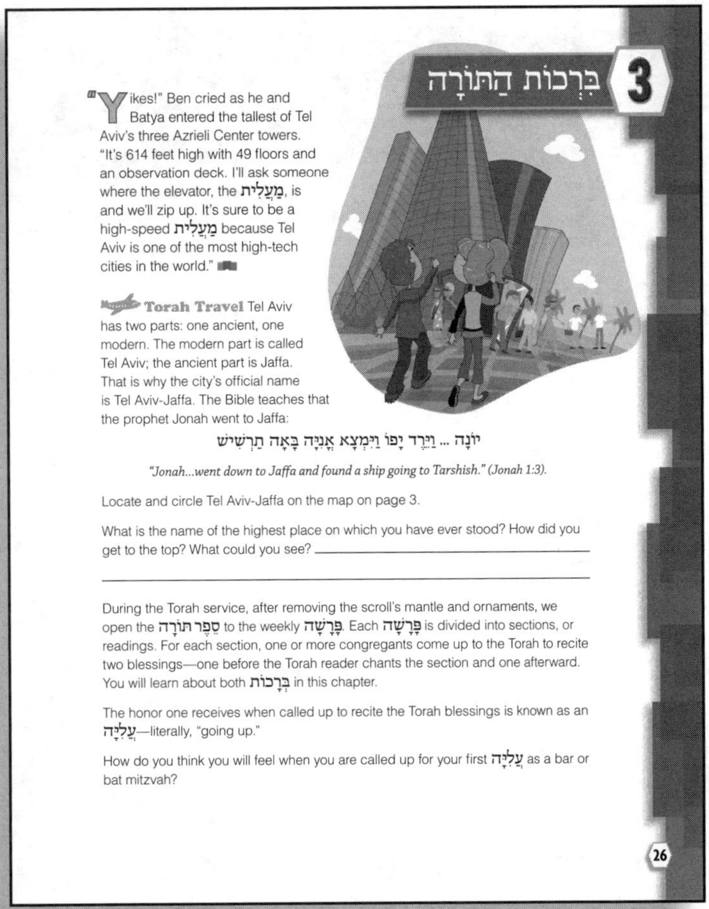

בְּרָכוֹת הַתּוֹרָה 3

"Yikes!" Ben cried as he and Batya entered the tallest of Tel Aviv's three Azrieli Center towers. "It's 614 feet high with 49 floors and an observation deck. I'll ask someone where the elevator, the מַעֲלִית, is and we'll zip up. It's sure to be a high-speed מַעֲלִית because Tel Aviv is one of the most high-tech cities in the world."

Torah Travel Tel Aviv has two parts: one ancient, one modern. The modern part is called Tel Aviv; the ancient part is Jaffa. That is why the city's official name is Tel Aviv-Jaffa. The Bible teaches that the prophet Jonah went to Jaffa:

יוֹנָה ... וַיֵּרֶד יָפוֹ וַיִּמְצָא אֳנִיָּה בָּאָה תַרְשִׁישׁ

"Jonah...went down to Jaffa and found a ship going to Tarshish." (Jonah 1:3).

Locate and circle Tel Aviv-Jaffa on the map on page 3.

What is the name of the highest place on which you have ever stood? How did you get to the top? What could you see? ____________________

____

During the Torah service, after removing the scroll's mantle and ornaments, we open the סֵפֶר תּוֹרָה to the weekly פָּרָשָׁה. Each פָּרָשָׁה is divided into sections, or readings. For each section, one or more congregants come up to the Torah to recite two blessings—one before the Torah reader chants the section and one afterward. You will learn about both בְּרָכוֹת in this chapter.

The honor one receives when called up to recite the Torah blessings is known as an עֲלִיָּה—literally, "going up."

How do you think you will feel when you are called up for your first עֲלִיָּה as a bar or bat mitzvah?

26

INTO THE TEXT

Before you begin this chapter, ask your education director or rabbi about the traditions your congregation follows when assigning עֲלִיּוֹת. Questions you might ask include: Can two or more people recite the Torah blessings together? Do we read the full פָּרָשָׁה each week? How many עֲלִיּוֹת do we have on Shabbat—seven or fewer?

As a class, read the Hebrew title of the chapter. Challenge students to derive its English meaning. *(Torah blessings)* Compliment your students for having learned the prayers recited when taking the Torah from the Ark, and tell them that they are now ready to learn the blessings recited before and after the Torah reading.

Invite a volunteer to act the part of Ben and read dramatically the first paragraph on page 26.

Torah Travel

Have students silently read the introduction to the verse from Jonah. Ask: Why is the city's official name Tel Aviv-Jaffa? *(because it has two parts, Tel Aviv and Jaffa)* What prophet took a ship from Jaffa thousands of years ago? *(Jonah)* Inform students that we read the Book of Jonah in synagogue every year on the afternoon of Yom Kippur. Read the Hebrew quote from Jonah. Have the class chorally read the English. Ask: How does this verse teach us that Jaffa is next to water? *(Jonah got on a ship in Jaffa.)*

Direct students to locate and circle תֵּל־אָבִיב־יָפוֹ on the map on page 3 and to individually write about the highest place on which they have ever stood. Have students describe that.

Digital Application

At home, or in class, have students click on Tel Aviv-Jaffa on the Contents map or on the prayers listed for Level 3 and then click on the camera to view photographs of Tel Aviv-Jaffa. Included are photos of (1) the skyline of Tel Aviv from Old Jaffa, (2) the Azrieli Towers, (3) a pharmacy inside a mall, (4) parasailing over the Mediterranean, (5) older rooftops and new skyscrapers in Tel Aviv, (6) minaret on a mosque in Old Jaffa. Consider showing students additional photos of Tel Aviv-Jaffa. The Internet has great photos of the colorful Carmel market, the old city of Jaffa, the modern city buildings, and the beach lined with tall hotels.

Note: The Hebrew in photo 3 is: סופר־פארם—Super-Pharm; בֵּית־מִרְקַחַת means pharmacy.

Ask students if they would prefer to visit the ancient city of Jaffa or the modern city of Tel Aviv, and to explain their choice.

Call on volunteers to read the last three paragraphs aloud, one sentence at a time. After each sentence, ask questions such as: When do we open the Torah? *(after removing the mantle and ornaments)* What is a mantle? *(the cloth covering)* What is a פָּרָשָׁה? *(the weekly Torah reading)*

Invite students to express how they think they will feel when they are called up for their first עֲלִיָּה. *(Answers may include: excited, nervous, happy.)*

Blessing Before the Torah Reading

Create word cards for the terms בַּעַל קְרִיאָה—male Torah reader—and בַּעֲלַת קְרִיאָה—female Torah reader. Teach students the Hebrew terms. Challenge students to determine which is the feminine and which is the masculine form. *(*בַּעַל קְרִיאָה *is masculine and* בַּעֲלַת קְרִיאָה *is feminine. The* ת *is a common feminine ending.)* Have students practice saying these terms by directing them to repeat the words after you, say the terms chorally with you, and then say the terms to a partner. Call on volunteers to create sentences. *(Possible sentences include: The* בַּעַל קְרִיאָה *is my friend's father; At my bat mitzvah I will be the* בַּעֲלַת קְרִיאָה*.)*

Create word cards for the words עוֹלֶה—a man who is called to the Torah—and עוֹלָה—a woman who is called to the Torah. Show students the Hebrew words and say that these are people who have the honor of being called to the Torah. Challenge students to determine which word is feminine and which is masculine *(*עוֹלֶה *is masculine and* עוֹלָה *is feminine. The* ■ָה *is a common feminine ending.)*. Have students practice saying the words and then use them in a sentence. *(Possible sentences include: My grandfather will be the first* עוֹלֶה *at my bar mitzvah; At my bat mitzvah I will be the second* עוֹלָה*.)*

Direct students to read silently the first two English paragraphs on page 27. Ask questions about the Torah blessings, such as, What prayer is recited at the start of most prayer services and is also the first two lines of the Torah blessing? *(*בָּרְכוּ*)*

Read lines 1–6 of the Torah blessing, one at a time, having students chorally repeat each line in Hebrew, and then read its English translation. Direct students to read these Hebrew lines with a partner. Challenge students to locate and read lines from this blessing by posing challenges such as: Read the line that is recited at the beginning of almost all blessings. *(line 3)* Read the line that praises God for giving us the Torah. *(line 6)*

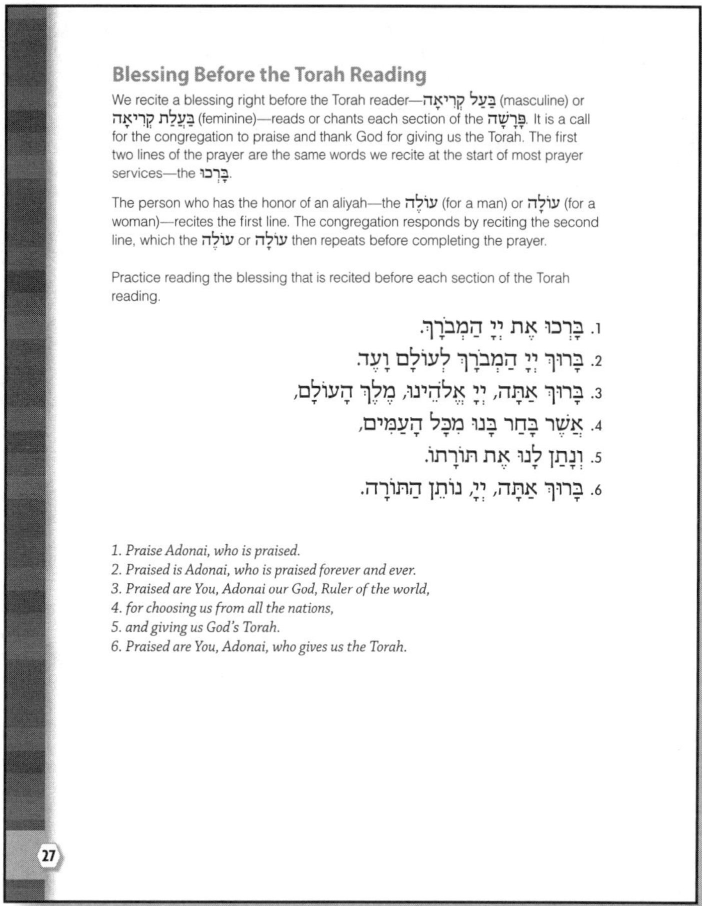
Blessing Before the Torah Reading

We recite a blessing right before the Torah reader—בַּעַל קְרִיאָה (masculine) or בַּעֲלַת קְרִיאָה (feminine)—reads or chants each section of the פָּרָשָׁה. It is a call for the congregation to praise and thank God for giving us the Torah. The first two lines of the prayer are the same words we recite at the start of most prayer services—the בָּרְכוּ.

The person who has the honor of an aliyah—the עוֹלֶה (for a man) or עוֹלָה (for a woman)—recites the first line. The congregation responds by reciting the second line, which the עוֹלֶה or עוֹלָה then repeats before completing the prayer.

Practice reading the blessing that is recited before each section of the Torah reading.

1. בָּרְכוּ אֶת יְיָ הַמְבֹרָךְ.
2. בָּרוּךְ יְיָ הַמְבֹרָךְ לְעוֹלָם וָעֶד.
3. בָּרוּךְ אַתָּה, יְיָ אֱלֹהֵינוּ, מֶלֶךְ הָעוֹלָם,
4. אֲשֶׁר בָּחַר בָּנוּ מִכָּל הָעַמִּים,
5. וְנָתַן לָנוּ אֶת תּוֹרָתוֹ.
6. בָּרוּךְ אַתָּה, יְיָ, נוֹתֵן הַתּוֹרָה.

1. Praise Adonai, who is praised.
2. Praised is Adonai, who is praised forever and ever.
3. Praised are You, Adonai our God, Ruler of the world,
4. for choosing us from all the nations,
5. and giving us God's Torah.
6. Praised are You, Adonai, who gives us the Torah.

27

Teach, or invite your cantor or music specialist to teach, your students how to chant the blessing before the Torah reading. Discuss with your students the traditions your congregation follows.

For example, tell students whether the עוֹלֶה or עוֹלָה must wear a tallit, or if the עוֹלֶה or עוֹלָה touches the Torah with *tzitzit* or with the Torah's belt before reciting the blessing.

Digital Application

Tell students that at home, before the next class, they should click on Tel Aviv-Yafo or וְזֹאת הַתּוֹרָה/ בִּרְכוֹת הַתּוֹרָה to enter Level 3. Next, they click on the Torah scroll and (Before reading) בִּרְכוֹת הַתּוֹרָה to practice reading the blessing before the Torah reading. Challenge students to read the blessing without mistakes. Remind students that pronouncing the words correctly is more important than how fast they recite the words. In the next class, ask students to read the blessing out loud with a partner.

Prayer Words

Practice reading these words from the blessing before the Torah reading.

chose (choosing)	בָּחַר
us	בָּנוּ
from all	מִכָּל
the nations	הָעַמִּים
and gave (and giving)	וְנָתַן
to us	לָנוּ
God's Torah	תּוֹרָתוֹ
gives	נוֹתֵן

Note: תּוֹרָתוֹ literally means "his Torah," but because God is neither masculine nor feminine, we translate תּוֹרָתוֹ as "God's Torah."

PRAYER PUZZLE

Complete the puzzle by writing the Hebrew word for each English word below. Do not include the vowels or any other dots.

Down
1. the nations
2. us
3. gives
5. to us

Across
2. chose (choosing)
4. from all
6. God's Torah
7. and gave (and giving)

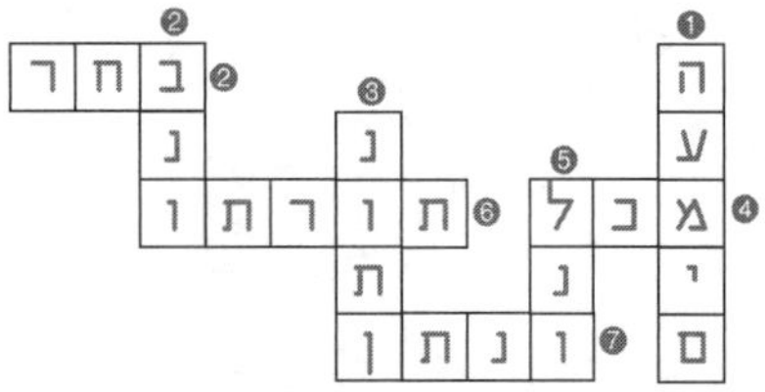

28

than having Moses pass along God's word? *(Responses may include: because it is more powerful hearing something firsthand; so that the Israelites would believe this is God's word; to form a greater connection between the Israelites and God.)* Why do you think Jewish tradition teaches us that in every generation each person must imagine that he or she left Egypt and stood at Mount Sinai to receive God's law? *(Possible responses include: so that we each feel a personal connection with God; so we each feel that it is our responsibility to live by the words of the Torah.)*

Prayer Words

Present word cards 24–31. As you display each card, call on students to read the word in Hebrew and to say its English meaning. Distribute word cards 24–31 among students. Challenge students to arrange the word cards on the ledge of the board in order of appearance in the Torah blessing.

What's That Word?

Divide the class into two teams. Ask a question about a prayer word. A member of each team comes to the board, writes the answer, and returns to his or her seat. The first team whose member writes the correct answer, and is then seated, earns a point. Be sure that each student has at least one turn. Suggested questions include: Which two words refer to "us"? (בָּנוּ, לָנוּ) Which two words are built on the same root letters? (נוֹתֵן, וְנָתַן) Which word tells us what we were given? (תּוֹרָתוֹ) The team with the most points is the winner.

Read aloud the note explaining why we translate the וֹ suffix of תּוֹרָתוֹ as "God's." Challenge students to name two other prayer words in *Kol Yisrael 3* that have an וֹ suffix that we translate as "God's." *(*לְעַמּוֹ*—to God's people;* בִּקְדֻשָּׁתוֹ*—in God's holiness)*

Explain that the word Torah means teaching. Have students work with a partner and list six teachings, *mitzvot*, or Jewish values, they consider important. Call on pairs to share their lists with the class.

Prayer Puzzle

Have students work with a partner to complete "Prayer Puzzle."

Receiving the Torah

Briefly tell your students the story of the Israelites receiving the Torah. You may wish to read selections from Exodus 19–24 or the story retold in *The Explorer's Bible, Volume 2* (Behrman House), pages 16–17. Ask: According to the account in Exodus, who hears God's commands? *(all of the Israelites)* Why do you think God speaks directly to the Israelites, rather

One or Many Chosen People?

Ask: How do you feel when you are chosen for a special task? *(excited, honored, nervous)* What are examples of such tasks? Why do you think certain people are selected for these special tasks? *(Possible responses include: they are qualified, they are dedicated, they have a relationship with the people who selected them.)* Some traditions teach that the Jewish people were chosen to receive the Torah. What does that mean? *(Answers might include: God has given the Jewish people certain tasks to carry out; the Jewish people were selected to follow God's teachings; the Jewish people are obligated to act according to the teachings of the Torah.)*

Divide the class into groups of 3–4 students. Have groups read, discuss, and then write responses for "One or Many Chosen People?"

Invite a representative from each group to describe things about the Jewish people that are unique or special and to explain how these things help us add goodness to the world. *(Suggestions may include: the Torah teaches us that we must be hospitable, which adds goodness by making others feel welcome when we include them in our community; the Torah teaches us to feed the hungry, which adds goodness to the world by reducing hunger in the world; the Torah teaches us that we are all responsible for one another, which adds goodness to the world by helping others when they are in a bad situation.)*

Encourage students to share something unique about themselves and how it helps them to contribute goodness to the world. *(Responses may include: because I play piano, I have been able to entertain others with my music; because I can read Hebrew, I help my little sister learn to read prayers; because I like to cook, I help prepare family meals.)*

Invite students to identify ways they can contribute in the future to make the world a better place. *(Possible answers include: walk to raise money for medical research; make quilts for people in hospitals; visit elderly people living in a home for the aged.)*

One or Many Chosen People?

The blessing before the Torah reading thanks God for "choosing us from all the nations" (אֲשֶׁר בָּחַר בָּנוּ מִכָּל הָעַמִּים). Some traditions teach that the Jewish people were chosen to receive the Torah and to share its teachings with the other nations of the world.

Other peoples also have traditions about their relationship with God and why they were chosen to receive their own sacred texts.

Describe something about the Jewish people that is unique or special and how it helps us add goodness to the world.

____

____

Describe something about yourself that is unique or special and how it helps you contribute goodness to the world.

____

____

Choice Voices

These phrases from the Bible express that God chose us from among the nations. Read the biblical quotes. Circle the Hebrew word for **chose** each time it appears.

1. בְּךָ בָּחַר יְיָ אֱלֹהֶיךָ לִהְיוֹת לוֹ לְעַם סְגֻלָּה
2. הָעָם בָּחַר לְנַחֲלָה לוֹ
3. כִּי־יַעֲקֹב בָּחַר לוֹ יָהּ יִשְׂרָאֵל לִסְגֻלָּתוֹ
4. וּבָחַר עוֹד בְּיִשְׂרָאֵל

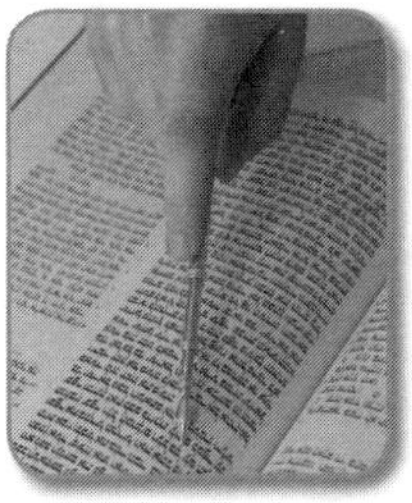

29

Choice Voices

Read line 1 aloud, and have students chorally repeat this line with you. Continue reading one line at a time, having students read the line chorally after you. Direct students to read the lines with a partner and then to circle independently the Hebrew word for "chose" in each line.

Photo Op

Call on volunteers to describe the book in the photo. *(Descriptions may include: it has two columns; it is all Hebrew; the Hebrew in the two columns appears to be in different fonts.)*

Explain that this is a photograph of a תִּקּוּן. Inform students they will learn more about a תִּקּוּן on page 31.

> **Putting It in ConTEXT**
>
> The Hebrew words in a Torah scroll and in a printed book of the Torah are the same, but the words *look* different. The words of a Torah scroll are written without vowels and without punctuation. Every letter is handwritten by a scribe—סוֹפֵר—in calligraphy. Nine of the letters are decorated with crowns that are drawn as three vertical lines on top of the letter:
>
> Like a scribe, draw the nine crowned letters in the numbered spaces.
>
> א ב ג ד ה ו ז ח ט י כ ך ל מ ם נ ן ס ע פ ף צ ץ ק ר ש ת
>
> 1. ג 2. ז 3. ט 4. נ 5. ן 6. ע 7. צ 8. ץ 9. ש
>
> Practice reading these words from Deuteronomy.
>
> כִּי עַם קָדוֹשׁ אַתָּה לַיהוָֹה אֱלֹהֶיךָ וּבְךָ בָּחַר יְהוָֹה...
>
> *You are a holy people to Adonai your God, for Adonai chose you... (Deuteronomy 14:2)*
>
> Now try to read the same words as they appear in the Torah scroll—סֵפֶר תּוֹרָה.
>
> כי עם קדוש אתה ליהוה אלהיך ובך בחר יהוה
>
> Turn to page 5 and circle the verse below as it appears in the אֵין כָּמוֹךָ blessing.
>
> (*Remember:* יְיָ *can be written* יְהוָֹה.) Then read the verse as it is written below.
>
> *Adonai will rule forever and ever (Exodus 15:18)* יהוה ימלך לעלם ועד
>
> 30

learning it from a text that has the vowels and musical notes, called trope. Then, they practice reciting each verse without the vowels and trope.

Challenge students to read the unvocalized phrase at the bottom of the page. *(יְיָ יִמְלֹךְ לְעֹלָם וָעֶד)* Direct students to turn to page 5 and circle these words from Exodus 15:18 *(line 3, words 5–8)* and to chorally read this line again. Inform students that Exodus 15:18 is in פָּרָשַׁת בְּשַׁלַּח.

Putting It in ConTEXT

Take your students to the sanctuary and open a Torah for all to see. Alternatively, show students the parchment from inside a mezuzah, or direct students to look at the copy of a תִּקּוּן on page 31. Have students identify differences between the Hebrew writing in the Torah or a mezuzah from the printed Hebrew in their text book. *(Responses may include: unlike the Hebrew in the text book, the Hebrew in the Torah and mezuzah does not have vowels or punctuation; the Hebrew in the Torah and mezuzah has extra markings at the top of some letters; unlike the letters in our text book, some of the letters in the Torah and mezuzah, such as the* ד *or* ר*, are not uniformly written.)*

Prepare, and display, a word card for the term סוֹפֵר—scribe (feminine: סוֹפֶרֶת). Have students read silently the opening paragraphs of "Putting It in ConTEXT." Point to the word card and call on a student to describe what a סוֹפֵר does. *(A* סוֹפֵר *is a scribe who writes a Torah by hand.)* Direct students to circle the nine letters that the סוֹפֵר writes with a crown. *(*ג, ז, ט, נ, ן, ע, צ, ץ*, and* ש*)* Invite three students to each write three of the letters, with their crowns, on the board while the rest of the class draws the nine crowned letters in their text.

Read aloud the Hebrew from Deuteronomy 14:2. Have students chorally read this biblical verse. Challenge students to identify some of its words, such as the word that has to do with holiness (קָדוֹשׁ); the word that means "chose" (בָּחַר); and the word that means "nation" or "people" (עַם).

Inform students that Deuteronomy 14:2 is in פָּרָשַׁת רְאֵה.

Divide the class into groups of 3–4 students. Have groups practice reading the vocalized verse from Deuteronomy until they can read it fluently. Next, have groups practice reading the same words, unvocalized, as they appear in the Torah. Call on volunteers to cover the vocalized verse and to read the unvocalized verse. Inform students that this is how a בַּעַל קְרִיאָה or בַּעֲלַת קְרִיאָה prepares to read from the Torah. First, they must master the Hebrew verse,

Help Is on the Way

Have students read silently "Help Is on the Way." Ask students the Hebrew name of the book in which the Torah text appears twice. *(תִּקּוּן)*

Ask your education director, cantor, or rabbi for a תִּקּוּן, and bring the תִּקּוּן to class. Show your students the inside pages of the תִּקּוּן. Turn to Exodus 15 (שְׁמוֹת ט"ו) and challenge students to find the words יְיָ יִמְלֹךְ לְעֹלָם וָעֶד. These words comprise the final phrase in the poem "The Song of the Sea" and are found in the center of the last line of the poem (Exodus 15:18).

Torah, Torah

Have students work with a partner to locate and underline the six words of the שְׁמַע in each of the columns depicted on page 31. *(vocalized text: line 6, first six words; unvocalized text: all of line 6)* Direct students to individually write how the two columns are similar and how they are different. Call on volunteers to share their descriptions. *(Responses might include: they are similar because the two columns have the same words or because the columns have the same open spaces; they are different because they are printed in different fonts or because only one of the columns has vowels and trope marks.)*

Challenge students to name the prayer that appears immediately after the שְׁמַע. *(וְאָהַבְתָּ)*

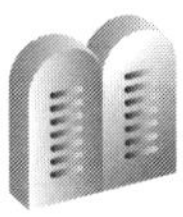

Torah Tunes

If your students know how to chant the וְאָהַבְתָּ, distribute prayer books. Ask students to open to the וְאָהַבְתָּ (*Mishkan T'filah*, page 116; *Siddur Sim Shalom*, page 112; *Kol Haneshamah*, page 277). Direct students to look for trope marks, the marks that are not vowels, in the וְאָהַבְתָּ. Call on volunteers to draw the trope marks for various words in the וְאָהַבְתָּ, such as אֵת, וְהָיוּ, and הַדְּבָרִים. As a class, chorally chant the וְאָהַבְתָּ. Inform students that if they will be chanting Torah for their bar or bat mitzvah, they will be using these trope marks to learn the tune for their reading. They will also use these same trope marks, although sung somewhat differently, as they learn to chant their haftarah.

Help Is on the Way

When Torah readers prepare to read from the Torah, they often practice in a תִּקּוּן a book in which the Torah text appears twice—in two different columns—on each page. In the right-hand column the text is set in regular Hebrew print with vowels, punctuation, and musical notations, or trope marks; in the left-hand column, the text looks just like it does on a Torah scroll.

Torah, Torah

Underline the six words of the שְׁמַע in each column in the תִּקּוּן.

How are the two columns similar?

They have the same words from the Torah

How are they different?

Only the column on the right has numbers, trope marks, and vowels.

Bonus Points: Which prayer appears immediately after the שְׁמַע?

וְאָהַבְתָּ

31

Language Link

When someone moves from a country outside of Israel to live in יִשְׂרָאֵל, we say he or she is making עֲלִיָּה, meaning that the person is **going up** to the holy land of יִשְׂרָאֵל. Like a person who receives an עֲלִיָּה to the Torah, an **immigrant** is called an עוֹלֶה (masculine) or עוֹלָה (feminine).

These Hebrew words—עֲלִיָּה, עוֹלֶה, and עוֹלָה—are all built on the root עלה. Words that are built on the root עלה have **going up** as part of their meaning.

Why do you think Jewish tradition teaches that, like having an עֲלִיָּה, immigrating to Israel brings us to a higher spiritual level? ______________________

____

The following two words are also built on the root עלה.

elevator מַעֲלִית degree (of heat or cold) מַעֲלָה

What do a מַעֲלִית and a מַעֲלָה have in common? both go up (and down)

Draw a line from the words that are built on the root עלה to the jet.

עֲלִיָּה תּוֹרָתוֹ מַעֲלָה יִשְׂרָאֵל עוֹלָה מַעֲלִית

32

Divide the class into two teams, א and ב. Tell Team א the beginning of a sentence that Team א must complete by using the word עֲלִיָּה, עוֹלֶה, or עוֹלָה. Possible sentences include: When a person moves to Israel, we say that person is making ________. *(עֲלִיָּה)* Rachel was very excited to be called to the Torah as an ________. *(עוֹלָה)* Have teams take turns finishing sentences. A team earns a point each time they finish a sentence correctly. The team with the most points wins.

Language Link

Write the following words on the board, עֲלִיָּה, עוֹלֶה, and עוֹלָה, or hold up word cards you have made. Challenge students to identify the root letters these words are built on. (עלה) Ask students to explain the meaning of the words. *(עֲלִיָּה—the honor one receives when called up to recite the Torah blessings; עוֹלֶה—a male who has the honor of an עֲלִיָּה; עוֹלָה—a female who has the honor of an עֲלִיָּה)*

Direct students to read the first paragraph of "Language Link" and to underline additional meanings for עֲלִיָּה, עוֹלֶה, and עוֹלָה. *(עֲלִיָּה—When someone moves from a country outside of Israel to live in יִשְׂרָאֵל; עוֹלֶה—an immigrant to Israel [masculine]; עוֹלָה—an immigrant to Israel [feminine])*

Call on a volunteer to explain how the two meanings of עֲלִיָּה are similar. *(they both have to do with going up)* Point out that when we use עֲלִיָּה in regard to immigration, we say "*making* עֲלִיָּה," and when we use עֲלִיָּה in regard to a Torah honor, we say "*having* an עֲלִיָּה." Have students write individually why they think Jewish tradition teaches that immigrating to Israel brings us to a higher spiritual level. *(Answers may include: a person who lives in Israel might find greater meaning in the prayers that mention Israel; our connection to our past may become stronger when we live in the same places our ancestors lived thousands of years ago; we may have a greater sense of belonging to the Jewish community when we are living in a place that is the homeland for Jews all over the world.)* Invite students to share what they have written.

Have the class chorally read the Hebrew words for elevator and degree. Call on students to say what a מַעֲלִית and מַעֲלָה have in common. *(They both go up and down.)*

Direct students to draw a line from the words that are built on the root עלה to the jet. *(עֲלִיָּה, מַעֲלָה, עוֹלָה, and מַעֲלִית)* Challenge students to read and translate the two remaining words. *(תּוֹרָתוֹ—God's Torah; יִשְׂרָאֵל—Israel)*

Blessing After the Torah Reading

Write on the board: Torah of truth. Call on volunteers to share why they think we call the Torah "Torah of truth." *(Possible answers include: the Torah teaches us to be true to other people and to God; the values we learn from the Torah are true; the words of the Torah are true.)* Inform students that the phrase "Torah of truth," תּוֹרַת אֱמֶת, is from the Bible and is found in a verse from the prophet Malachi (Malachi 2:6).

Write the phrase חַיֵּי עוֹלָם on the board and explain that it means "eternal life." Have students discuss with a partner how rereading the Torah, year after year, and passing its lessons on from generation to generation help give the Jewish people "eternal life." Call on volunteers to share their answers. *(Possible answers include: by reading the Torah each year, we are always learning its teachings and keeping its teachings alive; if every generation passes the Torah on to the next generation, the Torah will be alive forever.)*

Have students write their own answers to the questions on page 33.

Read lines 1–4 of the blessing after the Torah reading, one at a time, having students chorally repeat each line in Hebrew, and then read its English translation. Direct students to read these Hebrew lines with a partner. Challenge students to locate and read lines from this blessing by posing challenges such as: Read the line that is recited at the beginning of almost all blessings. *(line 1)* Read the line that praises God for giving us the Torah. *(line 4)* Read the two lines in the blessing after the Torah reading that are also in the blessing before the Torah reading. *(Lines 1 and 4)*

Teach, or invite your cantor or music specialist to teach, your students how to chant the blessing before the Torah reading. Inform your students about the traditions your congregation follows.

For example, tell students if the עוֹלֶה or עוֹלָה touches the Torah with *tzitzit* or with the Torah's belt before reciting this blessing.

Blessing After the Torah Reading

The blessing after each section of the פָּרָשָׁה praises God for giving us the Torah of truth and for the eternal life the Torah gives us.

Why do you think we call the Torah "Torah of truth"?

____

____

How does rereading the Torah, year after year, and passing its lessons on from one generation to the next, help give the Jewish people "eternal life"?

____

____

Practice reading the blessing after the Torah reading.

1. בָּרוּךְ אַתָּה, יְיָ אֱלֹהֵינוּ, מֶלֶךְ הָעוֹלָם,
2. אֲשֶׁר נָתַן לָנוּ תּוֹרַת אֱמֶת,
3. וְחַיֵּי עוֹלָם נָטַע בְּתוֹכֵנוּ.
4. בָּרוּךְ אַתָּה, יְיָ, נוֹתֵן הַתּוֹרָה.

1. Praised are You, Adonai our God, Ruler of the world,
2. who gave us the Torah of truth,
3. and planted eternal life in us.
4. Praised are You, Adonai, who gives us the Torah.

Congratulations!

It is a custom to congratulate people who have just had an עֲלִיָּה or other Torah honor. One popular expression of congratulations is יְיַשֵׁר כֹּחַ ("Strength to you"). Another is חֲזַק וּבָרוּךְ ("Be strong and be blessed").

33

Digital Application

Tell students that at home, before the next class, they should click on בִּרְכוֹת הַתּוֹרָה /וְזֹאת הַתּוֹרָה or Tel Aviv-Yafo to enter Level 3. Next, they click on the Torah scroll and (After reading) בִּרְכוֹת הַתּוֹרָה to practice reading the blessing after the Torah reading. Challenge students to read the blessing without mistakes. Remind students that pronouncing the words correctly is more important than how fast they recite them. In the next class, ask students to read the blessing out loud with a partner.

Congratulations!

Have students practice saying an enthusiastic יְיַשֵׁר כֹּחַ. Divide the class into two groups, א and ב.

Direct Group א to chant the blessing after the Torah reading and Group ב to congratulate them with a hearty יְיַשֵׁר כֹּחַ (often said as *yasher ko'ach*). Ask the groups to switch, so that Group ב chants the blessing and Group א congratulates them. Repeat this using the phrase חֲזַק וּבָרוּךְ. Inform students which phrase is used commonly in your congregation.

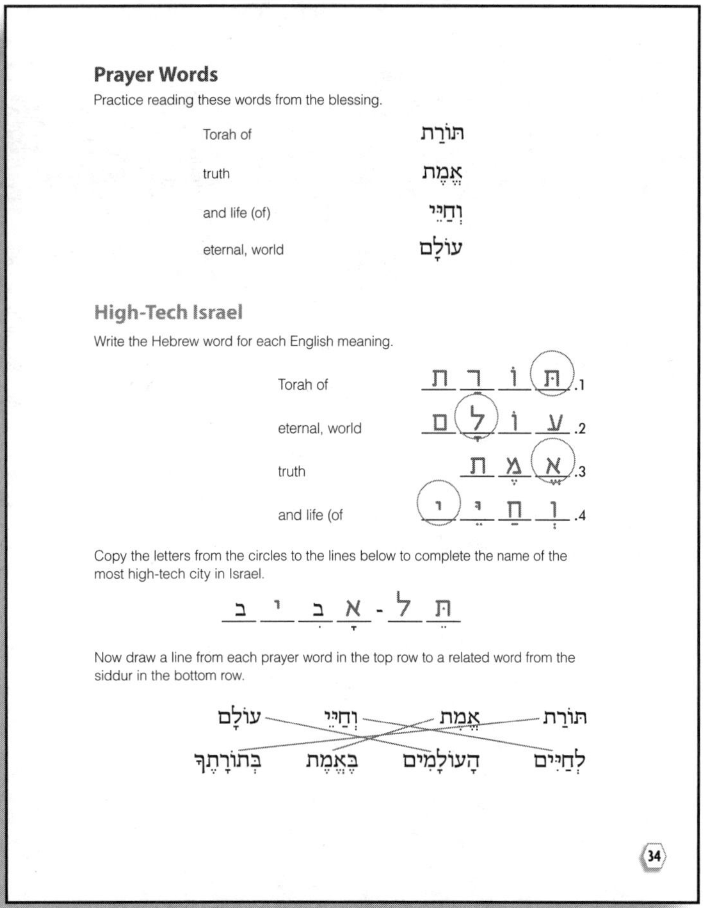

Prayer Words

Practice reading these words from the blessing.

Torah of	תּוֹרַת
truth	אֱמֶת
and life (of)	וְחַיֵּי
eternal, world	עוֹלָם

High-Tech Israel

Write the Hebrew word for each English meaning.

Torah of	1. ת ו ר ת
eternal, world	2. ע ו ל ם
truth	3. א מ ת
and life (of	4. ו ח י י

Copy the letters from the circles to the lines below to complete the name of the most high-tech city in Israel.

תּ ל - אָ ב י ב

Now draw a line from each prayer word in the top row to a related word from the siddur in the bottom row.

עוֹלָם	וְחַיֵּי	אֱמֶת	תּוֹרַת
בְּתוֹרָתֶךָ	בֶּאֱמֶת	הָעוֹלָמִים	לְחַיִּים

34

bottom, right word, לְחַיִּים. Challenge students to translate part or all of the word לְחַיִּים. *(to life)* If your students have studied *Kol Yisrael 2*, they will be familiar with the word and its meaning.

Ask students to name occasions when people say לְחַיִּים. *(Responses may include: celebrations such as a wedding, bar mitzvah, or bat mitzvah)*

Prayer Words

Present word cards 32–35 to the class. Ask questions about the new vocabulary, such as: Which of these words has two meanings? (עוֹלָם) Which two words have "of" as part of their meaning? (תּוֹרַת, וְחַיֵּי) Challenge students to find and underline each of the prayer words on page 33. *(line 2, fourth and fifth words; line 3, first and second words)* Hold up each word card and ask students to read the line on page 33 that contains that word.

Digital Application

By clicking on the activities light bulb in Level 3 students can play "Matching" to review new vocabulary, including the following Hebrew words: בָּנוּ (us), תּוֹרַת (Torah of), אֱמֶת (truth), וְחַיֵּי (and life [of]), and עוֹלָם (eternal, world). At the next class, ask: Which word appears in the blessing *before* the reading of the Torah? *(בָּנוּ)*

What's Missing?

Display word cards 32–35 on the ledge of the board. Ask students to put their heads down and close their eyes. Remove one of the cards. Challenge students to say the Hebrew and the English for the missing card. Have the first student who correctly identifies and translates the missing word card place the card back on the ledge and then remove another card while the other students have their eyes closed. Continue until each student has had at least one turn. To expand the game add a few additional word cards.

High-Tech Israel

Have students individually write the Hebrew word for each English meaning and then copy the circled letters to complete the name of Israel's high-tech city. Call a volunteer to the board to write the name of the city.

Direct partners to read aloud the two rows of Hebrew words and to draw lines to connect the related words.

Direct students to pretend they are holding up a glass, and read chorally with enthusiasm the

וְזֹאת הַתּוֹרָה

Direct students to read the first two paragraphs of וְזֹאת הַתּוֹרָה with a partner. Ask recall and open-ended questions, such as: What is the Hebrew term for a Torah scroll? (סֵפֶר תּוֹרָה) What do you think it feels like to lift the Torah high for all to see? *(scary, awesome, exciting)* What do we look at as we sing וְזֹאת הַתּוֹרָה? *(the open Torah scroll, the words of the Torah)*

Create, and display, word cards for the terms הַגְבָּהָה, מַגְבִּיהַּ, and מַגְבִּיהָה. Invite students to use these Hebrew words in a sentence. A student might say, for example, "David is the מַגְבִּיהַּ today." Continue doing this until all students have used at least one term in a sentence. Divide the class into groups of 3–4 students. Ask the groups to read, discuss, and write responses to the two questions on page 35. Call on a representative from each group to share its responses.

(Possible responses to the first question include: knowing that Jews have read the same words for thousands of years connects us to our ancestors; it helps us to understand the lives of our ancestors who lived in the days of the Bible; so that each generation can teach the next generation what they have learned. Possible responses to the second question include: I think that the meaning of some parts of the Torah stays the same. For example, the words of the וְאָהַבְתָּ *have always instructed us to teach our children Torah; I think that the meaning changes for each generation and for each person. For example, when I read the story of Joseph and his brothers, I think about how it relates to my own family.)*

Read both lines of וְזֹאת הַתּוֹרָה, one phrase at a time, having students chorally repeat each phrase. Direct students to read these lines in Hebrew and in English with a partner. Challenge students to locate and read words from this passage by asking them questions such as: Which phrase means, "This is the Torah"? (וְזֹאת הַתּוֹרָה) Which word appears twice? (מֹשֶׁה)

Teach, or have your cantor or music specialist teach, students to chant וְזֹאת הַתּוֹרָה.

וְזֹאת הַתּוֹרָה

After we finish reading from the סֵפֶר תּוֹרָה (Torah scroll), an honoree comes to the בִּימָה, grasps the scroll by its wooden rollers, and raises it high. Looking at the open scroll, the congregation proudly sings וְזֹאת הַתּוֹרָה declaring that the words we read at the Torah service are the very same ones that Moses shared with the Israelites in the wilderness of Sinai almost 3,500 years ago.

The ritual of raising the Torah for the congregation to see is called הַגְבָּהָה. The person who raises the Torah is called מַגְבִּיהַּ (masculine) or מַגְבִּיהָה (feminine).

Why is it important that the Torah's words have remained the same for thousands of years, so that generations of Jews hear and study the same text?

____

____

Do you think that each generation of the Jewish people finds the same meaning in the words of the Torah, or different meanings? Explain your answer.

____

____

Practice reading וְזֹאת הַתּוֹרָה.

1. וְזֹאת הַתּוֹרָה אֲשֶׁר שָׂם מֹשֶׁה לִפְנֵי בְּנֵי יִשְׂרָאֵל,
2. עַל־פִּי יְיָ בְּיַד מֹשֶׁה.

1. This is the Torah that Moses set before the people of Israel,
2. the word of Adonai by the hand of Moses.

וְזֹאת הַתּוֹרָה

35

Digital Application

Tell students that at home, before the next class, they should click on בִּרְכוֹת הַתּוֹרָה/ וְזֹאת הַתּוֹרָה or Tel Aviv-Yafo to enter Level 3. Next, they click on the Torah scroll and וְזֹאת הַתּוֹרָה to practice reading the prayer that is recited as we lift the Torah. In the next class, ask students to read the blessing out loud with a partner.

Photo Op

Focus students on the photo of the man lifting the Torah. Ask: What honor has this person been given? *(הַגְבָּהָה)* Why do you think he is holding the Torah open? *(so everyone can see the words of Torah)* How many columns can you see? *(three)* Explain that it is traditional for the person lifting the Torah to open the Torah until at least three columns can be seen.

If your congregation follows a tradition such as holding up *tzitzit* or a pinkie toward the open Torah and then kissing the *tzitzit* or pinkie, demonstrate the action.

Prayer Words

Practice reading these words from וְזֹאת הַתּוֹרָה.

and this is	וְזֹאת
that, which	אֲשֶׁר
set, put	שָׂם
Moses	מֹשֶׁה
before	לִפְנֵי
by the hand of	בְּיַד

Picture That!

Draw a line to connect each Hebrew phrase to its English meaning.
Hint: If you need help, turn to page 35.

that Moses set	לִפְנֵי בְּנֵי יִשְׂרָאֵל
and this is the Torah	בְּיַד מֹשֶׁה
by the hand of Moses	אֲשֶׁר שָׂם מֹשֶׁה
before the people of Israel	וְזֹאת הַתּוֹרָה

Circle the Hebrew word that appears in two of these phrases.

Now choose one of the above phrases and draw a picture to illustrate it. Write the phrase in Hebrew next to the illustration.

36

My Reflections on the Prayer

If your students are creating a booklet of reflections on the prayers, give each student two pages of prompts to complete (see page 29). The first page should be devoted to בִּרְכוֹת הַתּוֹרָה and the second to וְזֹאת הַתּוֹרָה. In addition, remember to have students draw an illustration or symbol to represent each prayer. Add these new pages to their folder or binder of personal reflections.

הַגְבָּהָה Know-How

Teach, or invite someone expert in lifting the Torah to teach, your students the proper technique for doing הַגְבָּהָה. Guide your students as follows: (1) Roll the scroll open so three columns as well as a seam attaching two pieces of parchment are visible, (2) hold each wooden handle with one hand, (3) slide the Torah toward you until it is halfway off the table, (4) bend your knees, (5) push the handles downward, (6) lift the Torah straight up as you stand straight. Encourage students to practice הַגְבָּהָה using a lightweight Torah.

Prayer Words

Present the Hebrew and English of word cards 36–41. Invite a student to the front of the room.

Direct the student to stand in front of you, facing the class. As you stand behind the student, show the rest of the class one of the words. Challenge the student standing in front of you to guess which word is being displayed. The student may ask the class "yes" and "no" (or כֵּן and לֹא) questions about the word. For example, a student might ask, "Does the word have four letters?" Once the student has guessed the word and said its meaning, invite another student to guess a second word.

Divide the class into groups of 3–4 students. Direct students to work as a team to learn to read fluently and translate each of the new prayer words.

Digital Application

By clicking on the activities light bulb in Level 3 students can play "Tic-Tac-Toe" to review new vocabulary from Chapter 3. At the next class, ask: Which word is used to describe the honor of being called up to the Torah? *(עֲלִיָּה)*

Picture That!

Direct partners to read the Hebrew phrases to one another. Have students then work independently as they connect each Hebrew phrase to its English meaning, circle the Hebrew word that appears twice in the phrases, and then illustrate one of the phrases.

Invite students to share their illustrations with their classmates.

Prayer Chart

If you have created a chart of the Shabbat morning service (see page 25), write בִּרְכוֹת הַתּוֹרָה and וְזֹאת הַתּוֹרָה on two 4″ x 6″ index cards and add these new prayers to the chart.

Putting It in ConTEXT

Direct students to find and underline independently the words from the verses that also appear in וְזֹאת הַתּוֹרָה. Walk around the room to informally assess students' ability to identify the words from וְזֹאת הַתּוֹרָה. Note that the verses are from the following passages and פָּרָשׁוֹת in the Torah: Deuteronomy 4:44, פָּרָשַׁת וָאֶתְחַנַּן, and Numbers 9:23, פָּרָשַׁת בְּהַעֲלֹתְךָ.

Dressing the Torah

Before class, prepare one word card for each of the following: סֵפֶר תּוֹרָה—Torah scroll; בִּימָה—bimah/elevated platform; גְּלִילָה—honor of rolling and dressing Torah; גּוֹלֵל—male who dresses the Torah; גּוֹלֶלֶת—female who dresses the Torah; פָּרָשָׁה—portion of the Torah; פָּרָשׁוֹת—portions of the Torah. Display these cards on the ledge of the board.

Have students silently read "Dressing the Torah." Call on volunteers to come to the front of the room and identify and read the word card for: a male who dresses the Torah (גּוֹלֵל); the honor of dressing the Torah (גְּלִילָה); a female who dresses the Torah (גּוֹלֶלֶת).

If you have prepared word cards for synagogue terms, flash these cards to review the following terms: סוֹפֵר; בַּעַל קְרִיאָה; בַּעֲלַת קְרִיאָה; עֲלִיָּה; עוֹלֶה; עוֹלָה; הַגְבָּהָה; מַגְבִּיהַ; מַגְבִּיהָה. Add these Hebrew word cards to the display on the ledge of the board. Then use all the synagogue word cards to play a game of "The Secret Word." (see page 13)

Clue to Cyberspace

Have students work with a partner to complete "Clue to Cyberspace."

Tell students that at home they should click on the joystick in Level 3 to play "Stampede" to review the new prayer words. In the game, students help the lion cross a stampede of wild animals and then cross a river to match a Hebrew word to its English meaning. Remind students to use the clue—מֹשֶׁה—to score bonus points.

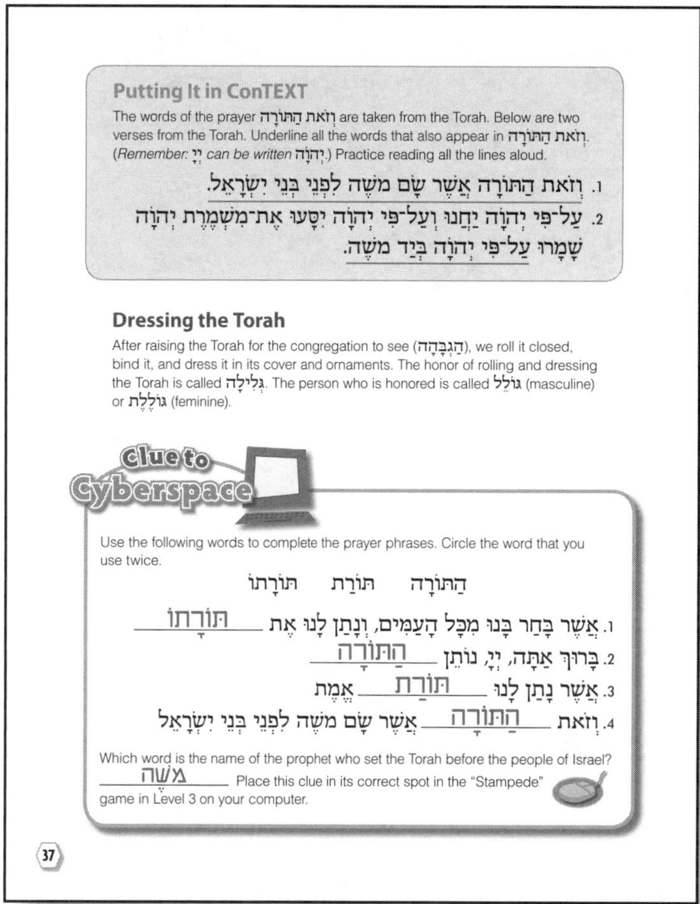

Putting It in ConTEXT

The words of the prayer וְזֹאת הַתּוֹרָה are taken from the Torah. Below are two verses from the Torah. Underline all the words that also appear in וְזֹאת הַתּוֹרָה. (*Remember:* יְיָ *can be written* יְהוָֹה.) Practice reading all the lines aloud.

1. וְזֹאת הַתּוֹרָה אֲשֶׁר שָׂם מֹשֶׁה לִפְנֵי בְּנֵי יִשְׂרָאֵל.
2. עַל־פִּי יְהוָֹה יַחֲנוּ וְעַל־פִּי יְהוָֹה יִסָּעוּ אֶת־מִשְׁמֶרֶת יְהוָֹה שָׁמָרוּ עַל־פִּי יְהוָֹה בְּיַד מֹשֶׁה.

Dressing the Torah

After raising the Torah for the congregation to see (הַגְבָּהָה), we roll it closed, bind it, and dress it in its cover and ornaments. The honor of rolling and dressing the Torah is called גְּלִילָה. The person who is honored is called גּוֹלֵל (masculine) or גּוֹלֶלֶת (feminine).

Clue to Cyberspace

Use the following words to complete the prayer phrases. Circle the word that you use twice.

הַתּוֹרָה   תּוֹרַת   תּוֹרָתוֹ

1. אֲשֶׁר בָּחַר בָּנוּ מִכָּל הָעַמִּים, וְנָתַן לָנוּ אֶת __תּוֹרָתוֹ__
2. בָּרוּךְ אַתָּה, יְיָ, נוֹתֵן __הַתּוֹרָה__
3. אֲשֶׁר נָתַן לָנוּ __תּוֹרַת__ אֱמֶת
4. וְזֹאת __הַתּוֹרָה__ אֲשֶׁר שָׂם מֹשֶׁה לִפְנֵי בְּנֵי יִשְׂרָאֵל

Which word is the name of the prophet who set the Torah before the people of Israel? __מֹשֶׁה__ Place this clue in its correct spot in the "Stampede" game in Level 3 on your computer.

37

Assessment

As students are working on any of the above activities, meet with them individually to assess reading fluency and knowledge of prayer content. Use the Prayer Mastery Assessment Chart on page 17 of the Teacher's Edition to keep track of student progress. You can also assess students' progress online at www.behrmanhouse.com. Click on the blue "Assessment" button at the bottom of the screen, select *Kol Yisrael 3*, and type in your class's serial number to see how students are doing in their digital application. Students can also e-mail their lesson summary to you directly or print out a lesson summary and bring it in to class.

What's Next?

As a class, brainstorm a list of prophets in the Bible. *(Prophets include: Jonah, Deborah, Elijah)* Explain that each week, after the Torah reading, we read a selection from the Prophets, called the haftarah. Inform students that in the upcoming chapter they will learn the blessings that are recited before and after the haftarah reading.

4 בְּרָכוֹת הַהַפְטָרָה

ABOUT THE PRAYER

We recite blessings both before and after chanting the haftarah. In these blessings, we praise God for the prophets of truth, the Torah, worship, and Shabbat. After chanting the haftarah and its blessings, we praise God's splendor with the words of יְהַלְלוּ and הוֹדוֹ. As we return the Torah to the Ark, we chant עֵץ חַיִּים and compare the Torah to a tree of life. יְהַלְלוּ comes from Psalms 148:13; Psalms 148:14 is the source of הוֹדוֹ; and Proverbs 3:17–18 and Lamentations 5:21 are the source of עֵץ חַיִּים.

LEARNING OBJECTIVES

Students will be able to:

- Recite בְּרָכוֹת הַהַפְטָרָה, יְהַלְלוּ, הוֹדוֹ, and עֵץ חַיִּים fluently.
- Define key words and the roots דבר, בחר, and אמר.
- Locate Haifa on a map of Israel.
- Explain that these prayers praise God for giving us the prophets, the Torah, worship, and Shabbat.
- Demonstrate the physical movements associated with returning the Torah to the Ark.
- Use synagogue terms, such as מַפְטִיר and דְּבַר תּוֹרָה.

ESSENTIAL QUESTION

How can we apply the teachings of the prophets to our lives today?

NEW WORDS AND PHRASES

Prayer Words:

prophets	נְבִיאִים
good	טוֹבִים
with their words	בְּדִבְרֵיהֶם
spoken	הַנֶּאֱמָרִים
in truth	בֶּאֱמֶת
his (God's) servant	עַבְדּוֹ
and righteousness (justice)	וָצֶדֶק
rock	צוּר
the One who is faithful	הַנֶּאֱמָן
the One who says	הָאוֹמֵר
for honor	לְכָבוֹד
thank (plural)	מוֹדִים
forever	תָּמִיד
(let us) praise	יְהַלְלוּ
name	שֵׁם
praise	תְּהִלָּה
tree of life	עֵץ חַיִּים
happy	מְאֻשָּׁר
its ways, its paths	דְּרָכֶיהָ
pleasantness	נֹעַם
renew	חַדֵּשׁ
our days	יָמֵינוּ

INSTRUCTIONAL MATERIALS

Text pages 38–51

word cards 42–63

Digital Application: Level 4—
בְּרָכוֹת הַהַפְטָרָה/עֵץ חַיִּים הִיא (see page 9 for a list of games and activities)

WHERE WE ARE

Batya and her father are camping out in the mountains near Haifa. By suggesting that they clean up their campground, Batya demonstrates that she knows right from wrong. In the days of the Bible, prophets instructed our ancestors so that they, like Batya, would know right from wrong. Nowadays, we continue to learn right from wrong as we study the words of these prophets each week when we read the haftarah.

INTRODUCING THE LESSON

Invite students to tell of a time when they spoke up against others or did something that was not popular

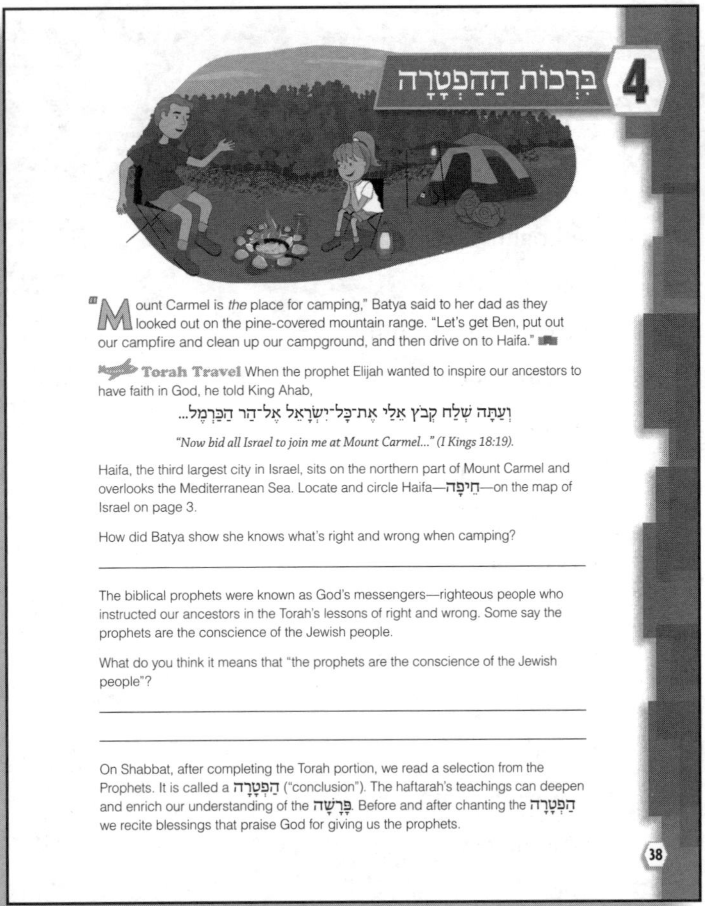

4 בִּרְכוֹת הַהַפְטָרָה

"Mount Carmel is *the* place for camping," Batya said to her dad as they looked out on the pine-covered mountain range. "Let's get Ben, put out our campfire and clean up our campground, and then drive on to Haifa."

Torah Travel When the prophet Elijah wanted to inspire our ancestors to have faith in God, he told King Ahab,

וְעַתָּה שְׁלַח קְבֹץ אֵלַי אֶת־כָּל־יִשְׂרָאֵל אֶל־הַר הַכַּרְמֶל...

"Now bid all Israel to join me at Mount Carmel..." (I Kings 18:19).

Haifa, the third largest city in Israel, sits on the northern part of Mount Carmel and overlooks the Mediterranean Sea. Locate and circle Haifa—חֵיפָה—on the map of Israel on page 3.

How did Batya show she knows what's right and wrong when camping?

____

The biblical prophets were known as God's messengers—righteous people who instructed our ancestors in the Torah's lessons of right and wrong. Some say the prophets are the conscience of the Jewish people.

What do you think it means that "the prophets are the conscience of the Jewish people"?

____

____

On Shabbat, after completing the Torah portion, we read a selection from the Prophets. It is called a הַפְטָרָה ("conclusion"). The haftarah's teachings can deepen and enrich our understanding of the פָּרָשָׁה. Before and after chanting the הַפְטָרָה we recite blessings that praise God for giving us the prophets.

38

because they knew it was the right thing to do. A student might describe, for example, sticking up for a classmate who was being bullied. Explain that, in biblical times, the prophets instructed our ancestors in the Torah's lessons of right and wrong. We continue to study these lessons of the prophets each week when we read the haftarah. In this chapter, students will learn to recite the blessings before and after the haftarah reading as well as the prayers that are recited when we return the Torah to the Ark.

INTO THE TEXT

Write the names of cities and places in Israel on the board or a large sheet of paper. Ask students what they know about any of these names. List their answers. *(Possible answers include: The Western Wall is in Jerusalem; Tel Aviv is very high-tech; the Negev desert is in the southern part of Israel.)* Call on a volunteer to read the introductory paragraph. Ask: What do we learn about the land around Haifa? *(there are tree covered mountains; it is not like the Negev)*

Digital Application

At home, or in class, have students click on Haifa on the Contents map or on the prayers listed for Level 4 and then click on the camera to view photographs of Haifa. Included are photos of (1) the Bahai Temple; (2) the Bahai gardens and Haifa's harbor; (3) the Carmelit, Haifa's underground funicular railway; (4) a view of Haifa and the harbor from the top of a mountain; (5) a vineyard. Consider showing students additional images of Haifa. The Internet is a great resource for photographs of Haifa. Since "Haifa" is also a person's name, narrow your results by searching for images of "Haifa Israel." If your students are creating travel guides for various places in Israel (see page 6), invite the students who are researching Haifa to describe highlights of what they have learned so far.

Torah Travel

Have students read silently the sentence about I Kings 18:19. Ask: Which prophet spoke up to King Ahab? *(Elijah)* What are some traditions that include the prophet Elijah? *(Answers may include: on Passover, we place Elijah's cup on the table and we open the door for Elijah; at the end of havdalah we sing* Eliyahu HaNavi, *Elijah the prophet.)* Inform students that this verse from Kings is found in the haftarah selection from פָּרָשַׁת כִּי תִשָּׂא. Lead the class in a choral reading of the biblical quote, in Hebrew and then in English. Ask: How do you think it would feel to stand on Mount Carmel, knowing that Elijah had once been in that place?

Direct students to locate and circle חֵיפָה on the map on page 3 and to write how Batya showed she knows what's right and wrong. *(She knew it was her responsibility to extinguish the fire and clean up their campground.)*

Have students read with a partner the fifth paragraph (beginning with "The biblical prophets...") Partners discuss, and then write, what they think it means that "the prophets are the conscience of the Jewish people." Invite students to share their answers with the class. *(Responses might include: the prophets reminded the Jewish people about what was right and wrong; the words of the prophets continue to guide us today to do the right thing.)*

Read aloud the final paragraph on page 38. Direct students to chorally join with you in reading the Hebrew terms הַפְטָרָה and פָּרָשָׁה. Focus students on the second sentence, which states that the haftarah's teachings deepen and enrich our understanding of the פָּרָשָׁה. Explain that most haftarah readings are connected to the פָּרָשָׁה by a shared theme or important idea. Uncovering the connection between the teaching of the haftarah and the Torah reading can give us a greater understanding of the פָּרָשָׁה. Encourage students to think about the connection between their haftarah and Torah reading as they prepare to speak about their פָּרָשָׁה when they celebrate becoming a bat or bar mitzvah.

It's an Honor

Before class, create word cards for מַפְטִיר, מַפְטִירָה, and הַפְטָרָה. To review synagogue terms, flash the word cards you prepared in Chapter 3. Display new words along with the word cards for עוֹלֶה—עוֹלָה—עֲלִיָּה; גּוֹלֵל—גּוֹלֶלֶת—גְּלִילָה; מַגְבִּיהַ—מַגְבִּיהָה—הַגְבָּהָה. Ask: If an עוֹלֶה and an עוֹלָה get an עֲלִיָּה, a גּוֹלֵל or גּוֹלֶלֶת does גְּלִילָה, and the מַגְבִּיהַ or מַגְבִּיהָה does הַגְבָּהָה, what do you think a מַפְטִיר or מַפְטִירָה does? *(chant the הַפְטָרָה)*

Read aloud the first paragraph of "It's an Honor." Have students chorally join with you as you read the Hebrew terms. Ask: In addition to the haftarah blessings, what other blessings does the מַפְטִיר or מַפְטִירָה recite? *(the blessings before and after the Torah—בִּרְכוֹת הַתּוֹרָה—because the מַפְטִיר or מַפְטִירָה is given the final עֲלִיָּה of the Torah reading)*

Have students write independently why they think it is often the bar or bat mitzvah who chants the הַפְטָרָה. Invite students to share their responses. *(Possible answers include: because it is a great honor to be chosen to recite a haftarah; because people sometimes recite a haftarah to celebrate a special occasion.)*

Read lines 1–4 of the blessing before the haftarah, one at a time, having students chorally

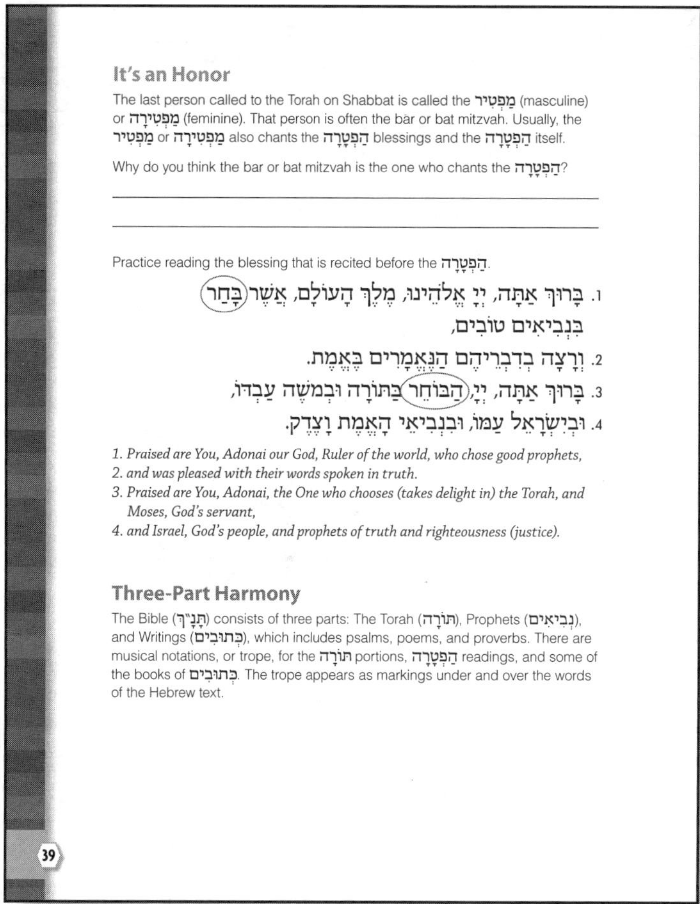

It's an Honor

The last person called to the Torah on Shabbat is called the מַפְטִיר (masculine) or מַפְטִירָה (feminine). That person is often the bar or bat mitzvah. Usually, the מַפְטִיר or מַפְטִירָה also chants the הַפְטָרָה blessings and the הַפְטָרָה itself.

Why do you think the bar or bat mitzvah is the one who chants the הַפְטָרָה?

Practice reading the blessing that is recited before the הַפְטָרָה.

1. בָּרוּךְ אַתָּה, יְיָ אֱלֹהֵינוּ, מֶלֶךְ הָעוֹלָם, אֲשֶׁר בָּחַר בִּנְבִיאִים טוֹבִים,
2. וְרָצָה בְדִבְרֵיהֶם הַנֶּאֱמָרִים בֶּאֱמֶת.
3. בָּרוּךְ אַתָּה, יְיָ, הַבּוֹחֵר בַּתּוֹרָה וּבְמֹשֶׁה עַבְדּוֹ,
4. וּבְיִשְׂרָאֵל עַמּוֹ, וּבִנְבִיאֵי הָאֱמֶת וָצֶדֶק.

1. Praised are You, Adonai our God, Ruler of the world, who chose good prophets,
2. and was pleased with their words spoken in truth.
3. Praised are You, Adonai, the One who chooses (takes delight in) the Torah, and Moses, God's servant,
4. and Israel, God's people, and prophets of truth and righteousness (justice).

Three-Part Harmony

The Bible (תַּנַ"ךְ) consists of three parts: The Torah (תּוֹרָה), Prophets (נְבִיאִים), and Writings (כְּתוּבִים), which includes psalms, poems, and proverbs. There are musical notations, or trope, for the תּוֹרָה portions, הַפְטָרָה readings, and some of the books of כְּתוּבִים. The trope appears as markings under and over the words of the Hebrew text.

39

repeat each line, and then read its English meaning. Direct students to read these lines with a partner.

Digital Application

Tell students that at home, before the next class, they should click on Haifa or בִּרְכוֹת הַהַפְטָרָה/עֵץ חַיִּים הִיא to enter Level 4. Next, they click on the Torah scroll and Before הַהַפְטָרָה to practice reading the blessing recited before reading the haftarah. In the next class, ask students to read the blessing out loud with a partner.

Teach, or have your cantor or music specialist teach, students to chant the blessing before the haftarah.

Three-Part Harmony

On the board, write תּוֹרָה, נְבִיאִים, and כְּתוּבִים, one word below another. Call on a volunteer to circle the first letter of each word and demonstrate how the term תַּנַ"ךְ is derived from these initial letters. Have students read silently "Three-Part Harmony." Ask: What do we call the musical notations? *(trope)* Where do these markings appear? *(under and over Hebrew words in the text)* Inform students that the

Prayer Words

Practice reading these words from the blessing recited before the הַפְטָרָה.

prophets	נְבִיאִים
good	טוֹבִים
with their words	בְדִבְרֵיהֶם
spoken	הַנֶּאֱמָרִים
in truth	בֶּאֱמֶת
his (God's) servant	עַבְדּוֹ
and righteousness (justice)	וָצֶדֶק

This is a street sign in Jerusalem. Write the name of the street in English:

Street of the prophets

Siddur Challenge

Write the number of each Hebrew word next to the matching English.

1. הַנֶּאֱמָרִים 2. וָצֶדֶק 3. טוֹבִים 4. בֶּאֱמֶת
5. נְבִיאִים 6. עַבְדּוֹ 7. בְדִבְרֵיהֶם

6 God's servant 1 spoken 7 with their words
3 good 5 prophets

Two important Hebrew words are left. Write each word on the right side below and its English meaning on the left.

in truth = בֶּאֱמֶת and righteousness (justice) = וָצֶדֶק

40

the haftarah blessing that is similar to the two Hebrew words they wrote at the bottom of the page. (בֶּאֱמֶת וָצֶדֶק—*truth and righteousness)* Ask: Who are these words describing? *(the prophets)*

Learning the Haftarah Blessings

It is important to note that the haftarah blessings are quite lengthy and can take students weeks or even months to master. It can become tedious to devote too much time in a single lesson to the decoding and chanting of these blessings. To keep students interested, teach them to chant three or four new lines each day. This may mean introducing the reading and chanting of the blessing after the haftarah while your students are still learning about the blessing before the haftarah. Begin a session by teaching a few new lines and reviewing the ones students have already learned. End a session by singing the blessing(s) one more time.

You may also find it helpful—or necessary!—to enlist the help of the cantor, musical director, or ritual director to help students learn the haftarah blessings. The digital application will be a big help, too.

trope, like punctuation marks, helps us know how to phrase a sentence when chanting it and when to pause or stop.

If your congregation chants this blessing according to the haftarah trope, tell your students that the musical notation, or trope, is the same that they will use when they chant their haftarah.

Prayer Words

Present word cards 42–48. As you display each card, call on students to read the word in Hebrew and to say its English meaning. Invite students to suggest ways to remember the meaning of each word. For example, the ◻ִים ending of נְבִיאִים makes it plural and we know נָבִיא means prophet, because we know of אֵלִיָּהוּ הַנָּבִיא. Distribute word cards 42–48 among students. Challenge students to arrange the word cards on the ledge of the board in order of appearance in the haftarah blessing.

Photo Op

Call on a volunteer to read the Hebrew name of the street. (הַנְּבִיאִים) Ask: Where else have you seen Hebrew without vowels? *(in the Torah)* Explain that in Israel most signs, newspapers, magazines, and books do not have vowels.

As a class, discuss what students learn about Israel from this photograph. *(Responses may include: street signs are in Hebrew, Arabic, and English; streets may be named after religious themes.)* Ask students why they think a street in Israel, but not in North America, would have this name. *(Responses may include: because Israel is a Jewish country; in North America the government and religion are separate.)* How do you think you would feel walking on streets with names like The Prophets or King David Street? *(Responses may include: proud to be Jewish; connected to my Jewish past.)*

Siddur Challenge

Direct students to work independently or with a partner to complete "Siddur Challenge." Call on a volunteer to read and translate the phrase from

At the Root

Write בְּדִבְרֵיהֶם on the board. Call a volunteer to guess the root letters of the word. (דבר) Invite a student to circle these letters in the word on the board.

Read aloud "At the Root." Direct students to join with you in reading the Hebrew words in this section. Have partners practice reading these words. Students independently circle the root letters and then look on page 15 for the word in כִּי מִצִּיּוֹן built on the root דבר. *(line 2, first word,* וּדְבַר*)* (The second #2 on the page) Challenge students to give the English meaning of this word. *(and the word of)*

Bible Speak

Write on the board: How is the word used? What does it have to do with "word" or "speak"?

Divide the class into three groups: א, ב, and ג. Direct Group א to read about (1) דְּבָרִים, Group ב to read about (2) דִּבְרֵי הַיָּמִים, and Group ג to read about (3) דְּבַר תּוֹרָה. Each group should prepare answers for the questions on the board regarding their specific word. If Group ב isn't sure of the meaning of "chronicles," explain that chronicles are written accounts of historical events. Call on a representative from each group to tell the class about its word.

Inform your students that דְּבָרִים literally means "words," and that the verse on page 41 is taken from פָּרָשַׁת דְּבָרִים.

Word Tree

Create a tree based on the root דבר, as you did for מלכ (see page 23). Include the words דִּבֵּר, בְּדִבְרֵיהֶם, דּוֹבְרֵי, מְדַבֶּרֶת, דְּבָרִים, כִּדְבָרֶיךָ, נְדַבְּרֵנוּ, דִּבְרֵי הַיָּמִים, הַדְּבָרִים, and דְּבַר תּוֹרָה found on page 41.

At the Root

בְּדִבְרֵיהֶם means **with their words**.

The root of בְּדִבְרֵיהֶם is דבר.

The root דבר tells us that **word** or **speak** is part of a word's meaning.

Circle the root letters דבר in the words below.

דִּבֵּר נְדַבְּרֵנוּ כִּדְבָרֶיךָ דְּבָרִים מְדַבֶּרֶת דּוֹבְרֵי

Bonus Points: Turn to the כִּי מִצִּיּוֹן prayer on page 15 and find the word built on the root דבר. Write it here. וּדְבַר

Bible Speak

1. The last book of the Torah, Deuteronomy, is called דְּבָרִים in Hebrew because דְּבָרִים is the first key word in the book. דְּבָרִים starts with these words:

   אֵלֶּה הַדְּבָרִים אֲשֶׁר דִּבֶּר מֹשֶׁה אֶל־כָּל־יִשְׂרָאֵל

   Circle the words that are built on the root דבר.

2. The last book of the Bible, Chronicles, is called דִּבְרֵי הַיָּמִים in Hebrew. Circle the part of the name that is built on the root דבר.

3. In synagogue, the prayer leader or the bat or bar mitzvah may speak about a lesson from the פָּרָשָׁה or הַפְטָרָה. The speech is called a דְּבַר תּוֹרָה. Circle the root letters in דְּבַר תּוֹרָה that let you know that **word** or **speak** is part of its meaning.

41

Torah Talk

Create a word card, as you did for other Torah related vocabulary, for דְּבַר תּוֹרָה—a word of Torah. Review all the Hebrew word cards (see pages 57 and 61) you have prepared that are related to the Torah and the Torah service.

Divide the class into two teams, א and ב. Call a member of Team א to the front of the room, and give that student one of the word cards. The student must act out the word silently, and the team has twenty seconds to guess the Hebrew term the student is presenting. If the team guesses correctly, the team earns 1 point, and Team ב gets a new word. If incorrect, the same word is given to a member of Team ב, and Team ב has twenty seconds to guess the word. Continue until all words have been presented, or you have played for a predetermined amount of time.

Language Link

Israel is a democracy. Israelis vote for their leaders in an election. The Hebrew word for **elections** is בְּחִירוֹת. The word בְּחִירוֹת is built on the root בחר. Words built on the root בחר have **choose** or **select** as part of their meaning.

Circle the words in the הַפְטָרָה blessing on page 39 that are also built on the root בחר.

Imagine that your class was planning a trip to Israel and had to choose where the class would go first. Circle your choice below and explain why.

Jerusalem / יְרוּשָׁלַיִם Tel Aviv / תֵּל-אָבִיב Negev / נֶגֶב Haifa / חֵיפָה

____

____

Just for Fun: A Hebrew word that may be used on election day is קַנְדִּידָט (masculine) / קַנְדִּידָטָה (feminine). What do you think it means in English?

candidate

Reader's Choice

Read these lines from the Prophets—נְבִיאִים.

1. וְאִם רַע בְּעֵינֵיכֶם לַעֲבֹד אֶת־יְהוָה בַּחֲרוּ לָכֶם הַיּוֹם אֶת־מִי תַעֲבֹדוּן...
2. וַיִּקַּח מַקְלוֹ בְּיָדוֹ וַיִּבְחַר־לוֹ חֲמִשָּׁה חַלֻּקֵי אֲבָנִים...
3. וְיִתְּנוּ־לָנוּ שְׁנַיִם פָּרִים וְיִבְחֲרוּ לָהֶם הַפָּר הָאֶחָד...

In each line, circle the word that is built on the root בחר.

The circled words have choose or select as part of their meaning.

42

Direct students to circle the words that are built on the root בחר and to write the meaning of these root letters. *(choose, select)*

The lines from the Prophets are found in Joshua 24:15, 1 Samuel 17:40, and I Kings 18:23.

Inform students that line 3, the quote from 1 Kings, is read as part of the haftarah for פָּרָשַׁת כִּי תִשָּׂא.

Word Tree

Consider creating a tree based on the root בחר, as you did for מלכ (see page 23). Include the words found on pages 39 and 42, such as בָּחַר, הַבּוֹחֵר, and בְּחִירוֹת.

Language Link

Show students word card 24. Call on a volunteer to read the word and say its meaning. *(*בָּחַר*—chose)* Remind students that this word is part of the Torah blessing in which we praise God for choosing us.

Have students read silently the opening paragraph of "Language Link." Ask: What is the Hebrew word for elections? (בְּחִירוֹת) What root is it built on? (בחר) What is part of the meaning of words built on the root בחר? *(choose, select)*

Direct students to circle the words in the הַפְטָרָה blessing on page 39 that are built on the root בחר. *(line 1—*בָּחַר*; line 3—*הַבּוֹחֵר*)* For an additional challenge, ask students to circle the word in the Torah blessing on page 27 that is built on this same root. *(line 4—*בָּחַר*)*

Suggest that students imagine the class is planning a trip to Israel. Students independently circle the name of the place they would like to visit and write a short explanation of their choice. Invite all students who chose Jerusalem to stand on the eastern side of your classroom, those who chose Tel Aviv to stand on the western side, students who chose Haifa to stand on the northern side, and those who chose the Negev to stand on the southern side. For fun, challenge students to guess how you decided where they should stand. *(loosely based on the geographic location of these places in Israel)* Show the class a map of Israel to demonstrate this.

Call on volunteers to read the words קַנְדִּידָט and קַנְדִּידָטָה and guess their meaning *(a male candidate and a female candidate)*. You may wish to have students practice using these words in short sentences, such as יוֹנָה קַנְדִּידָט (Jonah is a candidate) and רוּת קַנְדִּידָטָה (Ruth is a candidate).

Reader's Choice

Have students read these lines from the Prophets to a partner. Walk around the room, listening to the students, to do an informal assessment of students' decoding skills.

Blessings After the Haftarah Is Chanted

Have students read the first paragraph silently and circle the page number(s) of the version of the haftarah blessing that is recited in your congregation. Call on a volunteer to name the three qualities of God for which both versions express gratitude. *(faithfulness, compassion, and steadfastness)*

Ask students to give examples of how people might demonstrate each of these qualities. *(Possible suggestions include: Faithfulness—making a promise and sticking to the promise, being loyal to another person; Compassion—showing kindness to a person who is having a rough time, feeding the hungry; Steadfastness—being someone's friend through "thick and thin", letting a person know they can turn to you in any situation.)*

Allow students time to write about the attribute they consider most important. Ask for a show of hands from students who wrote about being faithful. Call on a few volunteers to share why they chose this attribute. Call on students to explain why they chose being compassionate or being steadfast as the most important attributes. *(Possible responses include: being faithful is most important because I need to know I can trust a person to do what he or she says; being compassionate is most important because we must make sure that people get the support and help that they need; being steadfast is most important because I need to know there is always at least one person I can rely on.)*

To help students connect these attributes to the description of God in the haftarah blessings, challenge students to find the English word in line 1 (page 43 or 44) that is a symbol for steadfast *(rock)*, to underline in line 2 (page 43 or 44) where God is described as faithful, and to underline in line 6 (page 44) where God is described as compassionate.

If your students are learning the Reform version (page 43), divide the class into three groups, **א**, **ב**, and **ג**. Assign each group two or three lines to master (lines 1–3, 4–5, or 6–8). Have the groups practice reading until all members can read the lines fluently and accurately. Direct students to

Blessings After the Haftarah Is Chanted

Several blessings are recited after the haftarah reading. This book gives two versions of these blessings. One is on this page; it is recited in Reform synagogues. The other is on pages 44–45; it is recited in Conservative synagogues. Both versions express gratitude for God's faithfulness, compassion, and steadfastness.

Think of what it means for a *person* to be "faithful, compassionate, and steadfast." Which attribute do you consider most important? Why?

____

____

Blessings recited after the haftarah in Reform synagogues

1. בָּרוּךְ אַתָּה, יְיָ אֱלֹהֵינוּ, מֶלֶךְ הָעוֹלָם, צוּר כָּל הָעוֹלָמִים,
2. צַדִּיק בְּכָל הַדּוֹרוֹת, הָאֵל הַנֶּאֱמָן, הָאוֹמֵר וְעֹשֶׂה,
3. הַמְדַבֵּר וּמְקַיֵּם, שֶׁכָּל דְּבָרָיו אֱמֶת וָצֶדֶק.
4. עַל הַתּוֹרָה, וְעַל הָעֲבוֹדָה, וְעַל הַנְּבִיאִים, וְעַל יוֹם הַשַּׁבָּת הַזֶּה,
5. שֶׁנָּתַתָּ לָּנוּ יְיָ אֱלֹהֵינוּ, לִקְדֻשָּׁה וְלִמְנוּחָה, לְכָבוֹד וּלְתִפְאָרֶת.
6. עַל הַכֹּל יְיָ אֱלֹהֵינוּ, אֲנַחְנוּ מוֹדִים לָךְ, וּמְבָרְכִים אוֹתָךְ.
7. יִתְבָּרַךְ שִׁמְךָ בְּפִי כָּל חַי תָּמִיד לְעוֹלָם וָעֶד.
8. בָּרוּךְ אַתָּה, יְיָ, מְקַדֵּשׁ הַשַּׁבָּת.

1. Praised are You, Adonai our God, Ruler of the world, Rock of all eternity,
2. righteous in all generations, the faithful God, the One who says and does,
3. the One who speaks and fulfills, for all God's words are truthful and just.
4. For the Torah, for worship, for the prophets, and for this Shabbat day,
5. that You have given to us, Adonai our God, for holiness and for rest, for honor and for glory.
6. For all of this, Adonai our God, we thank You, and praise You.
7. May Your name be praised forever by every living being.
8. Praised are You, Adonai, who makes Shabbat holy.

43

form new groups consisting of one or two students from each of the previous groups (**א**, **ב**, and **ג**). In these new groups, have the student(s) who practiced each set of lines help other group members master these lines. Continue until all students have mastered all eight lines.

Have students work with a partner to find and list five descriptions of God *(rock of all eternity; righteous in all generations; faithful; the One who says and does; the One who speaks and fulfills)* and four things for which we thank God that are mentioned in this blessing. *(Torah, worship, prophets, and Shabbat)* Have partners check their work with other pairs.

Teach, or have your cantor or music specialist teach, students to chant these verses. We suggest students learn to chant a few verses in each class session. Students will be less overwhelmed and have greater success. See note on page 62.

Digital Application

See the bottom of page 62 for the directions on practicing the Blessings After the Haftarah.

Blessings recited after the haftarah in Conservative synagogues

1. בָּרוּךְ אַתָּה, יְיָ אֱלֹהֵינוּ, מֶלֶךְ הָעוֹלָם, צוּר כָּל הָעוֹלָמִים,
2. צַדִּיק בְּכָל הַדּוֹרוֹת, הָאֵל הַנֶּאֱמָן, הָאוֹמֵר וְעֹשֶׂה,
3. הַמְדַבֵּר וּמְקַיֵּם, שֶׁכָּל דְּבָרָיו אֱמֶת וָצֶדֶק.
4. נֶאֱמָן אַתָּה הוּא יְיָ אֱלֹהֵינוּ, וְנֶאֱמָנִים דְּבָרֶיךָ,
5. וְדָבָר אֶחָד מִדְּבָרֶיךָ אָחוֹר לֹא יָשׁוּב רֵיקָם,
6. כִּי אֵל מֶלֶךְ נֶאֱמָן וְרַחֲמָן אָתָּה.
7. בָּרוּךְ אַתָּה, יְיָ, הָאֵל הַנֶּאֱמָן בְּכָל דְּבָרָיו.
8. רַחֵם עַל צִיּוֹן כִּי הִיא בֵּית חַיֵּינוּ, וְלַעֲלוּבַת נֶפֶשׁ תּוֹשִׁיעַ
9. בִּמְהֵרָה בְיָמֵינוּ. בָּרוּךְ אַתָּה יְיָ, מְשַׂמֵּחַ צִיּוֹן בְּבָנֶיהָ.

1. Praised are You, Adonai our God, Ruler of the world, Rock of all eternity,
2. righteous in all generations, the faithful God, the One who says and does,
3. the One who speaks and fulfills, for all God's words are truthful and just.
4. You are faithful, Adonai our God, and faithful are Your words,
5. and not one of Your words will return empty,
6. for You are a faithful and compassionate God and Ruler.
7. Praised are You, Adonai, faithful in all Your words
8. Have mercy on Zion, the source of our life; bring hope to the humbled spirit,
9. speedily in our time. Praised are You, Adonai, who gladdens Zion through her children.

צֶדֶק

44

Digital Application

Tell students that at home, before the next class, they should click on Haifa or בִּרְכוֹת הַהַפְטָרָה/עֵץ חַיִּים הִיא to enter Level 4. Next, they click on the Torah scroll. For the Reform version, students should click on After הַפְטָרָה and for the Conservative version they should click on Expanded בִּרְכוֹת הַהַפְטָרָה. Encourage students to practice reading the lines that they have learned so far. In the next class, ask students to read the blessing out loud with a partner. Direct students to practice additional lines at home on Level 4 as the lines are introduced in class.

Blessings recited in Conservative synagogues

If your students are learning the Conservative version (pages 44–45), divide the class into three groups, א, ב, and ג. Assign each group three lines to master (lines 1–3, 4–6, or 7–9). The groups should practice reading until all members can read the lines fluently and accurately. Direct students to form new groups consisting of one or two students from each of the previous groups (א, ב, and ג). In these new groups, have the student(s) who practiced each set of lines help other group members master these lines. Continue until all students have mastered all nine lines.

Teach, or have your cantor or music specialist teach, students to chant these verses. We suggest that students learn to chant a few verses at each class session. Students will be less overwhelmed, and experience greater success. See note on page 62.

Photo Op

As a class, read the photo's caption. Have a student say its English meaning *(righteousness, justice)* Call on volunteers to describe the photo and explain its connection to the caption. *(Possible responses include: there are people on a float from a helping organization; helping others is a form of righteousness and justice; people are supporting Yad Sarah, an organization that does righteous acts by loaning medical equipment and reaching out to the homebound.)*

If you have access to the Internet, invite students to visit the Yad Sarah site. The web address (www.yadsarah.org) is displayed on the float in the photo. Visit the site yourself, before you send students to the site. To encourage your students to explore the website, ask questions such as, Why does Yad Sarah loan medical equipment? After students have visited the website, ask them to explain why צֶדֶק is a good caption for this photo.

Blessings After the Haftarah Is Chanted

Divide the class into three groups, א, ב, and ג, as you did for the first half of the blessings after the haftarah. Assign each group three lines to master (lines 10–12, 13–15, or 16–18). The groups should practice reading until all members can read the lines fluently and accurately. Direct students to form new groups consisting of one or two students from each of the previous groups (א, ב, and ג). In these new groups, have the student(s) who practiced each set of lines help other group members master these lines. Continue until all students have mastered all nine lines.

Teach, or have your cantor or music specialist teach, students to chant these verses.

10. שַׂמְּחֵנוּ, יְיָ אֱלֹהֵינוּ, בְּאֵלִיָּהוּ הַנָּבִיא עַבְדֶּךָ, וּבְמַלְכוּת בֵּית דָּוִד מְשִׁיחֶךָ,
11. בִּמְהֵרָה יָבֹא וְיָגֵל לִבֵּנוּ, עַל כִּסְאוֹ לֹא יֵשֶׁב זָר,
12. וְלֹא יִנְחֲלוּ עוֹד אֲחֵרִים אֶת כְּבוֹדוֹ, כִּי בְשֵׁם קָדְשְׁךָ נִשְׁבַּעְתָּ
13. לוֹ שֶׁלֹּא יִכְבֶּה נֵרוֹ לְעוֹלָם וָעֶד. בָּרוּךְ אַתָּה, יְיָ, מָגֵן דָּוִד.
14. עַל הַתּוֹרָה, וְעַל הָעֲבוֹדָה, וְעַל הַנְּבִיאִים, וְעַל יוֹם הַשַּׁבָּת הַזֶּה,
15. שֶׁנָּתַתָּ לָנוּ יְיָ אֱלֹהֵינוּ, לִקְדֻשָּׁה וְלִמְנוּחָה, לְכָבוֹד וּלְתִפְאָרֶת.
16. עַל הַכֹּל יְיָ אֱלֹהֵינוּ, אֲנַחְנוּ מוֹדִים לָךְ, וּמְבָרְכִים אוֹתָךְ.
17. יִתְבָּרַךְ שִׁמְךָ בְּפִי כָּל חַי תָּמִיד לְעוֹלָם וָעֶד.
18. בָּרוּךְ אַתָּה, יְיָ, מְקַדֵּשׁ הַשַּׁבָּת.

10. Bring joy to us, Adonai our God, through Your servant Elijah the prophet, and the kingdom of the house of David, Your anointed one.
11. May he (Elijah) come speedily and gladden our hearts. May no stranger sit on his (David's) throne
12. nor permit others to inherit his honor, for by Your holy name, You promised
13. him that his light would not be extinguished forever and ever. Praised are You, Adonai, Shield of David.
14. For the Torah, and for worship, and for the prophets, and for this Shabbat day,
15. that You have given to us, Adonai our God, for holiness and for rest, for honor and for glory.
16. For all of this, Adonai our God, we thank You, and praise You.
17. May Your name be praised forever by every living being.
18. Praised are You, Adonai, who makes Shabbat holy.

45

Understanding the Prayer

Inform students that in the Conservative version of the blessing after the haftarah, we are actually reciting four blessings. Explain that the end of a blessing can be identified by the signature ending of — בָּרוּךְ אַתָּה, יְיָ. Challenge students to identify the four signature endings in the haftarah blessings. *(on pages 44–45: line 7, the last six words of line 9, the last five words of lines 13 and 18)*

Divide the class into four groups. Assign each group one of the four blessings. (lines 1–7, 8–9, 10–13, or 14–18) Give each group a set of questions to guide them as they reflect on their blessing. Questions might include: What is the Hebrew and the English signature ending? What word appears two or more times in the blessing? What is a main idea of this blessing?

Invite a representative from each group to tell the class about their blessing. Some things the groups may mention include: (1) Lines 1–7: The signature ending is הָאֵל הַנֶּאֱמָן בְּכָל דְּבָרָיו; the word faithful, נֶאֱמָן and נֶאֱמָנִים, appear five times; a main idea is that God is faithful and God's words are faithful. (2) Lines 8–9: The signature ending is מְשַׂמֵּחַ צִיּוֹן בְּבָנֶיהָ; the word צִיּוֹן appears twice; a main idea is that we pray on the behalf of צִיּוֹן (Israel). (3) Lines 10–13: The signature ending is מָגֵן דָּוִד; the name דָּוִד appears twice; a main idea is that the kingdom of David be restored (note: this group will most likely need your guidance). (4) Lines 14–18: The signature ending is מְקַדֵּשׁ הַשַּׁבָּת; the word שַׁבָּת appears twice; a main idea is that we thank God for the Torah, for worship, for the prophets, and for Shabbat.

Word Tree

If you have created word trees for the roots רחמ, קדש, and דבר, add the words רַחֵם, וְרַחֲמָן; מְקַדֵּשׁ, לִקְדֻשָּׁה, קָדְשְׁךָ; and הַמְדַבֵּר, מִדְּבָרֶיךָ, וְדָבָר, דְּבָרֶיךָ, דְּבָרָיו to the respective word trees.

> **Prayer Words**
>
> Practice reading these words from the blessings that are recited after the הַפְטָרָה.
>
> | | |
> |---|---|
> | rock | צוּר |
> | the One who is faithful | הַנֶּאֱמָן |
> | the One who says | הָאוֹמֵר |
> | for honor | לְכָבוֹד |
> | thank (plural) | מוֹדִים |
> | forever | תָּמִיד |
>
> **Finish the Phrases**
>
> Complete each prayer phrase with the missing Hebrew word. *Hint:* If you need help, turn to page 43 or to pages 44–45.
>
> 1. __הָאוֹמֵר__ וְעֹשֶׂה
> 2. אֲנַחְנוּ __מוֹדִים__ לָךְ
> 3. __צוּר__ כָּל הָעוֹלָמִים
> 4. __לְכָבוֹד__ וּלְתִפְאָרֶת
> 5. בְּפִי כָּל חַי __תָּמִיד__ לְעוֹלָם וָעֶד
> 6. הָאֵל __הַנֶּאֱמָן__
>
> *Challenge:* Draw a picture of the word you wrote in #3 above.
>
> 46

pages 44–45. *(The prayer phrases, according to their order on page 46, are found on the following lines of page 43: 2, 6, 1, 5, 7, 2, and on the following lines of pages 44–45: 2, 16, 1, 15, 17, and 2.)*

Prayer Chart

If you have created a chart of the Shabbat morning service (see page 25), write בִּרְכוֹת הַהַפְטָרָה on a 4″ x 6″ index card and add this new prayer to the chart. Your chart should now include the following: אַב הָרַחֲמִים, אֵין כָּמוֹךָ, לְךָ יְיָ, גַּדְּלוּ לַייָ, שְׁמַע, בָּרוּךְ שֶׁנָּתַן, כִּי מִצִּיּוֹן, וְזֹאת הַתּוֹרָה, בִּרְכוֹת הַתּוֹרָה and בִּרְכוֹת הַהַפְטָרָה.

Prayer Words

Present the Hebrew and English of word cards 49–54. Invite a student to act out one of the words. Have others guess the word. The student who guesses correctly acts out another word.

If your students have studied *Kol Yisrael 1* and 2, they will already be familiar with the words מוֹדֶה/מוֹדָה (thank) and כְּבוֹדוֹ (God's glory) which are related to these prayer words. Call on students to name the new prayer words that are related to מוֹדֶה/מוֹדָה (מוֹדִים) and כְּבוֹדוֹ (לְכָבוֹד).

The next time your students are in the sanctuary, point out the נֵר תָּמִיד. Challenge students to derive the English meaning of this term. Based on their previous knowledge, students may suggest "forever candle." Explain that the נֵר תָּמִיד is often referred to as the Eternal Light and that, according to tradition, the נֵר תָּמִיד is a symbol that God's Presence is always with us.

Digital Application

In Level 4 of the digital application, have students click on the activities light bulb and then "Matching." Here, students will match Hebrew words with their English meanings. (לְכָבוֹד—for honor, מוֹדִים—thank (plural), תָּמִיד—forever, נְבִיאִים—prophets, טוֹבִים—good) In the next class session, challenge students to name the word used to describe the prophets. *(*טוֹבִים*)*

Finish the Phrases

Have students complete each prayer phrase and draw a picture representing the word צוּר. Walk around the room to informally assess students' ability to identify and copy the new prayer words.

Divide the class into two groups. Have students check and correct their own work as groups take turns chorally reading the completed phrases.

Direct students to practice reading these phrases with a partner. For an extra challenge, have partners underline these phrases on page 43 or

At the Root

Write the root letters אמר on the board. Challenge students to find the word in line 2 (page 43 or 44) that is built on this root. *(הָאוֹמֵר)* Write the word הָאוֹמֵר on the board. Invite a volunteer to circle its three root letters. As a class, discuss what the prayer might mean when it calls God הָאוֹמֵר, "The One who says." Invite students to suggest ways that God might "speak." *(Responses may include: God is called הָאוֹמֵר because the Torah has accounts of God speaking to people; God may "speak" to us as we study and interpret words of Torah; when our conscience tells us what is right or wrong, that may be God "speaking" to us.)*

Remind students that God speaks throughout the Bible. Read students Genesis 1:1–3, the beginning of the Creation story, which tells how God spoke and then there was light; and Genesis 17:16, in which God promises Abraham that God will give Sarah a son. Write the phrase הָאוֹמֵר וְעוֹשֶׂה—"the One who says and does"—on the board. Ask: How are these both examples of God being הָאוֹמֵר וְעוֹשֶׂה? *(Possible responses include: Through speaking God creates. God says there will be light, and then light is created; Whatever promises God makes, God fulfills. God promises Abraham that Sarah will have a son, and then Sarah has a son.)*

Putting It in ConTEXT

Have students follow along as you read the Hebrew quote from Isaiah, and then chorally read the English translation. Ask questions such as: What problem was Isaiah describing? *(people do not have water to drink)* What other difficulties arise when there isn't enough water? *(Responses may include: plants and animals don't have water to survive; farmers can't grow their crops; people fight over the water that is available.)* Do you think Isaiah's words are still true today? If so, why? *(Responses may include: Yes, because there are countries that are having a drought and lack proper drinking water; Yes, because people who don't have clean water get very sick from drinking unsafe water.)* According to Isaiah, who will help the needy people? *(God)*

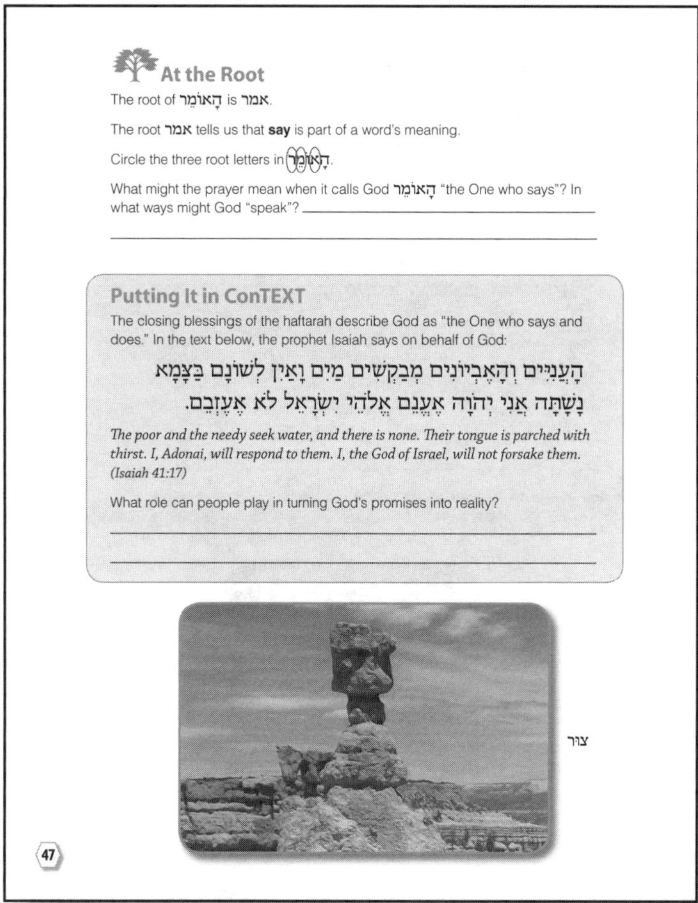

At the Root

The root of הָאוֹמֵר is אמר.

The root אמר tells us that **say** is part of a word's meaning.

Circle the three root letters in הָאוֹמֵר.

What might the prayer mean when it calls God הָאוֹמֵר "the One who says"? In what ways might God "speak"? ______

______

Putting It in ConTEXT

The closing blessings of the haftarah describe God as "the One who says and does." In the text below, the prophet Isaiah says on behalf of God:

הָעֲנִיִּים וְהָאֶבְיוֹנִים מְבַקְשִׁים מַיִם וָאַיִן לְשׁוֹנָם בַּצָּמָא
נָשָׁתָּה אֲנִי יְהֹוָה אֶעֱנֵם אֱלֹהֵי יִשְׂרָאֵל לֹא אֶעֶזְבֵם.

The poor and the needy seek water, and there is none. Their tongue is parched with thirst. I, Adonai, will respond to them. I, the God of Israel, will not forsake them. (Isaiah 41:17)

What role can people play in turning God's promises into reality?

______

______

צוּר

47

Divide the class into groups of 3–4 students. Remind students that in Judaism, we see ourselves as God's partners. Direct groups to discuss and then record how we, as God's partners, can turn God's promises into reality. Call on a representative from each group to share its responses. *(Responses may include: donate money to organizations that provide food for the hungry; volunteer in a soup kitchen.)*

If your students will engage in mitzvah projects as part of bat and bar mitzvah preparation, have students describe their projects. Your education director or rabbi may be able to provide you with a list of suggested mitzvah projects. Consider inviting post-bar and bat mitzvah students to speak to your class about their projects.

Photo Op

As a class, read the photo's caption. Have a student say its English meaning *(rock)* Ask: What are some adjectives we might use to describe God that we could also use to describe this rock? *(Possible responses include: amazing, awesome, unique)* You may wish to tell your students that they can visit awesome rocks like this one in Timna Park in the Negev.

Returning the Torah Scroll to the Ark

Before putting the Torah back in the Ark, the congregation stands and the prayer leader recites the יְהַלְלוּ prayer, which praises God.

1. יְהַלְלוּ אֶת שֵׁם יְיָ, כִּי נִשְׂגָּב שְׁמוֹ לְבַדּוֹ.

1. Praise the Name of Adonai, for God's Name alone is exalted.

The congregation responds by reciting the הוֹדוֹ prayer, which says God praises us.

2. הוֹדוֹ עַל אֶרֶץ וְשָׁמָיִם. וַיָּרֶם קֶרֶן לְעַמּוֹ,
3. תְּהִלָּה לְכָל־חֲסִידָיו, לִבְנֵי יִשְׂרָאֵל עַם־קְרֹבוֹ, הַלְלוּ־יָהּ!

2. God's splendor is on heaven and earth. God has raised the horn of God's people (made them safe),
3. giving praise to all of God's faithful, to the Children of Israel, the people close to God. Halleluyah!

Line 3 says our people are "close to God." What do you think that means?

____

____

After reciting the הוֹדוֹ prayer, some congregations sing Psalm 29 when they return the סֵפֶר תּוֹרָה to the Ark.

סִפְרֵי תּוֹרָה

48

sections of the Torah. By having more than one Torah, we can have each Torah rolled to the verses that will be read that day. If we had only one Torah, we would have to spend a lot of time during the service rolling the Torah from one section to the next. If you have not yet done so, point out the נֵר תָּמִיד, discuss the meaning of this term, and the symbolism of the נֵר תָּמִיד. (see page 68)

Experiencing Torah

As you did with אֵין כָּמוֹךָ and אַב הָרַחֲמִים, have your students practice reciting יְהַלְלוּ and הוֹדוֹ, either in your classroom using a miniature Ark or with a Torah in the congregation's chapel.

Motion for all students to stand as the Ark is opened and they chant יְהַלְלוּ and הוֹדוֹ.

Digital Application

Tell students that at home, they should click on Haifa or בִּרְכוֹת הַהַפְטָרָה/עֵץ חַיִּים הִיא to enter Level 4. Next, they click on the Torah scroll and יְהַלְלוּ, הוֹדוֹ to practice reading these prayers.

Returning the Torah Scroll to the Ark

Ask: What are some ways that we can praise God? *(Responses may include: recite prayers, name great things that God does for us.)* Explain that as we prepare to put the Torah back in the Ark, we praise God with words from the book of Psalms. Using the ancient verses of Psalms 148:13–14, the leader invites the congregation to praise God, and the congregation does so.

Read lines 1–3 of יְהַלְלוּ and הוֹדוֹ, one at a time, having students chorally repeat each line in Hebrew, and then read its English translation. Direct students to read the Hebrew with a partner.

Ask guiding questions, such as: Whom are we praising? *(God)* Where do we see God's greatness? *(on heaven and earth)* What might be an example of God's greatness? *(Responses may include: nature, knowledge, fire)* According to the הוֹדוֹ prayer, how does God help the people? *(makes them safe)* Who are God's faithful people? *(the Children of Israel)*

Have students write independently what they think it means that our people are "close to God." *(Responses may include: we can pray directly to God because we are close to God; we feel close to God when we partner with God to make the world a better place; we feel close to God when we study Torah and learn Jewish values.)*

Teach, or have your music specialist or cantor teach, students to chant יְהַלְלוּ and הוֹדוֹ. Inform students who, according to your congregation's tradition, carries the Torah during these prayers.

Photo Op

Have the class chorally read the caption of the photo and guess its meaning. *(Torah scrolls)* Take your students to the synagogue's sanctuary and count how many סִפְרֵי תּוֹרָה are in the Ark. As a class, count chorally, "One סֵפֶר תּוֹרָה, two סִפְרֵי תּוֹרָה, three סִפְרֵי תּוֹרָה," and so on. Ask students why they think the congregation has more than one Torah. Explain that on special Shabbatot and on holidays, we read from two, or even three,

Prayer Words

Show students word card 18. Call on a volunteer to read the word and say its meaning. (*שְׁמוֹ—God's Name*). Challenge students to identify another word in יְהַלְלוּ that is related to שְׁמוֹ. (שֵׁם) Display word cards 55–57 on the ledge of the board. Ask students to identify the letters that are in both יְהַלְלוּ and תְּהִלָּה. *(הלל)* Inform students that these words are both built on the root letters הלל. Part of the meaning of words built on these root letters is praise. (For those students who are interested, explain that the second ל from the root letters has dropped out and been replaced by a dot in the ל of תְּהִלָּה.) If students are familiar with the Hallel service, ask them to guess the meaning of the word הַלֵּל. *(praise)*

Direct students to find a second word in line 3 that is built on the root letters הלל. (הַלְלוּ־יָהּ)

Inform students that the יָהּ ending refers to Adonai. Challenge students to explain the meaning of הַלְלוּ־יָהּ, Halleluyah. *(Praise Adonai!)* Explain that Halleluyah is often translated as "Praise the Lord!"

Rhyme Time

Have students complete "Rhyme Time" individually. Walk around the room to assess informally students' ability to identify rhyming sounds and to write their own name in Hebrew. Ask partners to read the words aloud as they check their work together.

Call on a volunteer to read the word that rhymes with תְּהִלָּה. *(תְּפִלָּה)* Inform students that תְּפִלָּה is the Hebrew word for "prayer." You may wish to use the term תְּפִלָּה as part of your everyday classroom vocabulary. For example, before your students participate in a school prayer service, tell them that they will join with other classes for תְּפִלָּה.

Photo Op

Ask the class to chorally read the photo caption (*name*). Engage students in a discussion about their names, English and Hebrew. Consider beginning the conversation by telling students the story of your own name. Invite students to share the history of their names. Students may tell, for example, how their name was chosen, something about the person for whom they were named, or the meaning of their name. Encourage students to find out more at home about their name or the person after whom they were named. At the next class, invite students to share any additional interesting information they learned about their name.

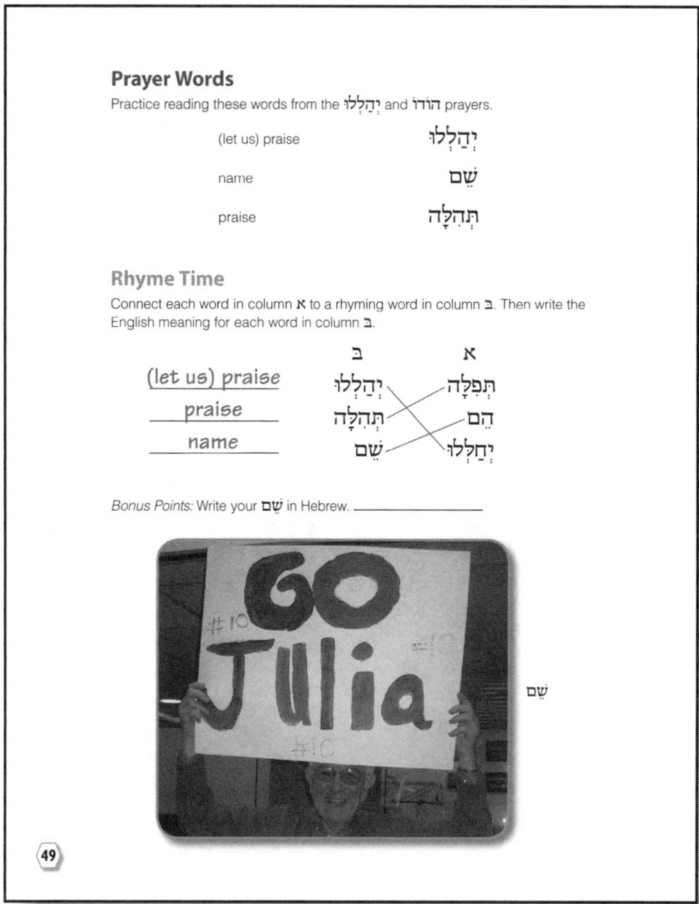

Prayer Words

Practice reading these words from the יְהַלְלוּ and הוֹדוּ prayers.

(let us) praise	יְהַלְלוּ
name	שֵׁם
praise	תְּהִלָּה

Rhyme Time

Connect each word in column א to a rhyming word in column ב. Then write the English meaning for each word in column ב.

	ב	א
(let us) praise	יְהַלְלוּ	תְּפִלָּה
praise	תְּהִלָּה	הֵם
name	שֵׁם	יְחַלְלוּ

Bonus Points: Write your שֵׁם in Hebrew. ________

שֵׁם

49

עֵץ חַיִּים הִיא

The Torah is often called a tree of life. Just as a tree sustains life through its fruit, oxygen, and shade, the Torah keeps us alive and strong through its teachings, such as the values of justice, peace, and rest on Shabbat. The Torah not only helps keep our bodies and spirits healthy, it also gives us a sense of purpose by telling us to improve the world.

The roots of the Torah are strong and deep, going back thousands of years to our ancestors who first received it at Mount Sinai. Its branches are forever expanding as each new generation studies the Torah and adds its understandings to our tradition.

Name another item in nature to which you might compare the Torah and explain why you made this choice.

____

____

____

When the Torah scroll is placed inside the Ark, the congregation remains standing and recites the כִּי לֶקַח and עֵץ חַיִּים prayers.

כִּי לֶקַח טוֹב נָתַתִּי לָכֶם, תּוֹרָתִי אַל תַּעֲזֹבוּ.

For I have given you precious teaching; do not abandon My Torah.

1. עֵץ חַיִּים הִיא לַמַּחֲזִיקִים בָּהּ, וְתֹמְכֶיהָ מְאֻשָּׁר.
2. דְּרָכֶיהָ דַרְכֵי נֹעַם, וְכָל נְתִיבוֹתֶיהָ שָׁלוֹם.
3. הֲשִׁיבֵנוּ יְיָ אֵלֶיךָ וְנָשׁוּבָה, חַדֵּשׁ יָמֵינוּ כְּקֶדֶם.

1. *It (the Torah) is a tree of life to those who uphold it, and those who support it are happy.*
2. *Its ways are ways of pleasantness and all its paths are peace.*
3. *Bring us back to You, Adonai, and we will return; renew our days as of old.*

50

עֵץ חַיִּים הִיא

Invite two volunteers to the board. Have one draw an illustration of a tree and the other draw a Torah. Direct students to work with a partner and to refer to the illustrations as they write one way that the Torah is like a tree. *(Responses may include: they are both found all over the world; they are both important to the Jewish people.)* Invite students to share their responses with the class. Direct partners to read the first two paragraphs about the עֵץ חַיִּים הִיא and to list the three comparisons between Torah and a tree that are described in these paragraphs. *(They both help to keep us alive; they both have strong roots; they both have branches that grow.)*

Inform your students that the handles on a סֵפֶר תּוֹרָה are called עֲצֵי חַיִּים, trees of life. Use this term when your students participate in a Torah service. If your congregation has a Tree of Life wall sculpture that celebrates lifecycle occasions, reinforce the concept of an עֵץ חַיִּים by bringing your students to view the sculpture and read some of the inscriptions.

Direct students to independently write about another item in nature to which the Torah can be compared. *(Answers may include: water—both come from heaven down to earth; sunlight—both give us energy and help us to see the world; wind—both guide us in a specific direction.)* Have students share their answers in groups of 3–4. Give each student a sheet of construction paper. Ask students to draw an illustration of their analogy and to then write a short explanation comparing the Torah to the item in nature they have chosen. Display students' work.

Read aloud the first phrase of כִּי לֶקַח. Have the class chorally read this phrase after you. Call on pairs of students to read the phrase. Repeat this with the second phrase of כִּי לֶקַח, and then with the complete line. Have the class chorally read the English meaning for this line. Repeat this for all three lines of עֵץ חַיִּים.

Divide the class into four groups: א, ב, ג, and ד. Assign each group one line to master. The groups should practice reading until all members can read the line fluently and accurately. Direct students to form new groups consisting of one or two students from each of the previous groups (א, ב, ג, and ד). In these new groups, have the student(s) who practiced each line help other group members master that line. Continue until all students have mastered all four lines.

Teach, or have your cantor or music specialist teach, students to chant these verses.

Experiencing Torah

As you did with יְהַלְלוּ and הוֹדוֹ, have your students practice reciting כִּי לֶקַח and עֵץ חַיִּים either in your classroom using a miniature Ark or with a Torah in the congregation's chapel. Remind students to remain standing as these prayers are chanted and the Torah is returned to the Ark.

Prayer Chart

If you have created a chart of the Shabbat morning service (see page 25), write יְהַלְלוּ, הוֹדוֹ, and עֵץ חַיִּים on 4″ x 6″ index cards and add these new prayers to the chart.

My Reflections on the Prayer

If your students are creating a booklet of reflections on the prayers, give each student three pages of prompts to complete (see page 29). The pages should be devoted to (1) בִּרְכוֹת הַהַפְטָרָה, (2) יְהַלְלוּ and הוֹדוֹ, and (3) עֵץ חַיִּים. Remember to have students draw an illustration or symbol to represent each prayer. Add these new pages to their folder or binder of personal reflections.

Prayer Words

Present word cards 58–63. Call on students to read each word in Hebrew and say its English meaning. Have students suggest ways to remember the meaning of each word. For example, I say the *"oo"* sound in מְאֻשָּׁר when I am *happy*. Distribute word cards 58–63 among students.

Challenge students to arrange the word cards on the ledge of the board in order of their appearance in עֵץ חַיִּים.

Digital Application

Tell students to click on the activities light bulb in Level 4 and play "Crossword" to review four new Prayer Words (תְּהִלָּה—praise; נֹעַם—pleasantness; מְאֻשָּׁר—happy; שֵׁם—name) and the names of places in Israel. At the next class, play a game of *Mishpaḥah* Madness (see page 14) to review prayer words (word cards 42–63) from this chapter.

Clue to Cyberspace

Have students work with a partner to complete "Clue to Cyberspace."

Tell students that at home, before the next class, they should click on the joystick to play the Lion's Bird House game. In the first two boards, they must smash the eggs containing words that are not part of the הַפְטָרָה blessings or יְהַלְלוּ, and then smash the word from the prayer. Remind students to use the clue—עֵץ חַיִּים—to score bonus points on the third board of this online game in Level 4—בִּרְכוֹת הַהַפְטָרָה/עֵץ חַיִּים הִיא.

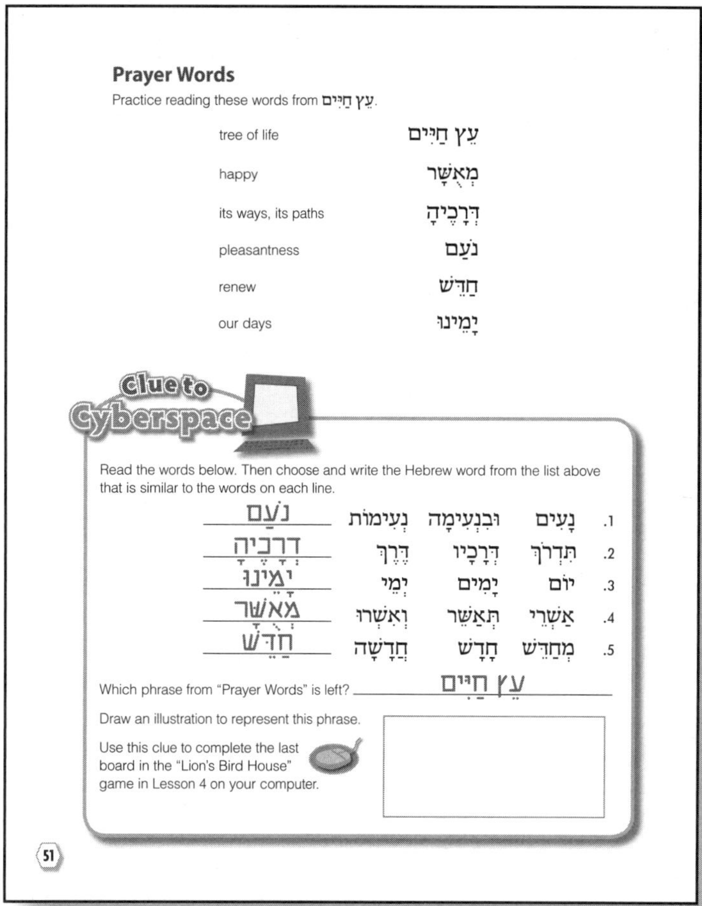

Prayer Words

Practice reading these words from עֵץ חַיִּים.

tree of life	עֵץ חַיִּים
happy	מְאֻשָּׁר
its ways, its paths	דְּרָכֶיהָ
pleasantness	נֹעַם
renew	חַדֵּשׁ
our days	יָמֵינוּ

Clue to Cyberspace

Read the words below. Then choose and write the Hebrew word from the list above that is similar to the words on each line.

.1	נָעִים	וּבִנְעִימָה	נְעִימוֹת	נֹעַם
.2	תִּדְרֹךְ	דְּרָכָיו	דֶּרֶךְ	דְּרָכֶיהָ
.3	יוֹם	יָמִים	יְמֵי	יָמֵינוּ
.4	אַשְׁרֵי	תְּאַשֵּׁר	וְאִשְּׁרוּ	מְאֻשָּׁר
.5	מְחַדֵּשׁ	חָדָשׁ	חֲדָשָׁה	חַדֵּשׁ

Which phrase from "Prayer Words" is left? עֵץ חַיִּים

Draw an illustration to represent this phrase.

Use this clue to complete the last board in the "Lion's Bird House" game in Lesson 4 on your computer.

51

Assessment

As students are working on any of the above activities, meet with them individually to assess reading fluency and knowledge of prayer content. Use the Prayer Mastery Assessment Chart on page 17 of the Teacher's Edition to keep track of student progress. You can also assess students' progress online at www.behrmanhouse.com. Click on the blue "Assessment" button at the bottom of the screen, select *Kol Yisrael 3*, and type in your class's serial number to see how students are doing in their digital application. Students can also e-mail their lesson summary to you directly or print out a lesson summary and bring it in to class.

What's Next?

Ask: Why do you think that, according to Jewish tradition, we are obligated to praise God? *(Responses may include: to remind us of what God does for us; so we remember to be grateful for what we have.)* Inform students that in the upcoming chapter they will learn the עָלֵינוּ, which begins by stating that it is our duty to praise God.

עָלֵינוּ 5

ABOUT THE PRAYER

The עָלֵינוּ prayer is a pledge of our loyalty to God, in which we praise God as the One Creator and Ruler. It was added to the Rosh Hashanah service in the third century CE and about eight hundred years later became part of the daily prayer service.

LEARNING OBJECTIVES

Students will be able to:

- Explain that the עָלֵינוּ is a pledge of loyalty to God.
- Locate Masada on a map of Israel.
- Recite עָלֵינוּ fluently and demonstrate its traditional choreography.
- Define key words found in עָלֵינוּ.
- Describe how fulfilling *mitzvot,* such as giving צְדָקָה, affirm our loyalty to God.

ESSENTIAL QUESTION

How can we demonstrate loyalty to God?

NEW WORDS AND PHRASES

Prayer Words:

it is upon us (our duty)	עָלֵינוּ
to praise	לְשַׁבֵּחַ
to God	לַאֲדוֹן
of all	הַכֹּל
and we	וַאֲנַחְנוּ
bend the knee	כּוֹרְעִים
Ruler of the rulers of rulers	מֶלֶךְ מַלְכֵי הַמְּלָכִים
and it is said	וְנֶאֱמַר

INSTRUCTIONAL MATERIALS

Text pages 52–59

word cards 64–71

Digital application: Level 5—עָלֵינוּ (see page 9 for a list of games and activities)

WHERE WE ARE

Batya and Ben are with their fellow Israeli Scouts—the צוֹפִים—at the ancient fortress of Masada in the Judean desert. As scouts, they promise to be loyal and trustworthy. Just as scouts pledge to be loyal to their people and their country, so we declare our loyalty to God and our desire for a peaceful, better world when we recite עָלֵינוּ.

INTRODUCING THE LESSON

Ask students to name people, groups, organizations, or places to which they are loyal. *(Responses may include: parents; a baseball team, friends.)* Tell students that the prayer they are about to study, עָלֵינוּ, declares our loyalty to God.

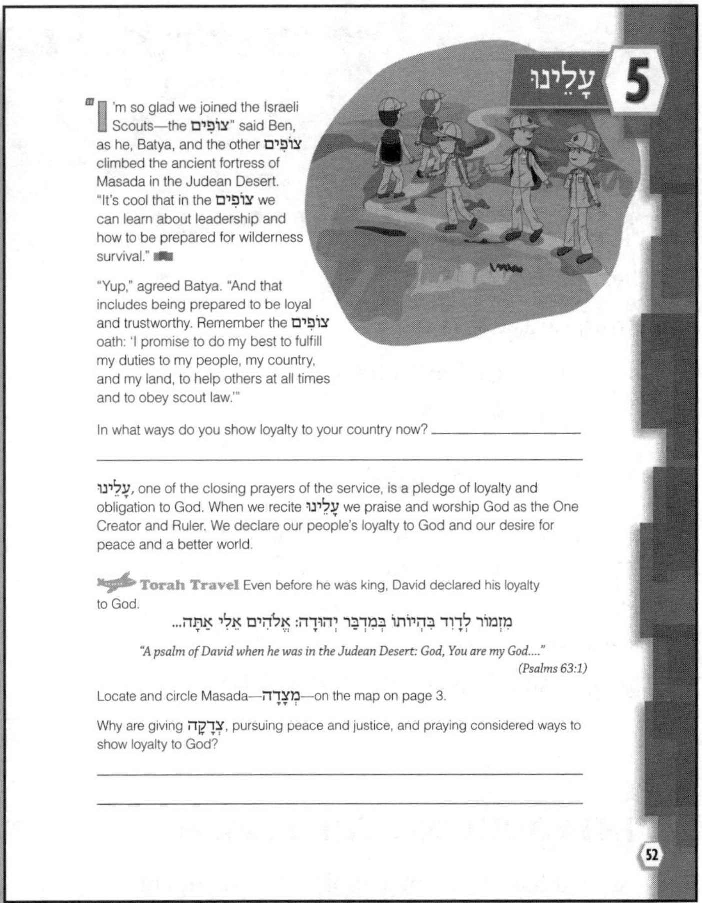

5 עָלֵינוּ

"I'm so glad we joined the Israeli Scouts—the צוֹפִים" said Ben, as he, Batya, and the other צוֹפִים climbed the ancient fortress of Masada in the Judean Desert. "It's cool that in the צוֹפִים we can learn about leadership and how to be prepared for wilderness survival."

"Yup," agreed Batya. "And that includes being prepared to be loyal and trustworthy. Remember the צוֹפִים oath: 'I promise to do my best to fulfill my duties to my people, my country, and my land, to help others at all times and to obey scout law.'"

In what ways do you show loyalty to your country now? ______________________

עָלֵינוּ, one of the closing prayers of the service, is a pledge of loyalty and obligation to God. When we recite עָלֵינוּ we praise and worship God as the One Creator and Ruler. We declare our people's loyalty to God and our desire for peace and a better world.

Torah Travel Even before he was king, David declared his loyalty to God.

מִזְמוֹר לְדָוִד בִּהְיוֹתוֹ בְּמִדְבַּר יְהוּדָה: אֱלֹהִים אֵלִי אַתָּה...

"A psalm of David when he was in the Judean Desert: God, You are my God...."
(Psalms 63:1)

Locate and circle Masada—מְצָדָה—on the map on page 3.

Why are giving צְדָקָה, pursuing peace and justice, and praying considered ways to show loyalty to God?

____

52

Have students circle מְצָדָה on the map on page 3.

Digital Application

At home, or in class, have students click on Masada on the Contents map or on the prayers listed for Level 5 and then click on the camera to view photographs of Masada. Included are photos of (1) the plateau on which Masada was built, (2) the cable car and the Snake Path, (3) an ancient synagogue, (4) ruins on Masada, (5) terraces on the side of the mountain, (6) Roman camps. Consider showing students additional images of Masada. The Internet is a great resource for photographs of Masada. If your students are creating travel guides for various places in Israel (see page 6), invite the students who are researching Masada to give highlights of what they have learned so far about this ancient fortress.

Direct students to discuss the closing question on page 52 with a partner. *(Possible responses include: because, according to Jewish tradition, these are the things God wants us to do; because these are values we learn from the Torah; because we are doing mitzvot.)*

INTO THE TEXT

Ask if students are or have ever been in a scout group. Together describe some of the things scouts do and learn. *(Responses may include: go on camping trips, sell cookies to raise money, learn to tie knots.)* Direct students to read the opening two paragraphs silently. Call on volunteers to say the Hebrew name for the Israeli Scouts (צוֹפִים) and to identify two things the צוֹפִים learn about. *(leadership and wilderness survival)* Have students suggest ways that the צוֹפִים might fulfill their oath. *(Suggestions may include: collecting food or clothing for the needy; cleaning a park by picking up litter; visiting the elderly)*

Have students individually write how they (or their families) show loyalty to their country. *(Responses may include: obey its laws; take care of the environment by recycling; say the Pledge of Allegiance; pay taxes; vote)*

Explain that at the end of every prayer service, we declare our loyalty to God as we recite the עָלֵינוּ. Direct students to read silently the paragraph that begins with the word עָלֵינוּ. Ask questions, such as: How do you feel when you make a pledge? *(Possible responses include: obligated to do what I say; more committed to what I have said.)* What kind of pledge is the עָלֵינוּ? *(one of loyalty and obligation to God)* What English phrase do we use to praise God? *(the One Creator and Ruler)* What desire do we express in the עָלֵינוּ? *(we want peace and a better world)*

Torah Travel

Remind or inform students that David was the first king over the *entire* kingdom of Israel. (Saul was the first king, but he ruled over a much smaller territory.) David lived and ruled in Jerusalem about 3,000 years ago. According to Jewish tradition, many of the psalms in the Bible were written by David.

Read aloud Psalms 63:1 in Hebrew. Have students chorally read the English. Ask: Where was David when he said these words? *(the Judean desert)* What ancient fortress is in this desert? *(Masada)* How does David declare his loyalty to God? *(He says, "God, You are my God.")*

A Prayer of Loyalty and Defiance

Have students read silently the first two paragraphs about עָלֵינוּ. Ask: How long ago was עָלֵינוּ included in the Rosh Hashanah service? *(about 1800 years ago)* For how many years has עָלֵינוּ been part of the daily service? *(about 800 years)* Why do we bow? *(as a sign of honor and respect for God)*

Ask students to name two other prayers in which we bow. *(*בָּרְכוּ *and* עֲמִידָה*)*

Read lines 1–5 of עָלֵינוּ, one at a time, having students chorally repeat each line in Hebrew, and then read its English translation. Direct students to read these Hebrew lines with a partner. Guide partners to practice lines 1 and 2 until they can read those lines fluently. After students are comfortable reading these lines, they should begin practicing lines 3–5.

Ask guiding questions, such as the following: Based on עָלֵינוּ, what are we obligated to do? *(praise God)* According to עָלֵינוּ are we unique or the same as all the other nations? *(unique)* In what ways do you think we are unique? *(Answers may include: we follow the teachings of the Torah; we have our own siddur.)* What do we do as we recite line 4? *(we bow)* What do we call God in line 5? *(the Ruler of the rulers of rulers)* What does this name tell us about the Jewish view of God? *(Responses may include: that God is more powerful than even the most powerful person; God rules over all people.)*

Teach, or ask your cantor or music specialist to teach, students to chant עָלֵינוּ. Demonstrate, and then have students practice, bending at the knee on the word כּוֹרְעִים (line 4), bowing on the words וּמִשְׁתַּחֲוִים וּמוֹדִים (line 4), and standing straight on the word לִפְנֵי (line 5).

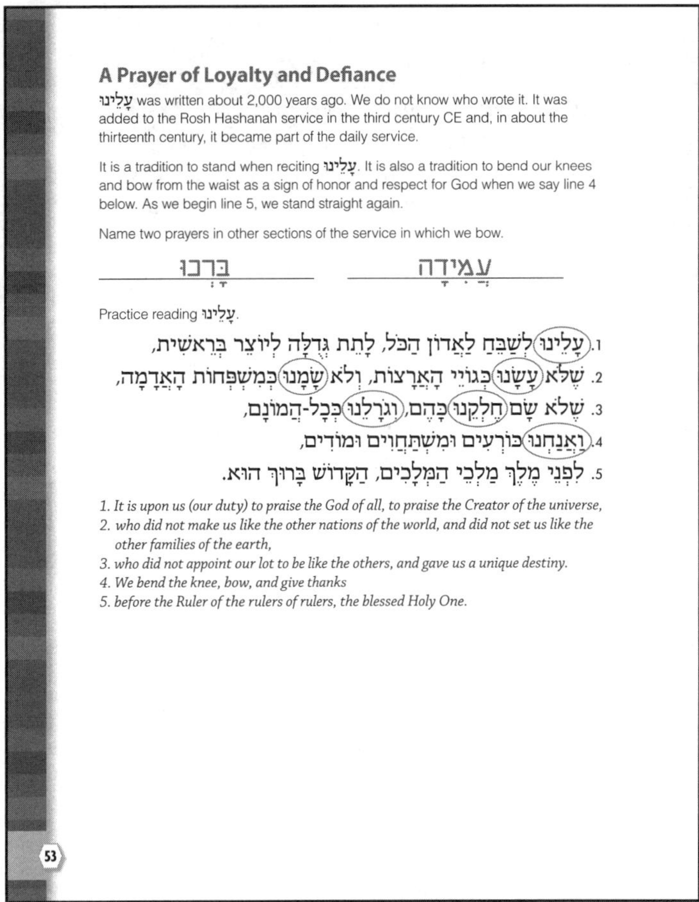

A Prayer of Loyalty and Defiance

עָלֵינוּ was written about 2,000 years ago. We do not know who wrote it. It was added to the Rosh Hashanah service in the third century CE and, in about the thirteenth century, it became part of the daily service.

It is a tradition to stand when reciting עָלֵינוּ. It is also a tradition to bend our knees and bow from the waist as a sign of honor and respect for God when we say line 4 below. As we begin line 5, we stand straight again.

Name two prayers in other sections of the service in which we bow.

בָּרְכוּ ______ עֲמִידָה ______

Practice reading עָלֵינוּ.

1. עָלֵינוּ לְשַׁבֵּחַ לַאֲדוֹן הַכֹּל, לָתֵת גְּדֻלָּה לְיוֹצֵר בְּרֵאשִׁית,
2. שֶׁלֹּא עָשָׂנוּ כְּגוֹיֵי הָאֲרָצוֹת, וְלֹא שָׂמָנוּ כְּמִשְׁפְּחוֹת הָאֲדָמָה,
3. שֶׁלֹּא שָׂם חֶלְקֵנוּ כָּהֶם, וְגֹרָלֵנוּ כְּכָל-הֲמוֹנָם,
4. וַאֲנַחְנוּ כּוֹרְעִים וּמִשְׁתַּחֲוִים וּמוֹדִים,
5. לִפְנֵי מֶלֶךְ מַלְכֵי הַמְּלָכִים, הַקָּדוֹשׁ בָּרוּךְ הוּא.

1. It is upon us (our duty) to praise the God of all, to praise the Creator of the universe,
2. who did not make us like the other nations of the world, and did not set us like the other families of the earth,
3. who did not appoint our lot to be like the others, and gave us a unique destiny.
4. We bend the knee, bow, and give thanks
5. before the Ruler of the rulers of rulers, the blessed Holy One.

53

Digital Application

Tell students that at home, before the next class, they should click on Masada or עָלֵינוּ to enter Level 5. Next, they click on the Torah scroll and עָלֵינוּ to practice reading lines 1–5 of the עָלֵינוּ.

In the next class, ask students to read these lines of the prayer out loud with a partner.

6. שֶׁהוּא נוֹטֶה שָׁמַיִם וְיֹסֵד אָרֶץ,
7. וּמוֹשַׁב יְקָרוֹ בַּשָּׁמַיִם מִמַּעַל וּשְׁכִינַת עֻזּוֹ בְּגָבְהֵי מְרוֹמִים.
8. הוּא אֱלֹהֵינוּ אֵין עוֹד, אֱמֶת מַלְכֵּנוּ אֶפֶס זוּלָתוֹ.
9. כַּכָּתוּב בְּתוֹרָתוֹ, וְיָדַעְתָּ הַיּוֹם וַהֲשֵׁבֹתָ אֶל לְבָבֶךָ,
10. כִּי יְיָ הוּא הָאֱלֹהִים בַּשָּׁמַיִם מִמַּעַל, וְעַל הָאָרֶץ מִתָּחַת, אֵין עוֹד.

6. God spreads out the heavens and establishes the earth,
7. God's glorious abode is in the heavens above and God's powerful Presence is in the highest of heights.
8. God is our God, there is no other. True that God is our Ruler, there is none besides God.
9. As it is written in God's Torah: Know on that day and take it to heart,
10. that Adonai is God in the heavens above, and on the earth below; there is no other.

11. וְנֶאֱמַר, וְהָיָה יְיָ לְמֶלֶךְ עַל כָּל הָאָרֶץ.
12. בַּיּוֹם הַהוּא יִהְיֶה יְיָ אֶחָד וּשְׁמוֹ אֶחָד.

11. And it is said: Adonai will rule all the land.
12. On that day, Adonai will be One and God's name will be One.

A Feeling of Belonging

Many of the words in עָלֵינוּ end with the suffix נוּ, meaning **us** or **our**. Circle all the words in עָלֵינוּ that end with נוּ. How many words did you circle? 8

Saying "us" and "our" rather than "me" and "my" reminds us that we are part of a community.

What do you think is the most important role of the synagogue community?

___

What do you like most about being part of your synagogue community?

___

54

A Feeling of Belonging

Have students complete "A Feeling of Belonging" with a partner. Call on students to share what they think is the most important role of the synagogue community *(Possible responses include: being a welcoming place for everyone who comes to the congregation; helping needy members of the community; teaching about Judaism to people of all ages)* and what they like most about being part of their synagogue community *(Responses may include: decorating the sukkah; feeling comfortable because I have been part of the community since pre-school; going to family dinners on Shabbat.)*

עָלֵינוּ

Read lines 6–12 of the עָלֵינוּ, one at a time, having students chorally repeat each line in Hebrew, and then read its English translation. Direct students to read these Hebrew lines with a partner.

Divide the class into three groups: א, ב, and ג. Assign each group two or three lines to master (lines 6–7, 8–9, or 10–12). The groups should practice reading until all members can read the lines fluently and accurately. Direct students to form new groups consisting of one or two students from each of the previous groups (א, ב, and ג). In these new groups, have the student(s) who practiced each set of lines help other group members master these lines. Continue until all students have mastered all seven lines.

Challenge students to underline each appearance of the words אָרֶץ, "earth," and שָׁמַיִם, "heavens." *(*אָרֶץ*—line 6, fifth word; line 10, eighth word; line 11, seventh word;* שָׁמַיִם*—line 6, third word; line 7, third word; line 10, fifth word)* Ask: What do these lines from the עָלֵינוּ tell us about the earth, or land, and the heavens? *(God spreads out the heavens; God establishes the earth; God is in the heavens; God is on the earth; God will rule all the land.)*

Teach, or have your cantor or music specialist teach, students to chant these verses.

Digital Application

Tell students that at home, before the next class, they should click on Masada or עָלֵינוּ to enter Level 5. Next, they click on the Torah scroll and עָלֵינוּ to practice reading all the lines of the עָלֵינוּ. In the next class, ask students to read this prayer out loud with a partner.

Word Tree

If you have created a word tree for the root מלכ, (see page 23), add מַלְכֵּנוּ, מֶלֶךְ מַלְכֵי הַמְּלָכִים, and לְמֶלֶךְ.

Prayer Words

Present the Hebrew and English of word cards 64–71. Invite a student to the front of the room.

Direct the student to stand in front of you, facing the class. As you stand behind the student, show the rest of the class one of the words. Challenge the student standing in front of you to guess which word is being displayed. The student may ask the class "yes" and "no" (or כֵּן and לֹא) questions about the word. For example, a student might ask, "Does the word have five or more letters?" Once the student has guessed the word and said its meaning, invite another student to guess a second word.

Display word card 51. Call on volunteers to read the word *(הָאוֹמֵר)*, give its English meaning *(the One who says)*, identify the prayer word to which it is related (וְנֶאֱמַר), state its English meaning *(and it is said)*, and name the three root letters on which these words are built (אמר).

Challenge students to identify the prayer word that is related to God's name, Adonai. (לַאֲדוֹן)

Remind students that God's name, Adonai, is not written the way we say it. We do not pronounce God's true name; rather we pronounce Adonai, which means "my God."

Have students work with a partner as they write the Hebrew for the English words listed, find these Hebrew words in the word search grid, and copy the letters they have not circled to reveal another name for God. Ask partners to check their work with another pair of students.

Digital Application

Tell students to click on the activities light bulb in Level 5 and play "Word Search" to review new vocabulary, which includes these Hebrew words: עָלֵינוּ (it is upon us [our duty]), לְשַׁבֵּחַ (to praise), לַאֲדוֹן (to God), הַכֹּל (of all), וַאֲנַחְנוּ (and we), כּוֹרְעִים (bend the knee), and וְנֶאֱמַר (and it is said). At the next class, display word cards 64–71. Ask: Which of these words or phrases was missing in the digital

Prayer Words

Practice reading these words from עָלֵינוּ.

it is upon us (our duty)	עָלֵינוּ
to praise	לְשַׁבֵּחַ
to God	לַאֲדוֹן
of all	הַכֹּל
and we	וַאֲנַחְנוּ
bend the knee	כּוֹרְעִים
Ruler of the rulers of rulers	מֶלֶךְ מַלְכֵי הַמְּלָכִים
and it is said	וְנֶאֱמַר

Write the Hebrew word for each English word below. Find and circle the Hebrew words hidden in the word search grid. Look from right to left and top to bottom. Then copy the letters you have *not* circled on to the lines below.

1. to God לַאֲדוֹן
2. bend the knee כּוֹרְעִים
3. and it is said וְנֶאֱמַר
4. to praise לְשַׁבֵּחַ
5. and we וַאֲנַחְנוּ
6. it is our duty עָלֵינוּ
7. of all הַכֹּל

ם	י	ע	ר	ו	כּ	
מ	ו	ע	ל	כּ	ה	ו
מ	נ	ל	ך	ל	ל	א
י	א	י	כ	שׁ	ל	נ
ל	מ	נ	מ	בּ	ה	ח
ם	ר	ו	י	ח	כ	נ
	ן	ו	ד	א	ל	ו

Another name for God is: מֶלֶךְ מַלְכֵי הַמְּלָכִים

55

Word Search? (מֶלֶךְ מַלְכֵי הַמְּלָכִים) What does this phrase mean? *(Ruler of the rulers of rulers)*

Collective Thanks

The word **וּמוֹדִים** tells us that **עָלֵינוּ** is a prayer of thanks as well as a declaration of loyalty. **וּמוֹדִים** means **and** (**we**) **give thanks**. The prefix **וּ** means **and**; the suffix **ִים** tells us that the verb is in the plural form.

Do you think it is significant that "and we give thanks" is in the plural form? Why or why not? ____________________

There are many other prayers of thanks. For example, each morning it is a tradition to recite a personal prayer of thanks to God, the מוֹדֶה/מוֹדָה אֲנִי.

How can it help us to start each day with words and thoughts of thanks and gratitude?

____

In modern Hebrew, the way to say **thanks a lot** is תּוֹדָה רַבָּה. Circle the word in that phrase that is in the same word family as מוֹדָה, מוֹדֶה, and וּמוֹדִים.

Name someone who has been kind or helpful to you. In the speech bubble, write "thanks a lot" in Hebrew.

תּוֹדָה רַבָּה

Thanksgiving in the Bible

Read these words of thanksgiving from the Bible.

In each line, find and circle the word of thanks, תּוֹדָה.

Remember: Sometimes a word includes prefixes.

1. וְקַטֵּר מֵחָמֵץ תּוֹדָה וְקִרְאוּ נְדָבוֹת הַשְׁמִיעוּ...
2. וַאֲנִי בְּקוֹל תּוֹדָה אֶזְבְּחָה-לָּךְ אֲשֶׁר נָדַרְתִּי אֲשַׁלֵּמָה...
3. וְהַתּוֹדָה הַשֵּׁנִית הַהוֹלֶכֶת לְמוֹאֵל וַאֲנִי אַחֲרֶיהָ...

56

Collective Thanks

Direct students to locate the word וּמוֹדִים on page 53. *(last word of line 4)* Call on a volunteer to read the English translation of lines 4 and 5. Have partners read the opening paragraph on page 56 and reflect on the significance of the phrase "and we give thanks" being in the plural form.

Invite students to share their responses with the class. *(Responses may include: It is significant because it reminds us that every person must express thanks; we join with others when we thank God; we are part of a community.)*

If your students have studied *Kol Yisrael 1*, ask them to tell about the מוֹדֶה/מוֹדָה אֲנִי prayer. *(Responses may include: When we recite* מוֹדֶה/מוֹדָה אֲנִי*, we thank God for the gift of a new day; boys say* מוֹדֶה אֲנִי *and girls say* מוֹדָה אֲנִי*.)*

Direct partners to finish reading the remaining paragraphs of "Collective Thanks" and to write how it can help us to start each day with words and thoughts of thanks. Call on volunteers to share their writings. *(Possible answers include: it makes us more aware of appreciating what we have; it reminds us of the importance of thanking others throughout the day; it reminds us not to take things for granted.)*

Ask a student to bring something, such as book, to your desk. Tell the student תּוֹדָה רַבָּה. Call on another student to translate תּוֹדָה רַבָּה. *(thanks a lot)* Thank that student by saying תּוֹדָה רַבָּה.

Thanksgiving in the Bible

Divide the class into groups of 3 students. Have students take turns reading the lines, so that all students read each line once. Direct students to circle the word תּוֹדָה in each of the three biblical quotes.

Line 1 is from Amos 4:5 ("And burn a thanksgiving offering of leavened bread, and loudly proclaim freewill offerings..."). Line 2 is from Jonah 2:10 ("But I will sacrifice to You with loud thanks, I will fulfill what I have vowed..."). Line 3 is from Nehemiah 12:38 ("And the second thanksgiving choir walked in the opposite direction, with me behind it..."). The verse from Jonah is part of the haftarah chanted on Yom Kippur afternoon.

Word Tree

Ask: Which word on page 56 is built on the root שלם? *(אֲשַׁלֵּמָה)* What is part of the meaning of words built on this root? *(wholeness)* If you have created a word tree for the root מלכ (see page 23), add the word הַמַּמְלָכָה.

Language Link

As a class, chorally read lines 11 and 12 on page 54. Direct students to locate the phrase בַּיּוֹם הַהוּא. Read aloud the first sentence of "Language Link." Have students join in with the Hebrew words in this sentence. Challenge students to name another prayer word that is related to the word בַּיּוֹם. *(word card 63—יָמֵינוּ—our days)*

Read aloud the days of the week, one day at a time, having students repeat chorally the Hebrew name of each day. Divide the class into groups of 3–4 students. Direct groups to practice saying the names of the days. Encourage group members to coach one another until all members can read the names fluently. For an added challenge, invite students to memorize the Hebrew names of the days. Consider preparing seven word cards, one for each day of the week. Distribute the cards to seven students. Challenge the students to stand, displaying their cards, according to the order of the days of the week.

Inform students that the literal translations of the days are as follows: יוֹם רִאשׁוֹן—a first day; יוֹם שֵׁנִי—a second day; יוֹם שְׁלִישִׁי—a third day; יוֹם רְבִיעִי—a fourth day; יוֹם חֲמִישִׁי—a fifth day; יוֹם שִׁשִּׁי—a sixth day; יוֹם שַׁבָּת—a day of rest. Ask students which Bible story is brought to mind by the Hebrew names of the days? *(the Creation story)* Consider reading selections to your students from chapter one of Genesis (verses 8, 13, 19, 23, and 31) which mention יוֹם שֵׁנִי—a second day, יוֹם שְׁלִישִׁי—a third day, יוֹם רְבִיעִי—a fourth day, and יוֹם חֲמִישִׁי—a fifth day, and יוֹם הַשִּׁשִּׁי—the sixth day.

Direct students to read and complete "Language Link" with a partner. Call on a student to say, in Hebrew, when we light candles. *(עֶרֶב שַׁבָּת)* Invite students to listen as you read the ending of Genesis 1:5, "There was evening and there was morning, a first day." Ask: Based on this verse, do you think the Jewish day begins in the morning or the evening? *(evening)* Why? *(Because according to the Creation story there was evening, then there was morning—the day began with the evening.)* What is the connection between the Creation

Language Link

The phrase בַּיּוֹם הַהוּא means **on that day**. In עָלֵינוּ it refers to the time when the world will be perfect. The Hebrew word for **day** is יוֹם.

Practice reading the days of the week in Hebrew.

Sunday (Day 1)	יוֹם רִאשׁוֹן
Monday (Day 2)	יוֹם שֵׁנִי
Tuesday (Day 3)	יוֹם שְׁלִישִׁי
Wednesday (Day 4)	יוֹם רְבִיעִי
Thursday (Day 5)	יוֹם חֲמִישִׁי
Friday (Day 6)	יוֹם שִׁשִּׁי
Saturday (Shabbat)	יוֹם שַׁבָּת

What Bible story in the Book of Genesis do the names of the days remind you of? Why?

The creation story. It tells about the seven days of creation

עֶרֶב שַׁבָּת means the **eve of Shabbat**, Friday night.

יוֹם שַׁבָּת means the **day of Shabbat**, Saturday.

Fill in the missing Hebrew word that tells when we light Shabbat candles.

שַׁבָּת עֶרֶב

Did you know that Sunday is a weekday in Israel? In fact, Jewish Israeli kids go to school יוֹם רִאשׁוֹן through יוֹם שִׁשִּׁי. The good news is that Jewish religious holidays, like רֹאשׁ הַשָּׁנָה and פֶּסַח, are also national holidays and days off from school!

57

story and the tradition of lighting Shabbat candles in the evening? *(We learn from the Creation story that the Jewish day begins in the evening. We mark the beginning of the Shabbat, around sunset, by lighting candles.)*

As a class, chorally name the days of the week, in Hebrew, that Israeli children attend school. Have students suggest other Jewish holidays when schools would be closed in Israel *(Yom Kippur, Sukkot, Shavuot)* Tell your students that you are going to ask them different questions and that they must respond in Hebrew. Suggested questions include: What day(s) do you play a sport? What day(s) do you take music lessons? What day(s) do you invite a friend over? For fun, have a student ask classmates a similar question. The student who answers the question in Hebrew is then invited to ask a new question.

Digital Application

In Level 5 of the digital application, have students click on the activities light bulb and then "Matching." Here, students will match the Hebrew and English names of the days of the week. In the next class session, challenge students to recite the days of the week in Hebrew.

Putting It in ConTEXT

Reread line 6 of עָלֵינוּ, which describes God as the Creator of the world.

נוֹטֶה שָׁמַיִם וְיֹסֵד אָרֶץ

This line comes from the book of the prophet Isaiah (51:13). Other lines in Isaiah (42:5) also describe God as the Creator of the world.

כֹּה־אָמַר הָאֵל יְהוָה בּוֹרֵא הַשָּׁמַיִם וְנוֹטֵיהֶם
רֹקַע הָאָרֶץ וְצֶאֱצָאֶיהָ...

Thus says God, Adonai, who created the heavens and stretched them out,
Who spread forth the earth and all that comes out of it ...

Circle the Hebrew words for **heaven** or **the heavens** in the three Hebrew lines from Isaiah above. How many words did you circle? 2

Underline the Hebrew words for **earth** or **the earth**. How many words did you circle? 2 *Hint:* Check out the photo caption on this page.

אֶרֶץ, שָׁמַיִם, וְצוֹפִים

Psst! The word הַצֹּפִים ("the scouts") appears in the Bible. Circle it below.

וַיִּרְאוּ הַצֹּפִים לְשָׁאוּל בְּגִבְעַת בִּנְיָמִן וְהִנֵּה הֶהָמוֹן נָמוֹג וַיֵּלֶךְ וַהֲלֹם.

(King) Saul's scouts in Gibeah of Benjamin saw masses of people scattering in all directions. (1 Samuel 14:16)

58

Students may also be surprised to learn about opportunities in Jewish scouting that are available for them in North America.

Prayer Chart

If you have created a chart of the Shabbat morning service (see page 25), write עָלֵינוּ on a 4″ x 6″ index card and add this new prayer to the chart.

אוֹי!

Play a game of אוֹי! (see page 13) to review the prayer words (word cards 64–71) from this chapter, along with words from previous chapters.

Putting It in ConTEXT

Have a student lead classmates in a choral reading of line 6, page 54, in both Hebrew and English. Call on students to explain the meaning of this line. *(Possible responses include: it is God who spreads out everything that is in the heavens and establishes everything that is on earth; it tells us that God created the heavens and the earth.)*

Direct students to chorally read the Hebrew verses from Isaiah on page 58. Alternatively, have students read these verses with a partner. Walk around the room to informally assess how well students can decode unfamiliar words. Then, read these verses chorally with your students.

Inform your students that the words in the עָלֵינוּ taken from Isaiah 51:13 are chanted as part of the haftarah of פָּרָשַׁת שֹׁפְטִים and that the second line on page 58 (Isaiah 42:5) is found in the haftarah of פָּרָשַׁת בְּרֵאשִׁית.

Have students circle independently the words for heaven and earth in the lines from Isaiah. Suggest that students read the caption of the photo if they need help recalling the Hebrew words for heaven and earth.

As a class, read aloud the verse from 1 Samuel in Hebrew and then in English. Direct students to circle the word הַצּוֹפִים in the verse.

Photo Op

Invite a volunteer to read the photo caption. Call on volunteers to describe the photo and to create a story that describes what the צוֹפִים might have been doing the day of the photo. A student may say, for example, that about twenty צוֹפִים and their leaders spent a day by a lake cleaning up the beachfront area. This photo was taken after a hard, but fun, day of work.

If you have access to the Internet, have your students research the Israeli Scouts and Jewish scouting in North America. The Israeli Scouts have a website in English that tells all about its history, its purpose, and its positive influence on Israeli youth. Inform students that presently there are thousands of Jewish and Arab Israelis who are active in the Israeli Scout movement.

My Reflections on the Prayer

If your students are creating a booklet of reflections on the prayers, give each student a page of prompts to complete (see page 29) devoted to עָלֵינוּ. Remember to have students draw an illustration or symbol to represent each prayer. Add this new page to their folder or binder of personal reflections.

Prayer Words

Make a word card for אֲדָמָה (earth) and review its meaning. Students may be familiar with the word if they studied the blessings over food in *Kol Yisrael 1*. Display the word אֲדָמָה along with the Hebrew of word cards 1, 5, 17, 20, 22, 33, 38, 40, 56, and 64–71 on the ledge of the board.

Divide the class into two teams. Have teams take turns choosing a word, reading the Hebrew, and giving its English translation. If the team reads and translates the word correctly, the team keeps the word card. Continue until all words have been read and correctly translated.

Have students play Tic-Tac-Toe, writing lightly in pencil, with a classmate. For an added challenge, ask students to say the meaning of the words as they read them. After playing both Tic-Tac-Toe boards, direct students to erase their boards and play another round with a new partner.

Clue to Cyberspace

Have students work with a partner to read and complete "Clue to Cyberspace."

Tell students that at home, before the next class, they should click on the joystick in Level 5 to play Carnival Duck. In the game they will review words from עָלֵינוּ. Remind students to use the clue—יְהוּדָה—to score bonus points in this online game in Level 5.

Tic-Tac-Toe

Play Tic-Tac-Toe with a classmate. Take turns reading a word or phrase. If you are correct, lightly write an X or an O in pencil in that box.

אֱמֶת	וַאֲנַחְנוּ	גְּדֻלָּה
אֵין	בַּשָּׁמַיִם	אֶחָד
מֶלֶךְ מַלְכֵי הַמְּלָכִים	עֹז	אֲדָמָה

כּוֹרְעִים	לִפְנֵי	וְנֶאֱמַר
הַכֹּל	שָׁם	לַאֲדוֹן
לְשַׁבֵּחַ	וּשְׁמוֹ	עָלֵינוּ

Clue to Cyberspace

Go down the steps of Masada by reading each line aloud and circling the words that do ***not*** appear in עָלֵינוּ.

1. עָלֵינוּ לְשַׁבֵּחַ לַאֲדוֹן (יִשְׂרָאֵל) הַכֹּל שֶׁלֹּא
2. עָשָׂנוּ כְּגוֹיֵי (הָרַחֲמִים) הָאֲרָצוֹת וַאֲנַחְנוּ כּוֹרְעִים
3. (וּבָאָרֶץ) וּמִשְׁתַּחֲוִים וּמוֹדִים לִפְנֵי מֶלֶךְ מַלְכֵי
4. הַמְּלָכִים וְנֶאֱמַר וְהָיָה (דְּבָרִים) בַּיּוֹם הַהוּא
5. יִהְיֶה (הַגְּבוּרָה) יְיָ אֶחָד וּשְׁמוֹ אֶחָד

On the lines below, write the first letter of each of the circled words to discover the Hebrew name of the desert in which Masada is located. Do not write any dots or vowels.

יְ ה וּ דָ ה

Use this clue to score bonus points in the "Carnival Duck!" game in Level 5 on your computer.

59

Assessment

As students are working on any of the above activities, meet with them individually to assess reading fluency and knowledge of prayer content. Use the Prayer Mastery Assessment Chart on page 17 of the Teacher's Edition to keep track of student progress. You can also assess students' progress online at www.behrmanhouse.com. Click on the blue "Assessment" button at the bottom of the screen, select *Kol Yisrael 3*, and type in your class's serial number to see how students are doing in their digital application. Students can also e-mail their lesson summary to you directly or print out a lesson summary and bring it in to class.

What's Next?

Ask: In which languages are the prayers in a siddur written? *(Responses may include: English, Hebrew, Russian, French, and Farsi)* Why do we have prayers in so many languages? *(so worshippers understand what they are saying)* Inform students that some of the prayers in the siddur are written in Aramaic, the language spoken by Jews about two thousand years ago. In the next chapter, they will study the קַדִּישׁ, which was written in the everyday language of our ancestors, Aramaic.

קַדִּישׁ 6

ABOUT THE PRAYER

The קַדִּישׁ praises God and expresses our hope for peace throughout the world. Every prayer services contains several versions of the קַדִּישׁ. The קַדִּישׁ often distinguishes the end of one part of a service from the beginning of the next. One version, the Mourner's קַדִּישׁ, is recited at the *end* of the service in memory of loved ones who have died. The קַדִּישׁ is written in Aramaic, the language spoken by Jews in the fifth century BCE and for about a thousand years after that. The קַדִּישׁ does not mention death.

LEARNING OBJECTIVES

Students will be able to:

- Recite the קַדִּישׁ fluently.
- Define key words and the root גדל.
- Locate Be'er Sheva on a map of Israel.
- Match Aramaic words of the קַדִּישׁ to related Hebrew words.
- Explain that the קַדִּישׁ, which is recited by mourners, praises God and does not mention death.
- Demonstrate how we bow when reciting עֹשֶׂה שָׁלוֹם at the end of the קַדִּישׁ.

ESSENTIAL QUESTION

How might reciting the קַדִּישׁ comfort mourners and strengthen their connection to God and the Jewish community?

NEW WORDS AND PHRASES

Prayer Words:

will be great	יִתְגַּדַּל
and will be holy	וְיִתְקַדַּשׁ
God's name	שְׁמֵהּ
in the world	בְּעָלְמָא
God's kingdom	מַלְכוּתֵהּ
the blessings	בִּרְכָתָא
peace	שְׁלָמָא

INSTRUCTIONAL MATERIALS

Text pages 60–69

word cards 72–78

Digital Application: Level 6—קַדִּישׁ (see page 9 for a list of games and activities)

WHERE WE ARE

Ben and Batya are visiting cousins in Be'er Sheva, a city that is home to many Jewish immigrants who made עֲלִיָּה in the hope of building better lives for themselves and their families.

Like the עוֹלִים, we all have times in our lives when we need hope and courage. The קַדִּישׁ expresses our hope for a kinder, more peaceful world.

INTRODUCING THE LESSON

Inform students that there is a specific prayer, the קַדִּישׁ, that is recited by a person who is in mourning. Invite students to name what they would expect the contents of this prayer to include.

Write students' suggestions on the board. Students will most likely guess that the prayer is about a person who has died or about death. Inform students that the קַדִּישׁ, the prayer they will study in this chapter, praises God's greatness and has no reference to death.

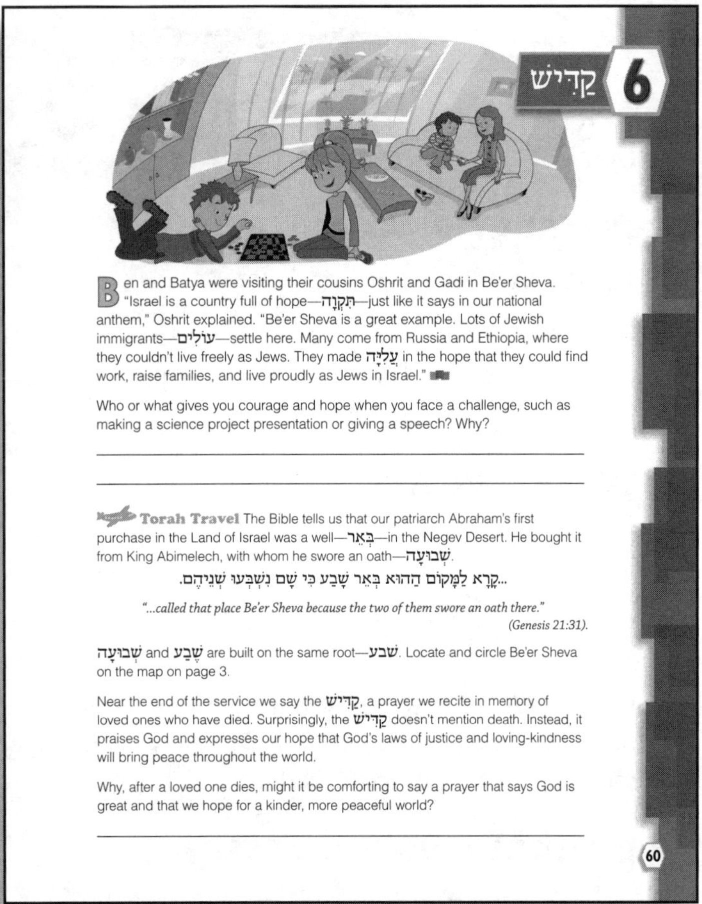

קַדִּישׁ 6

Ben and Batya were visiting their cousins Oshrit and Gadi in Be'er Sheva. "Israel is a country full of hope—תִּקְוָה—just like it says in our national anthem," Oshrit explained. "Be'er Sheva is a great example. Lots of Jewish immigrants—עוֹלִים—settle here. Many come from Russia and Ethiopia, where they couldn't live freely as Jews. They made עֲלִיָּה in the hope that they could find work, raise families, and live proudly as Jews in Israel."

Who or what gives you courage and hope when you face a challenge, such as making a science project presentation or giving a speech? Why?

Torah Travel The Bible tells us that our patriarch Abraham's first purchase in the Land of Israel was a well—בְּאֵר—in the Negev Desert. He bought it from King Abimelech, with whom he swore an oath—שְׁבוּעָה.

...קָרָא לַמָּקוֹם הַהוּא בְּאֵר שָׁבַע כִּי שָׁם נִשְׁבְּעוּ שְׁנֵיהֶם.

"...called that place Be'er Sheva because the two of them swore an oath there."
(Genesis 21:31).

שְׁבוּעָה and שֶׁבַע are built on the same root—שבע. Locate and circle Be'er Sheva on the map on page 3.

Near the end of the service we say the קַדִּישׁ, a prayer we recite in memory of loved ones who have died. Surprisingly, the קַדִּישׁ doesn't mention death. Instead, it praises God and expresses our hope that God's laws of justice and loving-kindness will bring peace throughout the world.

Why, after a loved one dies, might it be comforting to say a prayer that says God is great and that we hope for a kinder, more peaceful world?

60

the camera to view photographs of Be'er Sheva. Included are photos of (1) an ancient well with a stone waterway, (2) Ben Gurion University, (3) the Monument to the Negev Brigade, (4) a Bedouin camp, (5) salt along the Dead Sea, (6) floating in the Dead Sea. Consider showing students additional images of Be'er Sheva. The Internet is a great resource for these photos. If your students are creating travel guides for various places in Israel (see page 6), invite the students who are researching Be'er Sheva to give highlights of what they have learned so far about this city.

Have students read silently to the end of page 60. Ask: What are the main ideas expressed in the קַדִּישׁ? *(God is great; we hope that God's laws will help bring about a peaceful world.)* Why might a mourner find it comforting to recite the קַדִּישׁ? *(Students might suggest: it gives us hope that we will feel better in the future; it reminds us that there are still wonderful things in the world; it helps us to appreciate all that we do have.)*

Direct students to write a response to the final question on page 60.

INTO THE TEXT

Have partners read the opening paragraph on page 60. Ask questions, such as: Which song tells of our hope? *(Israel's national anthem—הַתִּקְוָה)* What is the meaning of עֲלִיָּה in this paragraph? *(immigrating to Israel)* What is another meaning of עֲלִיָּה? *(the honor of being called to the Torah)* Where did some of the Jews of Be'er Sheva live before making עֲלִיָּה? *(Ethiopia and Russia)* What do you think it was like for these עוֹלִים to move to Israel? *(Responses may include: wonderful, because they could finally live freely as Jews; scary, because Israel is very different from their homeland; challenging, because they needed to learn a new language and go to new schools)*

Have students write about a personal source of courage. Invite students to share their writings. *(Responses may include: my mother gives me courage because she tells me she knows I can succeed; when my friends give me a high five they make me feel like they believe in me.)*

Torah Travel

Direct students to follow along in the English, and chorally read the Hebrew words, as you read the paragraph introducing Genesis 21:31. Ask: Why do you think Abraham wanted to purchase a well? *(Possible answers include: there isn't a lot of rain in the Negev Desert; he needed to know he would have water for his family and animals.)* Remind students how nowadays Israel is called the Silicon Valley of water technology (see student text page 14). Inform students that while we don't know exactly when Abraham lived, we estimate that he lived about four thousand years ago.

Call on students to name four words on page 60 built on the root letters שבע. *(שְׁבוּעָה, שֶׁבַע, נִשְׁבְּעוּ, שָׁבַע)* Inform students that words built on these root letters have "oath" as part of their meaning. Direct students to circle בְּאֵר שֶׁבַע on the map on page 3.

Digital Application

At home, or in class, have students click on Be'er Sheva on the Contents map or on the prayers listed for Level 6 and then click on

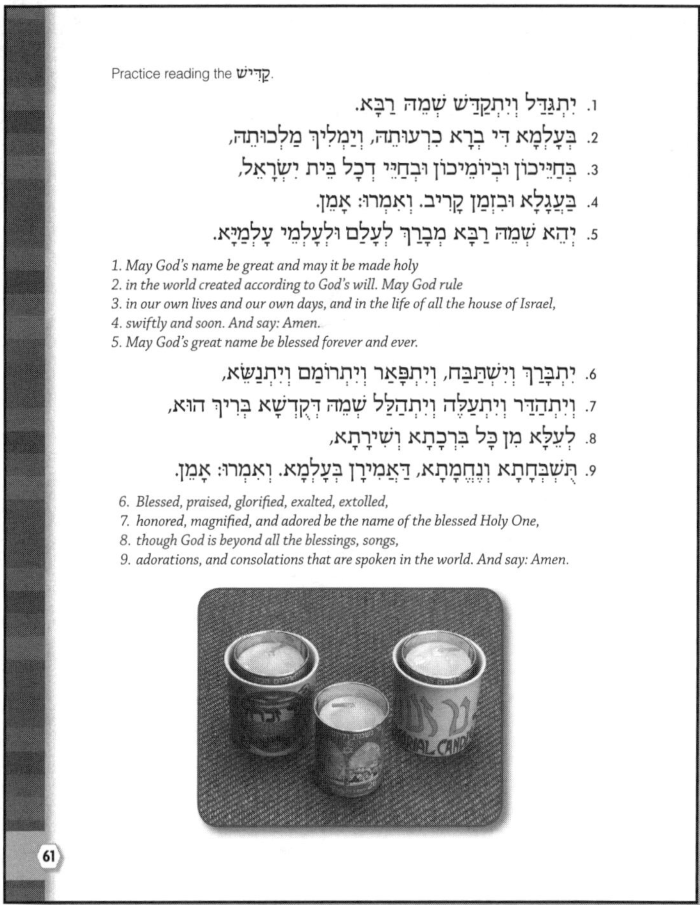

Practice reading the קַדִּישׁ.

1. יִתְגַּדַּל וְיִתְקַדַּשׁ שְׁמֵהּ רַבָּא.
2. בְּעָלְמָא דִּי בְרָא כִרְעוּתֵהּ, וְיַמְלִיךְ מַלְכוּתֵהּ,
3. בְּחַיֵּיכוֹן וּבְיוֹמֵיכוֹן וּבְחַיֵּי דְכָל בֵּית יִשְׂרָאֵל,
4. בַּעֲגָלָא וּבִזְמַן קָרִיב. וְאִמְרוּ: אָמֵן.
5. יְהֵא שְׁמֵהּ רַבָּא מְבָרַךְ לְעָלַם וּלְעָלְמֵי עָלְמַיָּא.

1. May God's name be great and may it be made holy
2. in the world created according to God's will. May God rule
3. in our own lives and our own days, and in the life of all the house of Israel,
4. swiftly and soon. And say: Amen.
5. May God's great name be blessed forever and ever.

6. יִתְבָּרַךְ וְיִשְׁתַּבַּח, וְיִתְפָּאַר וְיִתְרוֹמַם וְיִתְנַשֵּׂא,
7. וְיִתְהַדַּר וְיִתְעַלֶּה וְיִתְהַלַּל שְׁמֵהּ דְּקֻדְשָׁא בְּרִיךְ הוּא,
8. לְעֵלָּא מִן כָּל בִּרְכָתָא וְשִׁירָתָא,
9. תֻּשְׁבְּחָתָא וְנֶחֱמָתָא, דַּאֲמִירָן בְּעָלְמָא. וְאִמְרוּ: אָמֵן.

6. Blessed, praised, glorified, exalted, extolled,
7. honored, magnified, and adored be the name of the blessed Holy One,
8. though God is beyond all the blessings, songs,
9. adorations, and consolations that are spoken in the world. And say: Amen.

61

קַדִּישׁ

The קַדִּישׁ is packed with many unfamiliar words. Be gentle with your students! Introduce a limited number of new lines during one class session. If, for example, you are able to devote four sessions to the קַדִּישׁ, then have students study lines 1–3, 4–6, 7–9, and 10–13 over the four meetings.

Read three to four lines of the קַדִּישׁ, phrase by phrase, then line by line, having students chorally repeat each phrase and line. After each Hebrew line is practiced, have students chorally read aloud the English. Direct students to read the Hebrew lines with a partner. Walk around the room listening to students read. Take note of the words that are most difficult, such as כִּרְעוּתֵהּ, for students to decode. Devote a few minutes to practicing these challenging words. Write one of the words on the board, have students chorally, then in pairs, and then individually, read the word.

Repeat this for all challenging words. Encourage students to ask for assistance in reading difficult words. Remind them that asking questions is essential for learning.

At the next class sessions, repeat the above process, introducing three or four additional lines of the קַדִּישׁ.

After students have practiced reading all of the קַדִּישׁ, divide the class into three groups: א, בּ, and ג. Assign each group four or five lines to master (lines 1–5, 6–9, or 10–13). The groups should practice reading until all members can read the lines fluently and accurately. Direct students to form new groups consisting of one or two students from each of the previous groups (א, בּ, and ג). In these new groups, have the student(s) who practiced each set of lines help other group members master these lines. Continue until all students have mastered all thirteen lines.

Note: While groups are practicing, you may choose to work one-on-one with students who need more attention. *Be realistic about the level of fluency and accuracy you can expect from your students when they learn this prayer!* Remember, it can take years of practice to master it.

Digital Application

Tell students that at home, before the next class, they should click on Be'er Sheva or קַדִּישׁ to enter Level 6. Next, they click on the Torah scroll and קַדִּישׁ to practice reading lines 1–5 of the קַדִּישׁ. In the next class, ask students to read these lines of the prayer out loud with a partner.

Photo Op

Inform students that these are memorial candles, often referred to as *yahrtzeit* candles. A *yahrtzeit* candle burns for twenty-four hours and is lit on the anniversary of a loved one's death. It is also traditional to light a *yahrtzeit* candle at sundown on Yom Kippur, Shemini Atzeret, the last night of Passover, and Shavuot. Ask: How might lighting a yahrzeit candle bring comfort to a person who has lost a loved one? *(Responses may include: it signifies that the person will always be a part of our lives; it makes us think of how lucky we were to have had that person in our lives; we feel*

10. יְהֵא שְׁלָמָא רַבָּא מִן שְׁמַיָּא,
11. וְחַיִּים עָלֵינוּ וְעַל כָּל יִשְׂרָאֵל. וְאִמְרוּ: אָמֵן.
12. עֹשֶׂה שָׁלוֹם בִּמְרוֹמָיו, הוּא יַעֲשֶׂה שָׁלוֹם עָלֵינוּ,
13. וְעַל כָּל יִשְׂרָאֵל. וְאִמְרוּ: אָמֵן.

10. May there be great peace from heaven
11. and life for us and for all Israel. And say: Amen.
12. May God who makes peace in the heavens, make peace for us
13. and for all Israel. And say: Amen.

The Hebrew-Aramaic Connection

Did you notice anything unusual about the language of the קַדִּישׁ? Most of the words are in Aramaic, a language that is similar to Hebrew. Aramaic was spoken by the Jews at the time of Ezra the prophet in the fifth century BCE and for about a thousand years after that.

The last two lines of the קַדִּישׁ are written in Hebrew. What is the name of another prayer in which those same two lines appear? *Hint:* Its English meaning is the "Standing Prayer." עֲמִידָה

Many Aramaic words in the קַדִּישׁ are similar to Hebrew words that you already know. Be a world-class linguist and draw a line from each Hebrew word below to its related Aramaic word. *Hint:* Look for related roots.

ARAMAIC	HEBREW	
וְיַמְלִיךְ ✔	שָׁלוֹם	1. ✔
בְּרִיךְ ✔	קָדוֹשׁ	2. ✔
וְיִתְקַדַּשׁ ✔	שָׁמַיִם	3.
שְׁלָמָא ✔	יִמְלֹךְ	4. ✔
בְּעָלְמָא	הַגָּדוֹל	5.
שְׁמַיָּא	בָּרוּךְ	6. ✔
יִתְגַּדַּל	הָעוֹלָם	7.

62

comforted that we are doing something to honor the person we loved.)*

קַדִּישׁ

Focus students on lines 11–13. Challenge students to cover the English, and to translate the Hebrew of line 11, the last two words of line 12, and line 13. Call on a student to identify, in Hebrew, the two things we ask God for. *(*חַיִּים *and* שָׁלוֹם*)*

Teach, or have your cantor or music specialist teach, students to chant the קַדִּישׁ. We suggest that students learn to chant a few verses at each class session. Students will have greater success by learning a limited number of verses at a time.

Have your students practice chanting the קַדִּישׁ according to the traditions of your congregation.

Students should know which lines are chanted by the leader and which lines are chanted by the congregants. Demonstrate, and have students practice, the prayer movements of lines 12 and 13: bow to the left when saying עֹשֶׂה, bow to the right when saying הוּא, and to the center on the word עָלֵינוּ.

Reading Review

Divide the class into two teams: א and ב. Provide clues for teams to correctly identify a line from the קַדִּישׁ and then read it fluently. For example, ask a team to read the line that: has two words built on the root letters מלכ *(*מַלְכוּתֵהּ*,* וְיַמְלִיךְ*—line 2)*; has a word that is also the name of the prayer studied in Chapter 5 *(*עָלֵינוּ*—11)*; has three words built on the root letters עלמ *(*לְעָלַם*,* עָלְמַיָּא *,*וּלְעָלְמֵי*—line 5)*. Award a team one point for each line it identifies correctly and two additional points for each line it reads fluently and accurately. The team with the most points wins.

Digital Application

Tell students that at home, before the next class, they should click on Be'er Sheva or קַדִּישׁ to enter Level 6. Next, they click on the Torah scroll and קַדִּישׁ to practice reading the next lines of the קַדִּישׁ (1-8 on the second screen). In the next class, ask students to read the prayer out loud with a partner.

The Hebrew–Aramaic Connection

Direct students to work with a partner to read and complete "The Hebrew–Aramaic Connection." Have partners take turns reading the Hebrew and Aramaic words aloud. Each pair of students should check their work with another pair.

Play a short game to give students practice in reading these words. Divide the class into two teams. Prepare ten to twelve questions based on the word lists. Have teams take turns answering questions. Suggested questions include: What are the root letters on which both שָׁלוֹם and שְׁלָמָא are built? (שלמ) Which two words have bless or praise as part of their meaning? (בְּרִיךְ *and* בָּרוּךְ)

Which two words are built on the root letters גדל? (הַגָּדוֹל *and* יִתְגַּדַּל) A team earns a point for each correct answer. The team with the most points is the winner.

Prayer Words

Display Hebrew word cards 72–78 on the ledge of the board. Call on a volunteer to choose one word card and challenge classmates to say something about its meaning or to identify a related word. Encourage students to guess the general meaning of the word. After students have discussed the new word, tell students the full English meaning of the word. A student might, for example, show word card 74, שְׁמֵהּ. A classmate may note that it is similar to the words שֵׁם, "name," and שְׁמוֹ, "God's name," and suggest that "name" is part of its meaning. Inform students that שְׁמֵהּ is the Aramaic for שְׁמוֹ, God's name. Invite additional volunteers to choose and lead a discussion about the remaining word cards, one at a time.

Show students word cards 75, בְּעָלְמָא, and 77, בִּרְכָתָא. Ask: What ending do these words have in common? *(◼ָא)* Based on the English meaning of these words, what do you think the usual meaning of the ◼ָא suffix is? *(the)*

Challenge students to look over the קַדִּישׁ on pages 61 and 62 and circle all the words that have this ending. Inform students that in most of these words the ◼ָא suffix means "the." Have students identify the three consecutive lines in the קַדִּישׁ in which none of the words have the ◼ָא suffix. *(lines 11, 12, and 13)* Ask: What language do you think these lines are written in? *(Hebrew)* What is one clue we can use to judge if a prayer is in Hebrew or Aramaic? *(If there are a lot of words with the ◼ָא suffix, the prayer is in Aramaic. Otherwise, the prayer is in Hebrew.)*

Getting to the Root of a Word

Have students complete this activity independently. Walk around the room to informally assess how well students can identify words built on specific root letters. On page 62, students should put a check next to the following words: שָׁלוֹם, קָדוֹשׁ, יִמְלֹךְ, בָּרוּךְ, וַיַּמְלִיךְ, בְּרִיךְ, וְיִתְקַדַּשׁ, and שְׁלָמָא.

> **Prayer Words**
>
> Practice reading these words from the קַדִּישׁ.
>
> | | |
> |---|---|
> | will be great | יִתְגַּדַּל |
> | and will be holy | וְיִתְקַדַּשׁ |
> | God's name | שְׁמֵהּ |
> | in the world | בְּעָלְמָא |
> | God's kingdom | מַלְכוּתֵהּ |
> | the blessings | בִּרְכָתָא |
> | peace | שְׁלָמָא |
>
> **Getting to the Root of a Word**
>
> In the blank space next to each root below write a prayer word from above that is built on the same root.
>
> 1. ברכ ___בִּרְכָתָא___
> 2. מלכ ___מַלְכוּתֵהּ___
> 3. קדש ___וְיִתְקַדַּשׁ___
> 4. שלמ ___שְׁלָמָא___
>
> *Bonus Points:* Turn to the activity on page 62. Put a check next to each Hebrew and Aramaic word that is built on one of the roots below. *Hint:* ך is a final כ.
>
> מלכ   שלמ   ברכ   קדש
>
> Now, circle the root letters in each word that you checked.
>
> 63

Word Tree

If you have created word trees for the roots מלכ, שלמ, and דבר, add the words וַיַּמְלִיךְ, מַלְכוּתֵהּ; שְׁלָמָא; and וְיִתְקַדַּשׁ, דְּקֻדְשָׁא, קַדִּישׁ, to the respective word trees.

Prayer Chart

If you have begun a chart of the Shabbat morning service (see page 25), write קַדִּישׁ on a 4″ x 6″ index card and add this new prayer to the chart.

Language Link

The phrase בֵּית יִשְׂרָאֵל, in line 3 of the קַדִּישׁ, means **House of Israel.** בֵּית יִשְׂרָאֵל is not a place; it is the name of our people—the Jewish people. Many other Hebrew expressions that begin with the word בֵּית, meaning **house of**, *are* names of places. Here are just a few.

school (house of books)	בֵּית-סֵפֶר
cafe (house of coffee)	בֵּית-קָפֶה
hospital (house of the sick)	בֵּית-חוֹלִים
synagogue (house of assembly)	בֵּית-כְּנֶסֶת
court of law (house of law)	בֵּית-מִשְׁפָּט
factory (house of manufacturing)	בֵּית-חֲרֹשֶׁת

Hebrew Houses

Read the Hebrew phrases below then draw a line from each phrase to its illustration.

בֵּית-חֲרֹשֶׁת בֵּית-כְּנֶסֶת בֵּית-מִשְׁפָּט

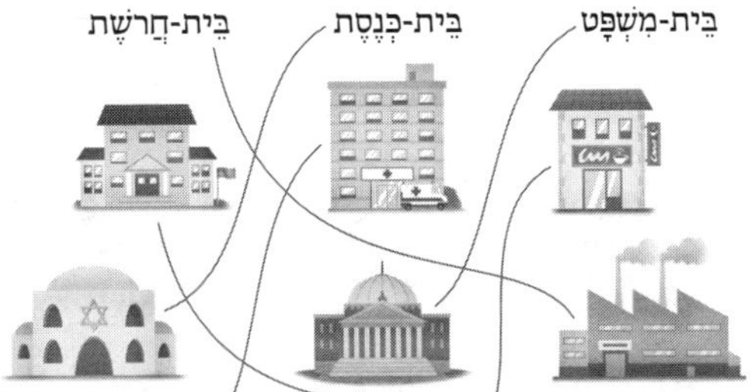

בֵּית-חוֹלִים בֵּית-קָפֶה בֵּית-סֵפֶר

The Hebrew word meaning "house of" is בֵּית

64

Hebrew Houses

Students work with a partner as they match each place name to its illustration.

Digital Application

In Level 6 of the digital application, have students click on the activities light bulb and then "Matching." Here, students will partner the Hebrew name of a building with a matching illustration. In the next class session, challenge students to say the Hebrew name of a place where they study (בֵּית־סֵפֶר) and a place where a community comes together for worship (בֵּית־כְּנֶסֶת).

Have your students return to Level 3, Tel Aviv, in the digital application. Direct students to click on the camera and read the Hebrew signs in the third photograph. Ask: Which word on the sign is similar to the words we have just studied? (בית־מרקחת) Write בית־מרקחת on the board. Add in the vowels; invite students to read the word בֵּית־מִרְקַחַת. Inform students that בֵּית־מִרְקַחַת means pharmacy. The other Hebrew sign is the name of the store: סופר־פארם—Super-Pharm.

Language Link

Have students locate the phrase בֵּית יִשְׂרָאֵל on page 61, line 3. Direct students to refer to the English translation of line 3 and say the meaning of בֵּית יִשְׂרָאֵל *(house of Israel)*. Ask students to name the person in the Bible who was called יִשְׂרָאֵל. *(Jacob)* Draw a simple house, or tent, on the board. Write the name יִשְׂרָאֵל on the house. Below the house, write the names of Jacob's children: Reuben, Simeon, Levi, Judah, Dan, Naphtali, Gad, Asher, Issachar, Zebulun, Dina, Joseph, and Benjamin. Alternatively, draw stick figures to represent Jacob's children. Inform students that Jacob, יִשְׂרָאֵל, had twelve sons and several daughters (we know the name of only one daughter, Dina). Explain that Jacob's children and their descendents are called בֵּית יִשְׂרָאֵל.

Direct students to read silently the opening paragraph of "Language Link." Invite a volunteer to read the English name of each of the places; lead the class in chorally reading its Hebrew name.

As a class, make up a story that uses these Hebrew names of places. Encourage students to be imaginative and have fun with the story. Begin the story by making up a sentence that includes the word בֵּית־סֵפֶר. Say for example, "I got lost on my way to my בֵּית־סֵפֶר." Go around the room, having each student add a new sentence, using the next Hebrew term on the list. The next student might say, "So I decided it would be fun to go to the בֵּית־קָפֶה and get a snack."

Continue until all students have had a chance to add a sentence.

Call on a volunteer to read the English meaning of בֵּית־כְּנֶסֶת that is written in parentheses *(house of assembly)*. Have students suggest why a synagogue would be called a "house of assembly." *(Responses may include: because it is a place where a community comes together, assembles; because it is a place where people come together to pray, study, and meet)*

More About the Kaddish

Read aloud the first paragraph on page 65. Invite students to chorally add the Hebrew words as you read the paragraph. Ask students to think about the contents of the קַדִּישׁ and to suggest why it is recited several times in each prayer service. *(Suggestions may include: because it gave people a chance to praise God in their everyday language; it allows us several opportunities to say that God is holy.)*

To reinforce the idea that the קַדִּישׁ appears in different versions and in many places, consider having students locate various versions of the קַדִּישׁ in your siddur. Some of the pages on which the קַדִּישׁ appears are as follows: *Mishkan T'filah*—pages 26, 90, 106, and 194; *Kol Haneshamah*—pages 55, 131, 173, and 381; *Siddur Sim Shalom* pages 10, 48, 106, and 184.

Direct students to read silently the rest of "More About the Kaddish." Ask open-ended and recall questions to review the information about the קַדִּישׁ. Suggested questions include: What is something new you learned from reading this page? What did you find most interesting on this page? What did you find most surprising? What other prayers and parts of a service are done only in the presence of a מִנְיָן? *(The Torah Service;* בָּרְכוּ*; the* קְדוּשָּׁה *of the* עֲמִידָה*).*

Have students write independently what they believe might be a good reason for mourners to recite the קַדִּישׁ only in the presence of a מִנְיָן. *(Responses may include: because the mourner may feel comforted by being part of a community; the mourner does not feel alone and receives emotional support from the community; the mourner is showing others his or her loyalty to God despite having suffered a loss.)* Invite students to share their responses with the class.

At the Root

Display word cards 19 (גַּדְּלוּ), 20 (הַגְּדֻלָּה), and 72 (יִתְגַּדַּל). Call on students to read and say the English meaning of each of these words. *(Respectively: glorify, the greatness, will be great)*

More About the Kaddish

So far, you have learned about the Mourner's קַדִּישׁ. But there are other versions of the קַדִּישׁ. One is the חֲצִי קַדִּישׁ, which means "Half Kaddish," even though it is only slightly shorter than the Mourner's קַדִּישׁ. The קַדִּישׁ divides a prayer service just like a bell between classes divides a school day. It indicates the end of one section of the service and the start of the next.

In some congregations, only the mourners and those observing *yahrtzeit*—the anniversary of a loved one's death—stand as they recite the Mourner's קַדִּישׁ. In others, everyone stands.

We are not sure who wrote the קַדִּישׁ or when it was written. It probably evolved over several centuries. About eight hundred years ago the קַדִּישׁ became the prayer recited by mourners.

Traditionally we recite the קַדִּישׁ only in the presence of a מִנְיָן —a group of ten or more Jews who are at least of bar or bat mitzvah age. As the mourners chant the prayer, the congregation praises God, hoping their words of faith will comfort and strengthen the mourners.

What might be a good reason to recite the Mourner's קַדִּישׁ only in the presence of a מִנְיָן?

___

At the Root

יִתְגַּדַּל means **May God's name be great**. The root of יִתְגַּדַּל is גדל.

The root גדל tells us that **great, big,** or **size** is part of a word's meaning.

Circle the root letters גדל in the words below.

גַּדְלָנוּת גַּדְלוּת גְּדוֹלוֹת גָּדוֹל גְּדוֹלָה מְגַדֵּל גֹּדֶל

65

Invite a volunteer to come to the board and write the three-letter root on which these words are built. *(*גדל*)* Challenge students to derive the meaning of the root גדל. *(big, great)*

Have students read and complete "At the Root."

Word Tree

Create a tree based on the root גדל, as you did for מלכ. Include the words יִתְגַּדַּל, גַּדְלָנוּת, מְגַדֵּל, גְּדוֹלָה, גָּדוֹל, גְּדוֹלוֹת, גַּדְלוּת, and גֹּדֶל found on page 65. Challenge students to skim pages 20, 22, and 53, and to identify one word on each page that is built on the root letters גדל. *(Respectively:* גַּדְּלוּ; הַגְּדֻלָּה; גְּדֻלָּה*)* Add these three words to the גדל word tree.

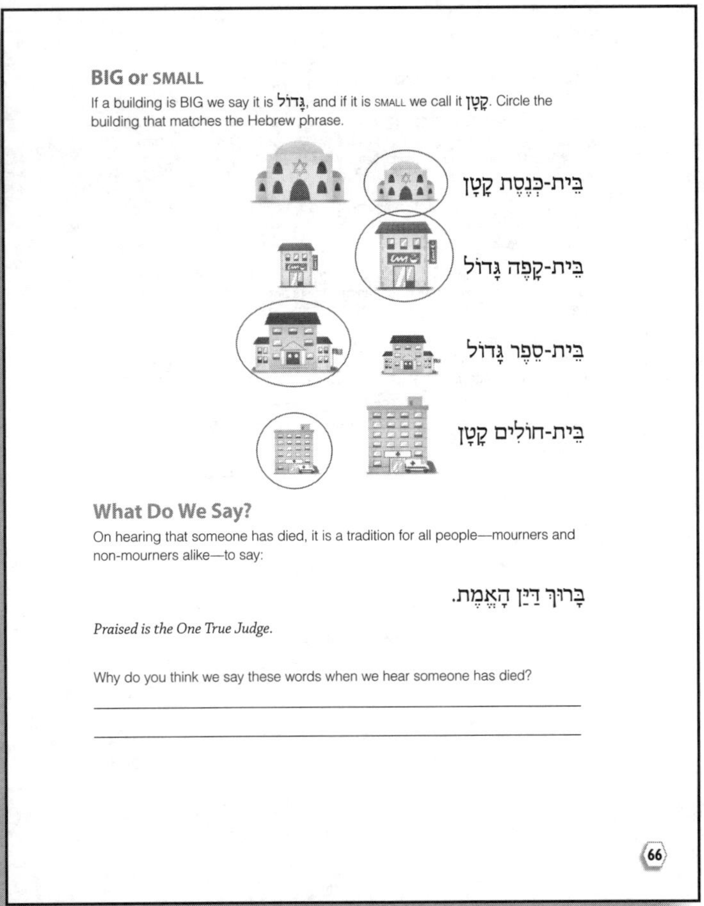

BIG or SMALL

If a building is BIG we say it is גָּדוֹל, and if it is SMALL we call it קָטָן. Circle the building that matches the Hebrew phrase.

בֵּית-כְּנֶסֶת קָטָן

בֵּית-קָפֶה גָּדוֹל

בֵּית-סֵפֶר גָּדוֹל

בֵּית-חוֹלִים קָטָן

What Do We Say?

On hearing that someone has died, it is a tradition for all people—mourners and non-mourners alike—to say:

בָּרוּךְ דַּיַּן הָאֱמֶת.

Praised is the One True Judge.

Why do you think we say these words when we hear someone has died?

66

Inform students that there is another sentence that is traditionally said to a mourner. In that sentence we ask God to comfort the mourner along with all the other mourners of Israel.

Digital Application

By clicking on the activities light bulb in Level 6 students can play "Tic-Tac-Toe" to review new vocabulary from Chapter 6, as well as previously learned prayer words. At the next class, ask: What are three Hebrew words that have "name" as all or part of their meaning? *(שֵׁם, שְׁמֵהּ, שְׁמוֹ)*

BIG or SMALL

Have students work with a partner as they read the Hebrew phrases aloud and circle the matching buildings. Give students the opportunity to use the terms גָּדוֹל and קָטָן by asking a variety of questions. Suggested questions include: What size בֵּית־סֵפֶר would you like to go to? *(בֵּית־סֵפֶר קָטָן; בֵּית־סֵפֶר גָּדוֹל)* In what size בֵּית־חוֹלִים would you expect to get better care? *(בֵּית־חוֹלִים גָּדוֹל; בֵּית־חוֹלִים קָטָן)*

Display, and review, word cards 6 (אַב, אָב—parent, father), 35 (עוֹלָם—eternal, world), 49 (צוּר—rock), and 56 (שֵׁם—name). Call on three or four volunteers to come to the board. Explain that you will say a phrase, such as צוּר קָטָן, and the students at the board will draw an illustration of the phrase. Phrases you might say include: אָב גָּדוֹל; עוֹלָם קָטָן; שֵׁם גָּדוֹל. Invite a new group of students to illustrate phrases that you call out.

What Do We Say?

Lead students in a choral reading of the Hebrew phrase, and its English translation, that is recited when hearing that someone has died. Ask: Who are we referring to as the One True Judge? *(God)* In our prayers and blessings, we are generally praising, thanking, or asking God for something. Which of these are we doing in this statement? *(praising God)* What are we praising God for? *(for being the One True Judge)*

Direct students to discuss with a partner why they think we say these words when we learn of a death. Invite partners to share their thoughts with the class. *(Suggestions may include: it may give us comfort to affirm our belief in God; it may remind us that we don't understand death; that sometimes we just have to accept things)*

Ask students why it might be helpful to know that there are these fixed words that we recite when hearing someone has died. *(Suggestions may include: because when we hear bad news we may not know what to say; we may feel more comfortable saying words that we know are "correct" than trying to think of something to say ourselves.)*

Taking Leave of Royalty

Write on the board: עֹשֶׂה שָׁלוֹם. Have students find the verse on page 62, made up of two lines, in the קַדִּישׁ that begins with these two words. *(lines 12–13)* Ask: Why do you think the קַדִּישׁ closes with a prayer for peace? *(Possible answers include: because we save our greatest wish for last; because we want peace to be the last thing we think of when we finish our prayer)* Inform students that many of our prayers end with the wish for שָׁלוֹם.

Have partners practice reading עֹשֶׂה שָׁלוֹם. Ask partners to read the paragraph about עֹשֶׂה שָׁלוֹם.

Ask: Which prayers, aside from the קַדִּישׁ, include עֹשֶׂה שָׁלוֹם? *(עֲמִידָה and בִּרְכַּת הַמָּזוֹן)* What other prayers are used in more than one context in our Shabbat and holiday services? *(Possible responses include: בָּרְכוּ—the call to prayer at the beginning of a service and the opening lines of the Torah blessing; שְׁמַע—recited before the וְאָהַבְתָּ and when we take the Torah from the Ark, and some people say it at night before they go to sleep and when they wake up.)*

Call on a volunteer to lead the class as they stand and practice reciting עֹשֶׂה שָׁלוֹם and bow left, right, and center.

Direct students to respond to the questions on page 67 independently. Invite students to share the lines they have written about peace.

Photo Op

Have the class chorally read the photo caption. Invite students to suggest why this is a representation of שָׁלוֹם. *(Responses may include: it shows a group of children who are cooperating with one another; it shows children from different backgrounds; it shows children of different races.)* Divide the class into groups of 4 to 5 students. Direct groups to recreate the same formation that they see in the photo, or a similar formation. Challenge groups to create a new formation and explain how that formation can be a symbol of peace.

Taking Leave of Royalty

Practice reading the last two lines of the קַדִּישׁ.

1. עֹשֶׂה שָׁלוֹם בִּמְרוֹמָיו, הוּא יַעֲשֶׂה שָׁלוֹם
2. עָלֵינוּ, וְעַל כָּל יִשְׂרָאֵל. וְאִמְרוּ: אָמֵן.

1. May God who makes peace in the heavens, make peace
2. for us and for all Israel. And say, Amen.

עֹשֶׂה שָׁלוֹם is the same sentence that concludes the עֲמִידָה and appears near the end of בִּרְכַּת הַמָּזוֹן (Grace After Meals). When we say עֹשֶׂה שָׁלוֹם at the end of the קַדִּישׁ and the עֲמִידָה, it is a tradition to take three steps backward, then bow to the left, to the right, and to the front. It is as if we are leaving the presence of a great ruler.

Who is the ruler whose presence we are leaving? God

If you could add another line about peace to עֹשֶׂה שָׁלוֹם, what would it be? Write it in English here:

שָׁלוֹם

67

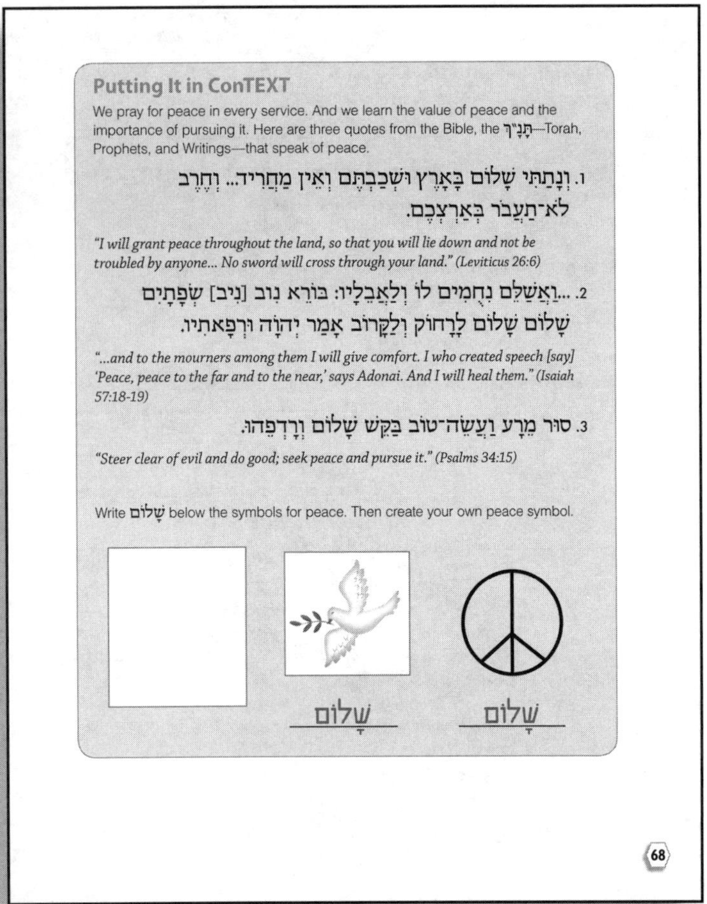

Putting It in ConTEXT

We pray for peace in every service. And we learn the value of peace and the importance of pursuing it. Here are three quotes from the Bible, the תָּנָ"ךְ—Torah, Prophets, and Writings—that speak of peace.

1. וְנָתַתִּי שָׁלוֹם בָּאָרֶץ וּשְׁכַבְתֶּם וְאֵין מַחֲרִיד... וְחֶרֶב לֹא־תַעֲבֹר בְּאַרְצְכֶם.

"I will grant peace throughout the land, so that you will lie down and not be troubled by anyone... No sword will cross through your land." (Leviticus 26:6)

2. ...וַאֲשַׁלֵּם נִחֻמִים לוֹ וְלַאֲבֵלָיו: בּוֹרֵא נוּב [נִיב] שְׂפָתָיִם שָׁלוֹם שָׁלוֹם לָרָחוֹק וְלַקָּרוֹב אָמַר יְהוָה וּרְפָאתִיו.

"...and to the mourners among them I will give comfort. I who created speech [say] 'Peace, peace to the far and to the near,' says Adonai. And I will heal them." (Isaiah 57:18-19)

3. סוּר מֵרָע וַעֲשֵׂה־טוֹב בַּקֵּשׁ שָׁלוֹם וְרָדְפֵהוּ.

"Steer clear of evil and do good; seek peace and pursue it." (Psalms 34:15)

Write שָׁלוֹם below the symbols for peace. Then create your own peace symbol.

שָׁלוֹם

שָׁלוֹם

68

opportunities for Jews and Palestinians to work and play together. Through the Peres Center for Peace, Jews and Palestinians work together on agricultural and economic projects, and children play various sports together. Ask students for other ideas for programs that could increase understanding and tolerance among diverse groups of people. *(Possible suggestions include: playing music together; research on protecting endangered animals; students creating a shared website.)*

Direct students to complete independently "Putting It in ConTEXT" by writing שָׁלוֹם below the peace symbols and then creating their own symbol. Invite volunteers to draw their symbol on the board.

Putting It in ConTEXT

Call on students to name the three sections of the תָּנָ"ךְ. *(Torah, Prophets, Writings)* Tell students that they are about to study three biblical verses about שָׁלוֹם, one from each section of the תָּנָ"ךְ.

Have partners read aloud the Hebrew verses and their English translation. Give each pair of students markers and construction paper. Direct pairs to choose one of the verses and to draw an illustration or symbol of the verse.

Invite students to read their verse aloud, present their illustration, explain their understanding of the verse, and describe what they find most meaningful or relevant about the verse. Students who chose the verse from Leviticus might for example, (1) display an illustration of a person sleeping comfortably, (2) explain that the verse describes peace as a time when people can live without fear because there will be no war and no weapons, and (3) say that they found the idea of not being troubled by anyone most meaningful. Continue until all pairs have presented.

Ask: Which of the verses on page 68 teaches us how we should act? *(Psalms 34:15)* What are some ways that we can "Steer clear of evil"? *(Suggestions may include: follow rules; be honest with others; listen to our own conscience.)* What are ways that we can "Do good"? *(Possible suggestions include: help a friend with homework; be a cooperative teammate; donate to the poor.)* How can we "Seek peace and pursue it." *(Suggestions may include: write letters to legislators to protest social injustice; support "peace" programs; respect others and work together peacefully to solve problems.)*

Inform your students that the first quote (Leviticus 26:6) is part of the Torah reading of פָּרָשַׁת בְּחֻקֹּתַי, and that the second quote (Isaiah 57:18–19) is read as part of the haftarah on Yom Kippur morning.

Tell students that there are a variety of programs designed to promote peace by creating positive relationships among diverse groups of people. If you have access to the Internet, direct your students to research programs in Israel, such as the Peres Center for Peace, that create

Prayer Puzzle

Display word cards 3 (מַלְכוּתֵךְ—Your sovereignty), 16 (בִּקְדֻשָּׁתוֹ—in [God's] holiness), 20 (הַגְּדֻלָּה—the greatness), 22 (בַּשָּׁמַיִם—in heaven), 35 (עוֹלָם—eternal, world), and 45 (הַנֶּאֱמָרִים—spoken) on the ledge of the board. Invite volunteers to read each Hebrew word and say its English meaning. Direct students to read these words aloud as they work with a partner to solve the "Prayer Puzzle." Call on students to say the meaning, or part of the meaning, of each of the Aramaic words.

מַה הַמִּילָה?—What's the Word?

Display word cards 72–78 on the ledge of the whiteboard or chalkboard. Have a student choose one of the word cards and quietly tell you which word he or she has chosen. Play a game of מַה הַמִּילָה? as described on page 15.

My Reflections on the Prayer

If your students are creating a booklet of reflections on the prayers, give each student a page of prompts to complete (see page 29) devoted to the קַדִּישׁ. Remember to have students draw an illustration or symbol to represent each prayer. Add this new page to their folder or binder of personal reflections.

Clue to Cyberspace

Have students work with a partner to read aloud and complete "Clue to Cyberspace."

Tell students that at home they should click on the joystick in Level 6 to play "Stampede" and review the prayer words from Lesson 6. In the game, students help the lion cross a stampede of wild animals and then cross a river to match a Hebrew word to a related Aramaic word. Remind students to use the clue—עָלֵינוּ—to score bonus points.

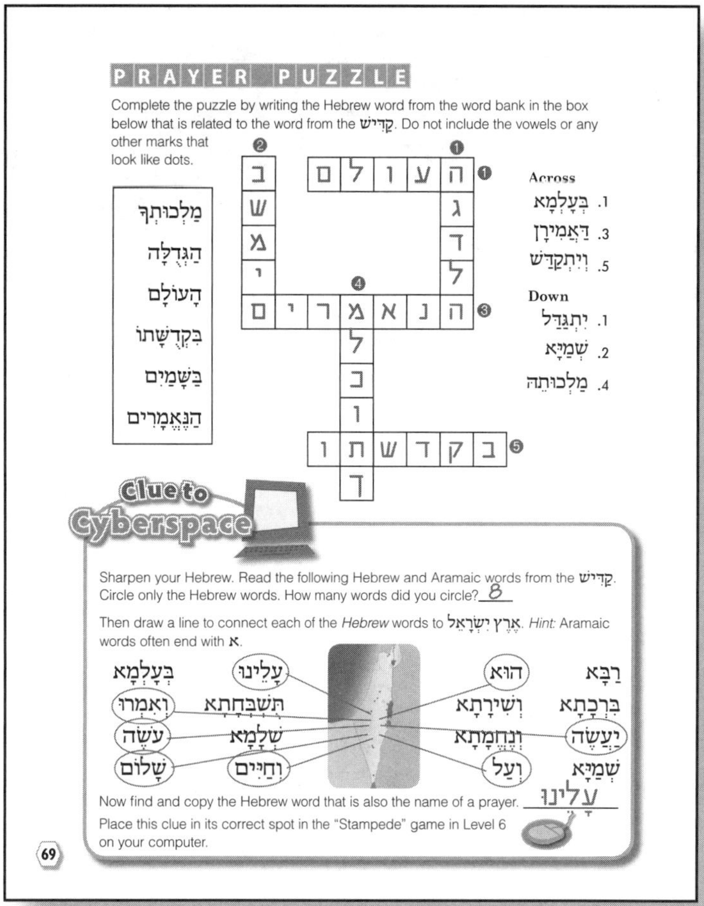

PRAYER PUZZLE

Complete the puzzle by writing the Hebrew word from the word bank in the box below that is related to the word from the קַדִּישׁ. Do not include the vowels or any other marks that look like dots.

מַלְכוּתְךָ
הַגְּדֻלָּה
הָעוֹלָם
בִּקְדֻשָּׁתוֹ
בַּשָּׁמַיִם
הַנֶּאֱמָרִים

Across
1. בְּעָלְמָא
3. דַּאֲמִירָן
5. וְיִתְקַדַּשׁ

Down
1. יִתְגַּדַּל
2. שְׁמַיָּא
4. מַלְכוּתֵהּ

Clue to Cyberspace

Sharpen your Hebrew. Read the following Hebrew and Aramaic words from the קַדִּישׁ. Circle only the Hebrew words. How many words did you circle? 8

Then draw a line to connect each of the *Hebrew* words to אֶרֶץ יִשְׂרָאֵל. *Hint:* Aramaic words often end with א.

בְּעָלְמָא עָלֵינוּ הוּא רַבָּא
וְאִמְרוּ תֻּשְׁבְּחָתָא וְשִׁירָתָא בִּרְכָתָא
עֹשֶׂה שְׁלָמָא וְנֶחֱמָתָא יַעֲשֶׂה
שָׁלוֹם וְחַיִּים וְעַל שְׁמַיָּא

Now find and copy the Hebrew word that is also the name of a prayer. עָלֵינוּ

Place this clue in its correct spot in the "Stampede" game in Level 6 on your computer.

69

Assessment

As students are working on any of the above activities, meet with them individually to assess reading fluency and knowledge of prayer content. Use the Prayer Mastery Assessment Chart on page 17 of the Teacher's Edition to keep track of student progress. You can also assess students' progress online at www.behrmanhouse.com. Click on the blue "Assessment" button at the bottom of the screen, select *Kol Yisrael 3*, and type in your class's serial number to see how students are doing in their digital application. Students can also e-mail their lesson summary to you directly or print out a lesson summary and bring it in to class.

What's Next?

Invite students to think about the many prayers and blessings they have learned this year. Ask: What are some of the things we express in these prayers? *(Responses may include: we ask God for peace; we affirm it is our duty to praise God; we thank God for giving us the Torah.)* What do you think might be expressed in the closing prayers of our service? *(Possible responses include: thanking God for words for prayers; saying that we believe in One God.)* Tell students that in the next chapter they will study two closing prayers that each praise God as our Ruler.

7 אֵין כֵּאלֹהֵינוּ/אֲדוֹן עוֹלָם

ABOUT THE PRAYER

אֵין כֵּאלֹהֵינוּ and אֲדוֹן עוֹלָם are hymns that describe God as our Sovereign and Ruler who is beyond compare. אֵין כֵּאלֹהֵינוּ is an acrostic in which we speak as a community about our God. When we recite אֲדוֹן עוֹלָם, we speak as individuals and affirm our personal connection to God. Both אֵין כֵּאלֹהֵינוּ and אֲדוֹן עוֹלָם are sung with spirit and joy at the conclusion of the Shabbat morning service.

LEARNING OBJECTIVES

Students will be able to:

- Recite אֵין כֵּאלֹהֵינוּ and אֲדוֹן עוֹלָם fluently.
- Define key words.
- Locate Tiberias and Lake Kinneret on a map of Israel.
- Describe the qualities of an acrostic and demonstrate that אֵין כֵּאלֹהֵינוּ is an acrostic.
- Offer reasons why we speak as a community in some prayers and we speak as individuals in others.
- Explain that both אֵין כֵּאלֹהֵינוּ and אֲדוֹן עוֹלָם are hymns that describe God as our Sovereign and Ruler who is beyond compare.

ESSENTIAL QUESTION

Despite our awareness that God is an awesome power beyond our understanding, why do we and how can we describe God in our prayers?

NEW WORDS AND PHRASES

Prayer Words:

there is none like	אֵין כּ־
who is like	מִי כּ־
we will give thanks to	נוֹדֶה ל־
You (God) are	אַתָּה הוּא
our God	אֱלֹהֵינוּ
our Sovereign	אֲדוֹנֵינוּ
our Ruler	מַלְכֵּנוּ
our Savior	מוֹשִׁיעֵנוּ
Sovereign	אֲדוֹן
(God) was	הָיָה
(God) is	הוֹוֶה
(God) will be	יִהְיֶה
without a beginning	בְּלִי רֵאשִׁית
without an end	בְּלִי תַכְלִית
my Redeemer	גֹּאֲלִי

INSTRUCTIONAL MATERIALS

Text pages 70–83

word cards 79–93

Digital Application: Level 7—
אֵין כֵּאלֹהֵינוּ/אֲדוֹן עוֹלָם (see page 10 for a list of games and activities)

WHERE WE ARE

Ben and Batya are on a class trip to Tiberias, a city situated on the western shore of Lake Kinneret. Tiberias was a seat of Jewish learning, law, and culture after the destruction of the Holy Temple. Batya is awed by the history of Tiberias, which is one of Judaism's holiest cities.

Just as Batya finds Tiberias awesome, we describe God as our Sovereign and Ruler, an awesome power beyond compare, as we joyfully sing אֵין כֵּאלֹהֵינוּ and אֲדוֹן עוֹלָם at the conclusion of the service.

INTRODUCING THE LESSON

Invite students to describe a situation in which they told someone, more than once and in more than one way, that what they did was great. A student might, for example, describe telling a teammate who scored the winning point for the team how great that person is, how much the person does for the team, and how amazing the play was. Ask: Why do you think that after all the prayers and blessings we have recited in our service, we conclude the service by praising God with two more hymns? *(Responses may include: because there*

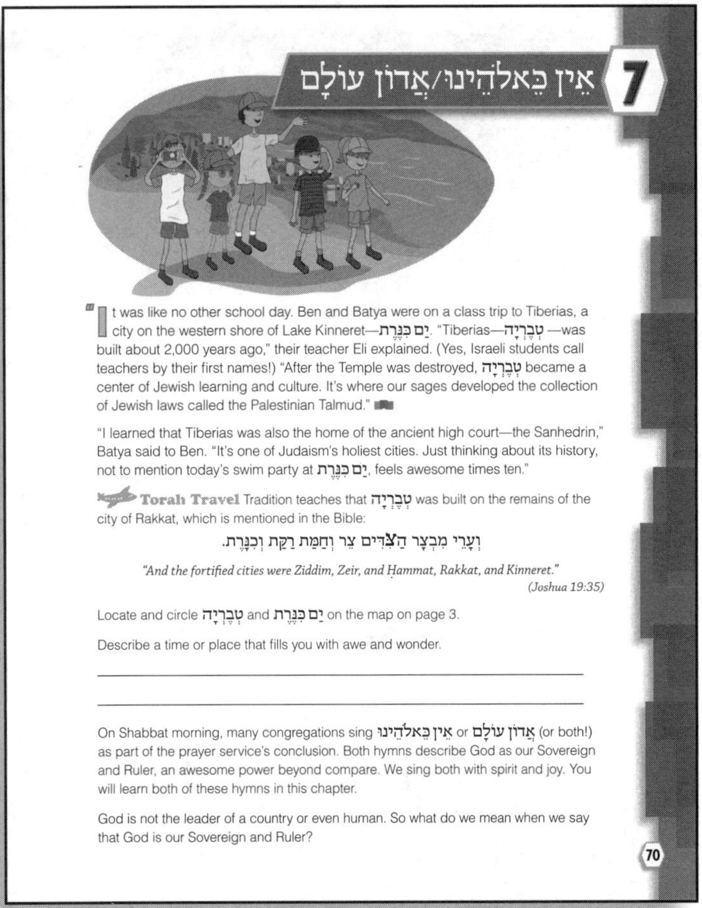

7 אֵין כֵּאלֹהֵינוּ/אֲדוֹן עוֹלָם

"It was like no other school day. Ben and Batya were on a class trip to Tiberias, a city on the western shore of Lake Kinneret—יַם כִּנֶּרֶת. "Tiberias—טְבֶרְיָה—was built about 2,000 years ago," their teacher Eli explained. (Yes, Israeli students call teachers by their first names!) "After the Temple was destroyed, טְבֶרְיָה became a center of Jewish learning and culture. It's where our sages developed the collection of Jewish laws called the Palestinian Talmud."

"I learned that Tiberias was also the home of the ancient high court—the Sanhedrin," Batya said to Ben. "It's one of Judaism's holiest cities. Just thinking about its history, not to mention today's swim party at יַם כִּנֶּרֶת, feels awesome times ten."

Torah Travel Tradition teaches that טְבֶרְיָה was built on the remains of the city of Rakkat, which is mentioned in the Bible:

וְעָרֵי מִבְצָר הַצִּדִּים צֵר וְחַמַּת רַקַּת וְכִנָּרֶת.

"And the fortified cities were Ziddim, Zeir, and Ḥammat, Rakkat, and Kinneret."
(Joshua 19:35)

Locate and circle טְבֶרְיָה and יַם כִּנֶּרֶת on the map on page 3.

Describe a time or place that fills you with awe and wonder.

On Shabbat morning, many congregations sing אֵין כֵּאלֹהֵינוּ or אֲדוֹן עוֹלָם (or both!) as part of the prayer service's conclusion. Both hymns describe God as our Sovereign and Ruler, an awesome power beyond compare. We sing both with spirit and joy. You will learn both of these hymns in this chapter.

God is not the leader of a country or even human. So what do we mean when we say that God is our Sovereign and Ruler?

70

Direct students to locate and circle טְבֶרְיָה and יַם כִּנֶּרֶת on page 3. Call on volunteers to describe their location. *(in the northeast of Israel; near the eastern border of Israel; not far from Haifa)*

Digital Application

At home, or in class, have students click on Tiberias on the Contents map or on the prayers listed for Level 7 and then click on the camera to view photographs of Tiberias. Included are photos of (1) Lake Kinneret, (2) residences along the shores of Lake Kinneret, (3) an aerial view, (4) a Galilee farming community, (5) agricultural fields, (6) wildflowers, and (7) sign posts in the Golan Heights. Consider showing the students additional images of Tiberias. The Internet is a great resource for these photos. If your students are creating travel guides for various places in Israel (see page 6), invite the students who are researching Tiberias to tell highlights of what they have learned so far about this city.

Ask students why Batya thought being in טְבֶרְיָה was awesome? *(it is a historic city; it is a holy city; it is next to an enormous lake)* Have students write about a time or place that *are so many things for which we want to praise God; because we want to show our appreciation; because it represents that there is no end to our praise for God .)* Inform students that they will be studying אֵין כֵּאלֹהֵינוּ and אֲדוֹן עוֹלָם, two hymns filled with praises of God.

INTO THE TEXT

Have students read the opening two paragraphs of page 70 with a partner. Ask questions, such as the following: What is the Hebrew name for Lake Kinneret? *(יַם כִּנֶּרֶת)* Why did Tiberias become a center for Jewish learning? *(after the Temple and Jerusalem were destroyed, Jews moved north to Tiberias, which had not been ravaged by the war)* [Note: More information on the move from Jerusalem to the north is found in *The History of the Jewish People*, Vol 1, Behrman House, pages 43–48.] What important collection of laws was developed in Tiberias? *(the Palestinian Talmud)* What was the name of the ancient high court? *(the Sanhedrin)* Why is Tiberias considered a holy city? *(because it was a center for Jewish learning and Jewish law)*

Torah Travel

As a class, read aloud the quote from Joshua 19:35. Direct students to underline the Hebrew name Rakkat *(רַקַּת)*, the city on which Tiberias was built, and to put a circle around the Hebrew name Kinneret *(כִּנֶּרֶת)*. Point out that כ and כּ are different forms of the same letter and that the change in the word's second vowel from "eh" to "ah" does not change its meaning. Therefore כִּנֶּרֶת and כִּנֶּרֶת both refer to the Kinneret.

Ask students if they have ever visited a city surrounded by a wall. Students may mention, for example, Quebec, Verona (Italy), or Jerusalem. Explain that a fortified city is one that is surrounded by protective walls. If you have access to the Internet, show your students images of walled cities. Inform your students that these walls are several feet wide, and one can still walk all around the Old City of Jerusalem atop its ancient walls.

fills them with wonder. Direct students to meet in groups of 4–5 students and share what they have written.

Have students read silently the paragraph about אֵין כֵּאלֹהֵינוּ and אֲדוֹן עוֹלָם. Tell students whether your congregation sings one or both of these hymns on Shabbat morning. Ask: How do both of these hymns describe God? *(as our Sovereign and Ruler, as an awesome power beyond compare)* What do you think we mean when we say that God is our Sovereign and Ruler? *(Possible responses include: we believe that there is no power greater than God; just as people in a kingdom follow the laws of its ruler, we follow the mitzvot given through Torah.)*

You're the Greatest

Read lines 1 and 2 of אֵין כֵּאלֹהֵינוּ, one phrase at a time, having students chorally repeat each phrase and then each line. Invite the class to chorally read the English meaning of lines 1 and 2.

Direct students to read these Hebrew lines with a partner. Repeat this by introducing the Hebrew, followed by the English, and then having partners practice reading lines 3 and 4, 5 and 6, 7 and 8, and 9 and 10. Challenge students to locate and read words from this passage by asking them questions such as: Which words are built on the root letters מלכ? (כְּמַלְכֵּנוּ, כְּמַלְכֵּנוּ, מַלְכֵּנוּ, למלכנו). Which word in line 3 is related to אֲדוֹנֵינוּ? (כַאדוֹנֵינוּ)

Provide an opportunity for students to practice distinguishing between the כּ and כ by saying כַאדוֹנֵינוּ—כּאדוֹנֵינוּ; כֵאלֹהֵינוּ—כֵּאלֹהֵינוּ; כְמוֹשִׁיעֵנוּ—כְּמוֹשִׁיעֵנוּ, כְמַלְכֵּנוּ—כְּמַלְכֵּנוּ. Invite students to stand with you in a circle. Tell students that if you say, for example, כְּמַלְכֵּנוּ, a student must respond by saying כְמַלְכֵּנוּ, and vice versa. Begin by saying one of the eight words that begin with either כּ or כ to a student. If the student responds correctly, the student remains standing in the circle. If a student responds incorrectly, he or she leaves the circle and sits down. Continue in a clockwise direction, saying one of these eight words and having a student say the related word.

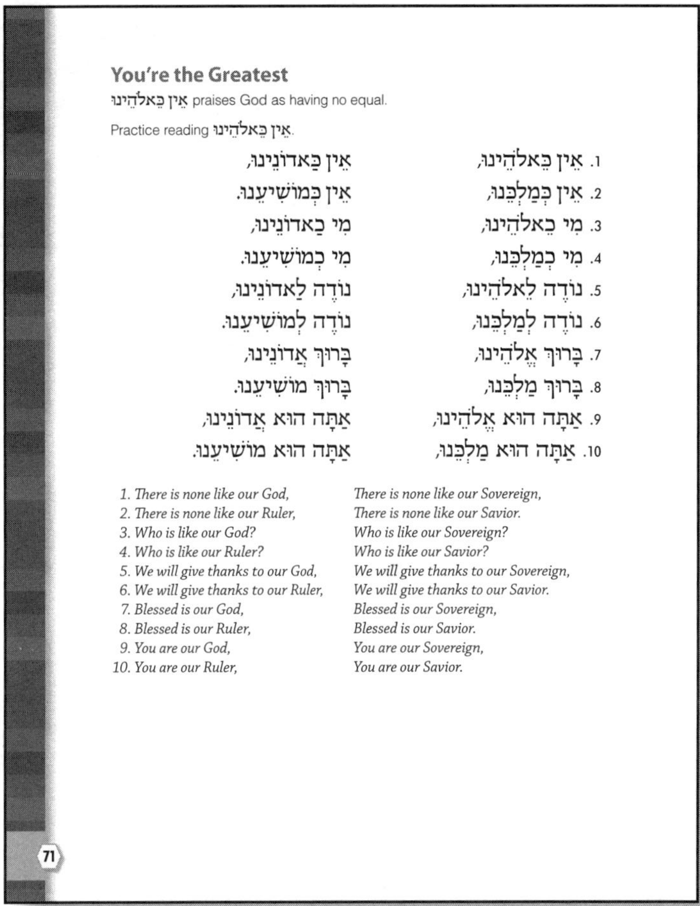

You're the Greatest

אֵין כֵּאלֹהֵינוּ praises God as having no equal.

Practice reading אֵין כֵּאלֹהֵינוּ.

1. אֵין כֵּאלֹהֵינוּ, אֵין כַּאדוֹנֵינוּ,
2. אֵין כְּמַלְכֵּנוּ, אֵין כְּמוֹשִׁיעֵנוּ.
3. מִי כֵאלֹהֵינוּ, מִי כַאדוֹנֵינוּ,
4. מִי כְמַלְכֵּנוּ, מִי כְמוֹשִׁיעֵנוּ.
5. נוֹדֶה לֵאלֹהֵינוּ, נוֹדֶה לַאדוֹנֵינוּ,
6. נוֹדֶה לְמַלְכֵּנוּ, נוֹדֶה לְמוֹשִׁיעֵנוּ.
7. בָּרוּךְ אֱלֹהֵינוּ, בָּרוּךְ אֲדוֹנֵינוּ,
8. בָּרוּךְ מַלְכֵּנוּ, בָּרוּךְ מוֹשִׁיעֵנוּ.
9. אַתָּה הוּא אֱלֹהֵינוּ, אַתָּה הוּא אֲדוֹנֵינוּ,
10. אַתָּה הוּא מַלְכֵּנוּ, אַתָּה הוּא מוֹשִׁיעֵנוּ.

1. There is none like our God, There is none like our Sovereign,
2. There is none like our Ruler, There is none like our Savior.
3. Who is like our God? Who is like our Sovereign?
4. Who is like our Ruler? Who is like our Savior?
5. We will give thanks to our God, We will give thanks to our Sovereign,
6. We will give thanks to our Ruler, We will give thanks to our Savior.
7. Blessed is our God, Blessed is our Sovereign,
8. Blessed is our Ruler, Blessed is our Savior.
9. You are our God, You are our Sovereign,
10. You are our Ruler, You are our Savior.

71

The students who remain standing after one or two rounds are the winners.

For fun, have students read אֵין כֵּאלֹהֵינוּ as a whip. Going around the room, have each student read one phrase. Continue until the class has read the entire hymn. Challenge your students to read all of the phrases correctly in under one minute.

Ask: How many times does the suffix נוּ appear in אֵין כֵּאלֹהֵינוּ? *(20)* What can we learn from the repeated appearance of "our," נוּ? *(Possible responses include: that we all feel a closeness to our God; that we are a community unified by the belief in our God; that we all share the belief that our God has no equal)*

Teach, or have your cantor or music specialist teach, students to chant אֵין כֵּאלֹהֵינוּ.

Word Tree

If you have created a word tree for the root מלכ, add the words לְמַלְכֵּנוּ, כְמַלְכֵּנוּ, כְּמַלְכֵּנוּ, and מַלְכֵּנוּ to the tree.

Prayer Words

Practice reading these words from אֵין כֵּאלֹהֵינוּ.

there is none like	אֵין כֵּ–
who is like	מִי כ–
we will give thanks to	נוֹדֶה ל–
You (God) are	אַתָּה הוּא
our God	אֱלֹהֵינוּ
our Sovereign	אֲדוֹנֵינוּ
our Ruler	מַלְכֵּנוּ
our Savior	מוֹשִׁיעֵנוּ

God's Majesty

Under each crown, write the English meaning of the word in the crown.

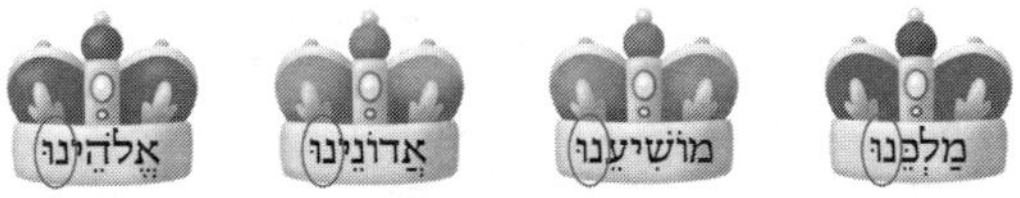

our God   our Sovereign   our Savior   our Ruler

Bonus points: In each of the four Hebrew words, circle the word ending that means **our**.

With a partner, find and underline the Hebrew word below that is related to נוֹדֶה ל-.

שָׁלוֹם   תּוֹדָה   יִשְׂרָאֵל   תּוֹרָה

Now, use this word to thank your partner for working with you.

72

Digital Application

Tell students that at home, before the next class, they should click on אֵין כֵּאלֹהֵינוּ/אֲדוֹן עוֹלָם or Tiberias to enter Level 7. Next, they click on the Torah scroll and אֵין כֵּאלֹהֵינוּ to practice reading this hymn. In the next class, ask students to read the hymn out loud with a partner.

Prayer Words

Present word cards 79–86. As you display each card, call on students to read the Hebrew and say its English meaning.

Write כּ—כ on the board. Hold up word cards 79 and 80 and challenge students to derive the meaning of כּ and כ. *(like)* Remind students that while putting a dot in כ changes its sound, the dot does not change the meaning of the prefix. Ask students to name a prayer that begins with מִי כָ־ *(מִי־כָמֹכָה)* and another that begins begins אֵין כָּ־. *(אֵין כָּמוֹךָ)*

Invite two students to the front of the class. Divide the rest of the class into two teams, א and ב.

Give one student word cards 79–82 and give the second student word cards 83–86. Direct the two students to each choose one word card and show classmates the Hebrew of that card. For example, one student might show word card 80, מִי כ־, and the other might show word card 85, מַלְכֵּנוּ. Call on team א to read the two word cards as a phrase *(מִי כְּמַלְכֵּנוּ)* and say its English meaning *(Who is like our Ruler?)*. If Team א answers correctly, they earn one point; each of the two students again choose a word card, and show the cards to Team ב. If Team א does not answer correctly, Team ב has a chance to read and translate the first set of word cards. Teams continue taking turns reading and translating the pairs of word cards. You may wish to tell students that you will play the game for a pre-set amount of time, such as five minutes.

God's Majesty

Have students work with a partner to complete "God's Majesty." As a class, review the correct answers, having students check and correct their own work. Lead the class in chorally saying the word they used to thank their partner, תּוֹדָה.

Challenge students to name other prayer words that are related to נוֹדֶה ל־. As a hint, tell students to think of other prayer words that mean "thank." *(מוֹדֶה, מוֹדָה, מוֹדִים)*

At the Heart of It All

Have students silently read the opening paragraph on page 73. Ask: What are the four ways we describe God in אֵין כֵּאלֹהֵינוּ? (אֱלֹהֵינוּ—*our God,* אֲדוֹנֵינוּ—*our Sovereign,* מַלְכֵּנוּ—*our Ruler,* מוֹשִׁיעֵנוּ—*our Savior)* What are some changes that may take place in a word when a prefix or suffix is added? *(the vowels may change;a final letter may drop out)*

Direct students to work independently as they connect each name of God to its related word and write the English meaning of the word in column 1. Walk around the room to assess how well students recognize related words and recall the meaning of the prayer words.

Read aloud the paragraph that lists additional names for God. Invite students to join with you in reading the Hebrew names included in the paragraph. Display word cards 49 and 70. Call on students to read the two word cards, which are additional names for God, and give their English meanings. *(*צוּר*—rock;* מֶלֶךְ מַלְכֵי הַמְּלָכִים*—Ruler of the rulers of rulers)*

Divide the class into five groups. Assign each group one of the following names of God: צוּר, אָבִינוּ, יוֹצְרֵנוּ, מֶלֶךְ מַלְכֵי הַמְּלָכִים, or רוֹעֵנוּ. Direct groups to list three things we learn about the Jewish understanding of God from this name. For example, from the name אָבִינוּ, our Parent, we learn that, according to Jewish tradition, God is like our parent. Therefore, (1) we have a personal relationship with God, (2) God loves us, and (3) God will treat us with compassion.

Invite a representative from each group to share its list with the class. Record on the board the students' lists, creating a compilation of things we learn about the Jewish view of God from these different names.

Ask students to suggest why we use human and earthly terms, such as shepherd or rock, to refer to God. Guide students to understand that since our language is based on our experience, and we

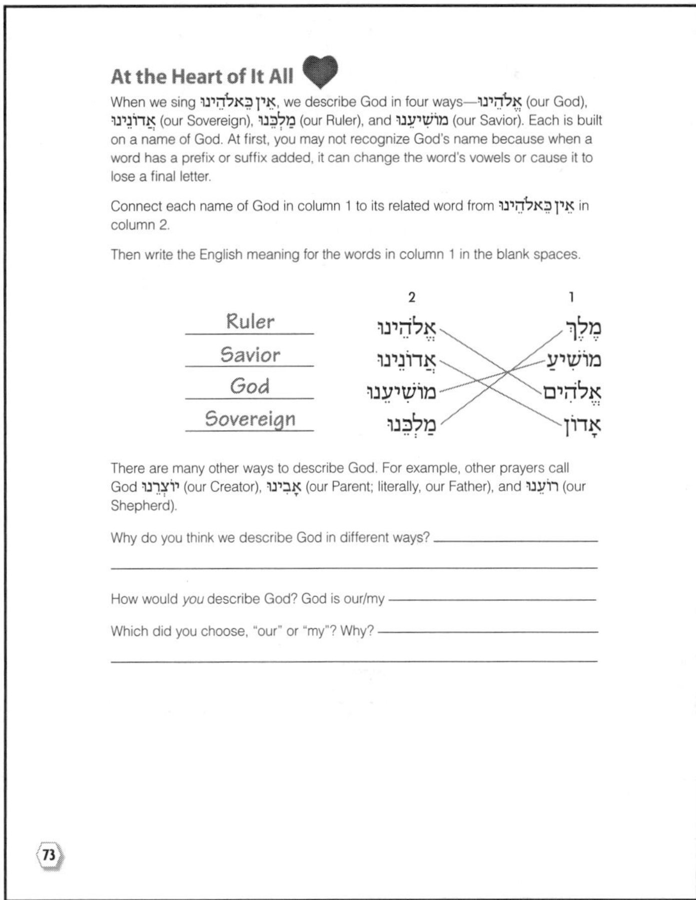

At the Heart of It All

When we sing אֵין כֵּאלֹהֵינוּ, we describe God in four ways—אֱלֹהֵינוּ (our God), אֲדוֹנֵינוּ (our Sovereign), מַלְכֵּנוּ (our Ruler), and מוֹשִׁיעֵנוּ (our Savior). Each is built on a name of God. At first, you may not recognize God's name because when a word has a prefix or suffix added, it can change the word's vowels or cause it to lose a final letter.

Connect each name of God in column 1 to its related word from אֵין כֵּאלֹהֵינוּ in column 2.

Then write the English meaning for the words in column 1 in the blank spaces.

	2	1
Ruler	אֱלֹהֵינוּ	מֶלֶךְ
Savior	אֲדוֹנֵינוּ	מוֹשִׁיעַ
God	מוֹשִׁיעֵנוּ	אֱלֹהִים
Sovereign	מַלְכֵּנוּ	אָדוֹן

There are many other ways to describe God. For example, other prayers call God יוֹצְרֵנוּ (our Creator), אָבִינוּ (our Parent; literally, our Father), and רוֹעֵנוּ (our Shepherd).

Why do you think we describe God in different ways? ________

How would *you* describe God? God is our/my ________

Which did you choose, "our" or "my"? Why? ________

73

can only describe what is familiar to us, we are limited to human and earthly terms when we describe God.

Direct students to write why they think we describe God in different ways. *(Possible responses include: to help us describe the different understandings of God; because to describe God in only a few ways would be limiting; because God is so many different things to us and does so many different things for us.)* Call on students to share their responses.

Have students write: (1) whether they would describe God as "our" or "my"; and (2) why they chose "our" or "my." Ask all students who wrote "our" to raise their hands. Invite a few students to share why they chose "our." Ask the students who wrote "my" to raise their hands and invite a few students to share the reason for their choice.

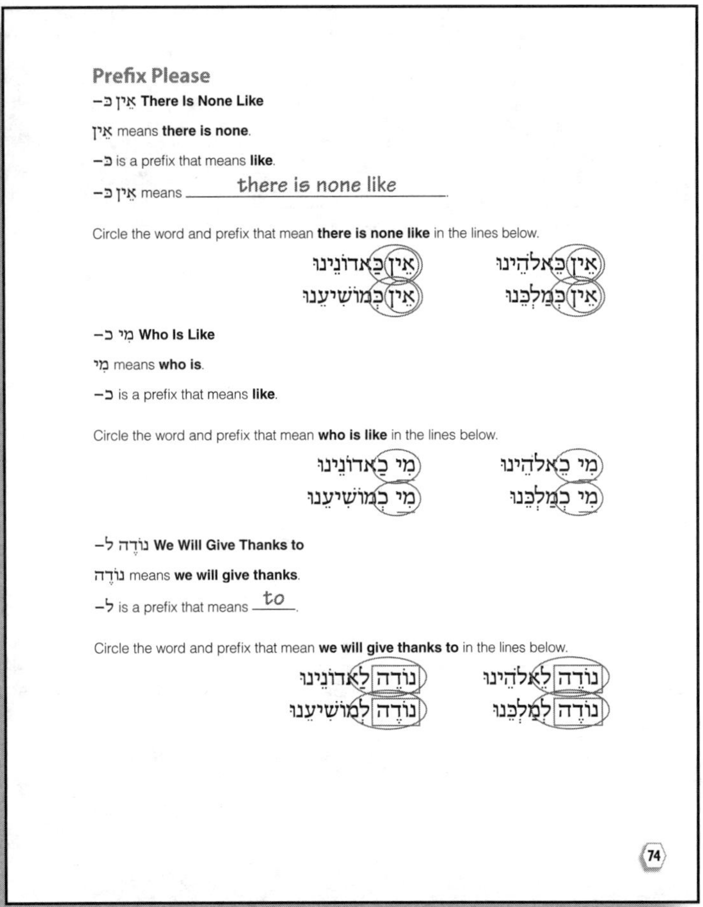

Prefix Please

אֵין כְּ– There Is None Like

אֵין means **there is none**.

–כְּ is a prefix that means **like**.

אֵין כְּ– means there is none like.

Circle the word and prefix that mean **there is none like** in the lines below.

אֵין כֵּאלֹהֵינוּ אֵין כַּאדוֹנֵינוּ

אֵין כְּמַלְכֵּנוּ אֵין כְּמוֹשִׁיעֵנוּ

מִי כְּ– Who Is Like

מִי means **who is**.

–כְּ is a prefix that means **like**.

Circle the word and prefix that mean **who is like** in the lines below.

מִי כֵאלֹהֵינוּ מִי כַאדוֹנֵינוּ

מִי כְמַלְכֵּנוּ מִי כְמוֹשִׁיעֵנוּ

נוֹדֶה לְ– We Will Give Thanks to

נוֹדֶה means **we will give thanks**.

–לְ is a prefix that means to.

Circle the word and prefix that mean **we will give thanks to** in the lines below.

נוֹדֶה לֵאלֹהֵינוּ נוֹדֶה לַאדוֹנֵינוּ

נוֹדֶה לְמַלְכֵּנוּ נוֹדֶה לְמוֹשִׁיעֵנוּ

74

Prefix Please

Direct students to turn to page 71. As a class, chorally sing the first two lines of אֵין כֵּאלֹהֵינוּ.

Call on a student to identify and translate the word-prefix combination that repeats in these lines. *(אֵין כְּ–—there is none like)* Challenge students to turn back to page 5 and to identify the two phrases that include this same word-prefix combination. *(Line 1 includes אֵין כָּמוֹךָ and וְאֵין כְּמַעֲשֶׂיךָ)*

Have students return to page 71 and chorally sing lines 3 and 4. Ask students to name the word-prefix combination that appears in these lines and to say its meaning. *(מִי כְּ–—who is like)*

Invite a volunteer to lead the class in singing lines 5 and 6 on page 71. Call on a student to identify and translate the word-prefix combination that repeats in these two lines. *(נוֹדֶה לְ–—we will give thanks to)* Challenge students to name prayer words that begin with the prefix –לְ, meaning "to." *(לָנוּ, לְעַמּוֹ, לַאֲדוֹן, לְשַׁבֵּחַ, לְכָבוֹד)*

Have students independently read and complete the activities on page 74. Walk around the room to assess informally how well students can identify the new prayer words and prefixes. Direct students to check their work with a classmate.

Prayer Chart

If you have begun a chart of the Shabbat morning service (see page 25), write אֵין כֵּאלֹהֵינוּ on a 4″ x 6″ index card. Inform students that אֵין כֵּאלֹהֵינוּ is usually sung before the עָלֵינוּ. Add this hymn to the chart below the עֵץ חַיִּים הִיא and above the עָלֵינוּ.

Crack the Code

Have students turn back to page 15 and chorally read, or chant, the two lines of כִּי מִצִּיּוֹן. Remind students that these two lines are an example of ancient Hebrew poetry (see page 33). Ask: How are the two phrases in this verse parallel, or similar, to one another? *(Both phrases describe that God's word, Torah, will come out of Jerusalem, also called Zion.)* Which words have meanings that are very similar to תּוֹרָה and מִירוּשָׁלָיִם? *(*וּדְבַר־יְיָ *and* מִצִּיּוֹן*)*

Inform students that אֵין כֵּאלֹהֵינוּ is an example of another kind of ancient Hebrew poetry. Direct students to read and complete "Crack the Code." Ask: What kind of poem is אֵין כֵּאלֹהֵינוּ? *(an acrostic—a poem in which a hidden message is spelled out in the first letter of each verse or line)* What is the hidden message in אֵין כֵּאלֹהֵינוּ? *(*אָמֵן*)* When do we say אמן? *(in response to someone's blessing, to say "we agree with your* בְּרָכָה*")*

Call on a volunteer to read aloud the last paragraph on page 75. Invite students to join in and chorally read the Hebrew words with the reader. Direct students to turn to page 71 and put a check next to the words בָּרוּךְ and אַתָּה. Write on the board: אָמֵן ← בָּרוּךְ אַתָּה. Call on students to explain why saying a blessing's ending followed by a blessing's beginning reminds us that our praise of God should go on forever. *(Responses may include: because as soon as we have praised God for one thing, we begin praising God for another; if we follow one blessing with another, the cycle of praising God is endless.)*

Consider having your students examine other acrostics in the siddur. For example, direct students to look at the first word of each verse in the אַשְׁרֵי (*Mishkan T'filah*, pages 185–186; *Kol Haneshamah*, pages 428–431; *Siddur Sim Shalom*, pages 151–152). Challenge students to derive why אַשְׁרֵי is an acrostic. *(The first letters of each verse are arranged in alef-bet order, from* א *to* ת*.)* Students may notice that there is no verse beginning with the letter נ. One explanation for the missing letter is that nun stands for נפל (falling), and the אַשְׁרֵי is an uplifting prayer.

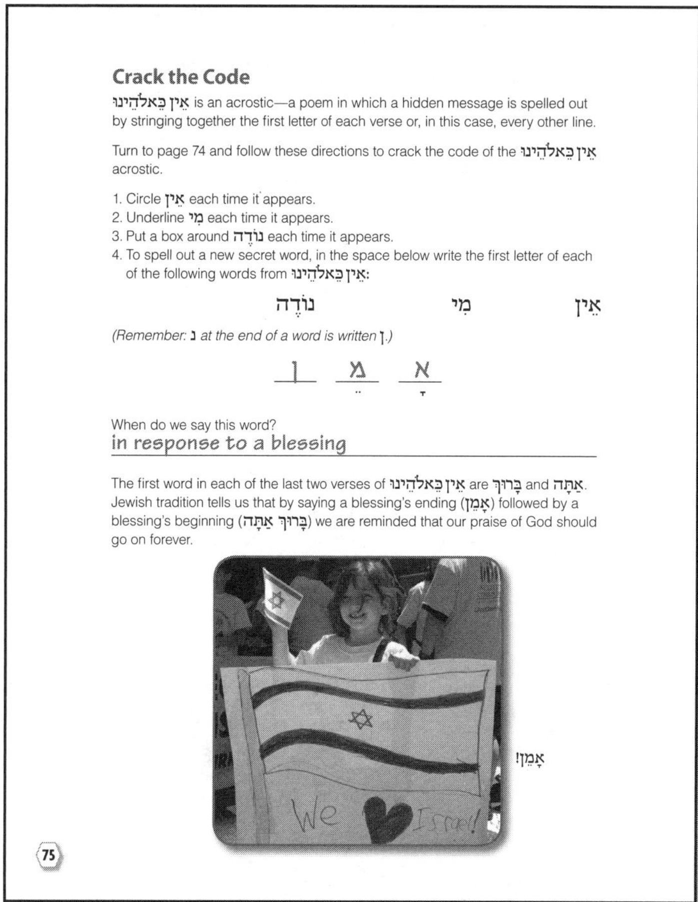

Crack the Code

אֵין כֵּאלֹהֵינוּ is an acrostic—a poem in which a hidden message is spelled out by stringing together the first letter of each verse or, in this case, every other line.

Turn to page 74 and follow these directions to crack the code of the אֵין כֵּאלֹהֵינוּ acrostic.

1. Circle אֵין each time it appears.
2. Underline מִי each time it appears.
3. Put a box around נוֹדֶה each time it appears.
4. To spell out a new secret word, in the space below write the first letter of each of the following words from אֵין כֵּאלֹהֵינוּ:

אֵין   מִי   נוֹדֶה

(Remember: נ at the end of a word is written ן.)

א   מ   ן

When do we say this word?
in response to a blessing

The first word in each of the last two verses of אֵין כֵּאלֹהֵינוּ are בָּרוּךְ and אַתָּה. Jewish tradition tells us that by saying a blessing's ending (אָמֵן) followed by a blessing's beginning (בָּרוּךְ אַתָּה) we are reminded that our praise of God should go on forever.

!אָמֵן

75

Photo Op

Invite students to say אָמֵן with enthusiasm. Ask: What might we be agreeing with when we say אָמֵן to this photo? *(Possible responses include: that we love Israel; that it is important to march on behalf of Israel; that it is our responsibility to join with the community to demonstrate our loyalty to Israel.)*

Call on students who have participated in parades for Israel to describe their experience. Ask: How did it feel to walk with a large group of people who shared the same commitment to Israel?

And Now, a Word about Israel

Some synagogues recite an additional verse at the end of אֵין כֵּאלֹהֵינוּ. It is a reminder of the days when our people made sacrifices and burned incense in Jerusalem's Temple.

אַתָּה הוּא שֶׁהִקְטִירוּ אֲבוֹתֵינוּ לְפָנֶיךָ אֶת קְטֹרֶת הַסַּמִּים.

It was in front of You that our ancestors burned the incense.

Circle the Hebrew word above that ends in the suffix meaning **our**.

Bonus Points: What does the word you circled mean? our fathers

Can you name two of אֲבוֹתֵינוּ? Write their names in Hebrew or English.

Jacob/יַעֲקֹב Isaac/יִצְחָק Abraham/אַבְרָהָם

Underline the Hebrew word above that means **You**.

Crazy Bonus Points: Draw a squiggly line under the two Hebrew words above that share the same root.

Off the Charts Bonus Points: What are the root letters in the two words?

ק ט ר

יְרוּשָׁלַיִם

76

And Now, a Word about Israel

Find out if your congregation recites this additional verse at the end of אֵין כֵּאלֹהֵינוּ. In general, Reform and Reconstructionist congregations do not, since they do not include references to Temple sacrifices in their services.

Direct students to read silently the opening paragraph on page 76. Call on a student to name what we are reminded of when we recite the additional verse of אֵין כֵּאלֹהֵינוּ. *(our ancestors making sacrifices and burning incense in the Holy Temple)*

Display word cards 6 (אַב, אָב—father, parent), 40 (לִפְנֵי—before), and 82 (אַתָּה הוּא—You [God] are). Call on students to read and say the English meaning of each prayer word or phrase.

Read aloud the additional verse from כֵּאלֹהֵינוּ אֵין. Challenge students to find the words that are the same or related to the words on display. (לְפָנֶיךָ, אֲבוֹתֵינוּ, אַתָּה הוּא)

Direct students to practice reading this verse with a partner and to complete the activities on page 76. Have partners check their answers with another pair of students. Call on students to say which of אֲבוֹתֵינוּ they named. *(Abraham, Isaac, or Jacob)*

Teach, or have your cantor or music specialist teach, your students to chant this verse. Lead students in singing אֵין כֵּאלֹהֵינוּ (page 71) followed by the additional verse.

Photo Op

Have students turn back to page 11 and compare the left-hand photo on page 11 to the photo on page 76. Invite students to comment on similarities and differences between the two photos. *(Similarities include that they both show: a golden dome [the Dome of the Rock]; stone structures; some trees and hills. Differences include: the photo on page 76 shows many smaller buildings, the one on page 11 shows the Western Wall and an open plaza; they show different views of the Dome of the Rock.)*

Inform students that, according to tradition, the Holy Temple, where our ancestors offered sacrifices, stood near or on the spot where the Dome of the Rock now stands. The Dome of the Rock is an Islamic mosque that was built around the year 690.

Language Link

Write on the board: אֲנִי־אַתָּה־הוּא. Challenge students to name prayers in which these words appear. *(Responses may include:* אֲנִי*—*מוֹדֶה/מוֹדָה אֲנִי; אַתָּה*—all blessings beginning with* בָּרוּךְ אַתָּה; הוּא*—appears several times in* עָלֵינוּ.*)* Call on students to say the English meaning of these words. *(I, you, and he)* Remind students that since God is neither male nor female, when הוּא appears in prayer to refer to God, we often translate הוּא as God.

Have students read the opening paragraph on page 77 with a partner. Challenge partners to write the English meaning of each of the six pronouns next to the pronoun. *(Right-hand column: I, you, he; left-hand column: I, you, she)*

Direct partners to read aloud Ben and Batya's Hebrew introductions of themselves and their classmates.

Divide the class into groups of three students. Have each group practice introducing themselves to one another and to the class. For example, in a group made up of רוּת, חָנָה, and יוֹנָה, רוּת might say אֲנִי רוּת, הִיא חָנָה, אַתָּה יוֹנָה. חנה might say אַתְּ רוּת, הוּא יוֹנָה, אֲנִי חָנָה. And יוֹנָה might say הִיא חָנָה, אֲנִי יוֹנָה, אַתְּ רוּת. Invite each group to the front of the room to introduce themselves to the class.

Have students complete individually the activities on page 77. Walk around the room to assess informally how well students can use the Hebrew pronouns.

Invite all your students to stand in a circle. Begin by turning to the student on your right and saying אֲנִי מוֹרֶה/מוֹרָה ________, מִי אַתָּה/אַתְּ? Coach the student to respond, for example, אֲנִי תָּמָר, and to then ask the student to her right מִי אַתָּה/אַתְּ?. Continue going around the circle until all students have identified themselves and asked their neighbor who they are. For fun, see how fast the class can go around the circle asking one another who they are and responding to the question.

Language Link

The last verse of אֵין כֵּאלֹהֵינוּ begins with the phrase אַתָּה הוּא, which means **You (God) are**. When the words are used individually, they are two separate pronouns meaning **you** and **he**. Below are the masculine and feminine forms of Hebrew singular pronouns.

F	M
אֲנִי	אֲנִי
אַתְּ	אַתָּה
הִיא	הוּא

Join Ben and Batya at יַם כִּנֶּרֶת. They and their classmates want to introduce themselves to you.

Now let's see who you remember. Fill in the blanks with אֲנִי ,הוּא ,הִיא, or the right name.

הִיא שָׂרָה הוּא דָוִד הִיא רָחֵל אֲנִי בֵּן הוּא דָנִי אֲנִי בָּתְיָה

Can you answer this question in Hebrew?

מִי אַתָּה/אַתְּ? אֲנִי ____________________

77

Digital Application

In Level 7 of the digital application, have students click on the activities light bulb and then "Matching." Here, students will pair a Hebrew sentence, such as אַתְּ שָׂרָה, with a matching illustration. In the next class session, ask students מִי אַתָּה/אַתְּ?. Using your students' names, ask additional questions, such as מִי תָּמָר?

> **God of Eternity**
>
> אֲדוֹן עוֹלָם praises God as having no equal, just as אֵין כֵּאלֹהֵינוּ does. In addition, it says that the God of the whole universe is also my personal God, who cares about me.
>
> Practice reading אֲדוֹן עוֹלָם.
>
> 1. אֲדוֹן עוֹלָם אֲשֶׁר מָלַךְ, בְּטֶרֶם כָּל יְצִיר נִבְרָא.
> 2. לְעֵת נַעֲשָׂה בְחֶפְצוֹ כֹּל, אֲזַי מֶלֶךְ שְׁמוֹ נִקְרָא.
> 3. וְאַחֲרֵי כִּכְלוֹת הַכֹּל, לְבַדּוֹ יִמְלוֹךְ נוֹרָא.
> 4. וְהוּא הָיָה, וְהוּא הֹוֶה, וְהוּא יִהְיֶה, בְּתִפְאָרָה.
> 5. וְהוּא אֶחָד וְאֵין שֵׁנִי, לְהַמְשִׁיל לוֹ לְהַחְבִּירָה.
> 6. בְּלִי רֵאשִׁית בְּלִי תַכְלִית, וְלוֹ הָעֹז וְהַמִּשְׂרָה.
> 7. וְהוּא אֵלִי וְחַי גֹּאֲלִי, וְצוּר חֶבְלִי בְּעֵת צָרָה.
> 8. וְהוּא נִסִּי וּמָנוֹס לִי, מְנָת כּוֹסִי בְּיוֹם אֶקְרָא.
> 9. בְּיָדוֹ אַפְקִיד רוּחִי, בְּעֵת אִישַׁן וְאָעִירָה.
> 10. וְעִם רוּחִי גְּוִיָּתִי, יְיָ לִי וְלֹא אִירָא.
>
> *1. Sovereign of the universe who ruled before any being was created,*
> *2. at the time when everything was created according to God's will, then God was called Ruler.*
> *3. After all else ends, God alone will rule in majesty.*
> *4. God was, God is, and God will be in glory.*
> *5. God is One and there is no one who is God's peer or who can join with God.*
> *6. Without a beginning, without an end, power and dominion are God's.*
> *7. God is my God and my living Redeemer, and my Rock in times of trouble and distress.*
> *8. God is my banner and my refuge, the portion of my cup on the day I call.*
> *9. I entrust my spirit into God's hand, when I sleep and when I wake.*
> *10. And with my spirit and my body, Adonai is with me and I shall not be afraid.*
>
> 78

God of Eternity

Have students read the introductory paragraph silently. Ask: How are the contents of אֲדוֹן עוֹלָם and אֵין כֵּאלֹהֵינוּ similar? *(They both praise God as having no equal.)* What does אֲדוֹן עוֹלָם say about God that is not included in אֵין כֵּאלֹהֵינוּ? *(God is my personal God, who cares about me.)*

What suffix appears in אֵין כֵּאלֹהֵינוּ that reminds us that God is *our* God? (נוּ) Does this suffix appear in אֲדוֹן עוֹלָם? *(no)* How many times does the word "my" appear in the English translation of אֲדוֹן עוֹלָם? *(9)* What do we learn from this? *(Possible responses include: that we see God as our own personal God; that we each have a personal connection to God.)*

Plan to introduce the reading of אֲדוֹן עוֹלָם over at least two class sessions. Have students study lines 1–5 at one session and 6–10 at the second.

Read lines 1–5 of אֲדוֹן עוֹלָם, phrase by phrase, then line by line, having students chorally repeat each phrase and line. After each Hebrew line is practiced, have students chorally read aloud the English. Direct students to read the Hebrew lines with a partner. Walk around the room listening to students read. Take note of the words that are most difficult, such as גְּוִיָּתִי, for students to decode. Devote a few minutes to practicing these challenging words. Write one of the words on the board, have students chorally, then in pairs, and then individually, read the word. Repeat this for all challenging words. Encourage students to ask for assistance in reading difficult words.

Remind them that asking questions is essential for learning. Tell them you know how hard these words are.

At the next class session, repeat the above process, introducing lines 6–10 of אֲדוֹן עוֹלָם.

After students have practiced reading all of אֲדוֹן עוֹלָם, divide the class into three groups: א, ב, and ג. Assign each group three or four lines to master (lines 1–4, 5–7, or 8–10). The groups should practice reading until all members can read the lines fluently and accurately. Direct students to form new groups consisting of one or two students from each of the previous groups (א, ב, and ג). In these new groups, have the student(s) who practiced each set of lines help other group members master these lines. Continue until all students have mastered all ten lines. Note: While groups are practicing, you may choose to work one-on-one with students who need individual attention.

Digital Application

Tell students that at home, before the next class, they should click on אֵין כֵּאלֹהֵינוּ/אֲדוֹן עוֹלָם or Tiberias to enter Level 7. Next, they click on the Torah scroll and אֲדוֹן עוֹלָם to practice reading this hymn. In the next class, ask students to read the hymn out loud with a partner.

Teach, or have your cantor or music specialist teach, your students to chant אֲדוֹן עוֹלָם.

Prayer Words

Present word cards 87–93. As you display each card, call on students to read the word in Hebrew and to say its English meaning. Divide the class into groups of three. Direct groups to practice reading these new prayer words and saying their meanings. Encourage students to coach one another, helping each other read the words fluently and memorize their meanings.

Divide the class into two teams, and play a quick game of Hebrew Baseball (see page 14) to reinforce the reading and meaning of word cards 87–93. You may use a word card more than once.

Distribute word cards 87–93 among students. Challenge students to arrange the word cards on the ledge of the board in order of their appearance in אֲדוֹן עוֹלָם.

Wish for the World

Have students read and complete "Wish for the World" with a partner. Partners should read aloud the Hebrew word for each English meaning. Call on a volunteer to say the Hebrew word, and its English meaning, for our greatest wish. *(*שָׁלוֹם*—peace)*. Challenge students to name prayers that express our wish for שָׁלוֹם. *(Possible answers include:* אֵין כָּמוֹךָ*;* שִׂים שָׁלוֹם*;* קַדִּישׁ*;* עֹשֶׂה שָׁלוֹם*)*

Was, Is, Will Be!

Display word cards 88, 89, and 90. Call on volunteers to read the Hebrew words and say their English meaning. Have students read chorally the Hebrew and English of line 4 on page 78. Ask: What do you think this verse means? *(Possible responses include: God has and will always exist in glory; God is eternal; we proclaim that God is always present.)*

Direct students to turn back to אֵין כָּמוֹךָ on page 5 and read line 3 aloud in Hebrew and English. (יְיָ מֶלֶךְ, יְיָ מָלָךְ, יְיָ יִמְלֹךְ לְעֹלָם וָעֶד—*Adonai is Ruler, Adonai ruled, Adonai will rule forever and ever.)* Ask how this line is similar to line 4 of אֲדוֹן עוֹלָם. *(They both speak of God in*

Prayer Words

Practice reading these words from אֲדוֹן עוֹלָם.

Sovereign	אֲדוֹן
(God) was	הָיָה
(God) is	הֹוֶה
(God) will be	יִהְיֶה
without a beginning	בְּלִי רֵאשִׁית
without an end	בְּלִי תַכְלִית
my Redeemer	גֹּאֲלִי

Wish for the World

Write the Hebrew word for each English meaning.

without a beginning	1. בְּלִי רֵאשִׁית
without an end	2. בְּלִי תַכְלִית
Sovereign	3. אֲדוֹן

Now copy the circled letters to reveal our greatest wish for the world.

שָׁלוֹם

Was, Is, Will Be!

Why do you think אֲדוֹן עוֹלָם says of God: הָיָה, הֹוֶה, יִהְיֶה (was, is, and will be)?

79

---

the past, present, and future.) Have students write a response to the final question on page 79. Call on volunteers to share their thoughts. *(Possible responses include: to emphasize that God is eternal; to declare our belief that God has always been and will always be with us.)*

Digital Application

In Level 7 of the digital application, have students click on the activities light bulb and then the phrase "Text Twist." Here, students will review prayer words introduced in Chapter 7. Invite students to play the online "Hebrew Twist," which challenges them to write the Hebrew prayer word for an English word or phrase by unscrambling Hebrew letters. Encourage students to play several rounds, record their point scores, and keep track of their personal best.

!אוֹי

Play a game of !אוֹי (see page 13) to review the prayer words (word cards 79–93) from this chapter along with words from previous chapters.

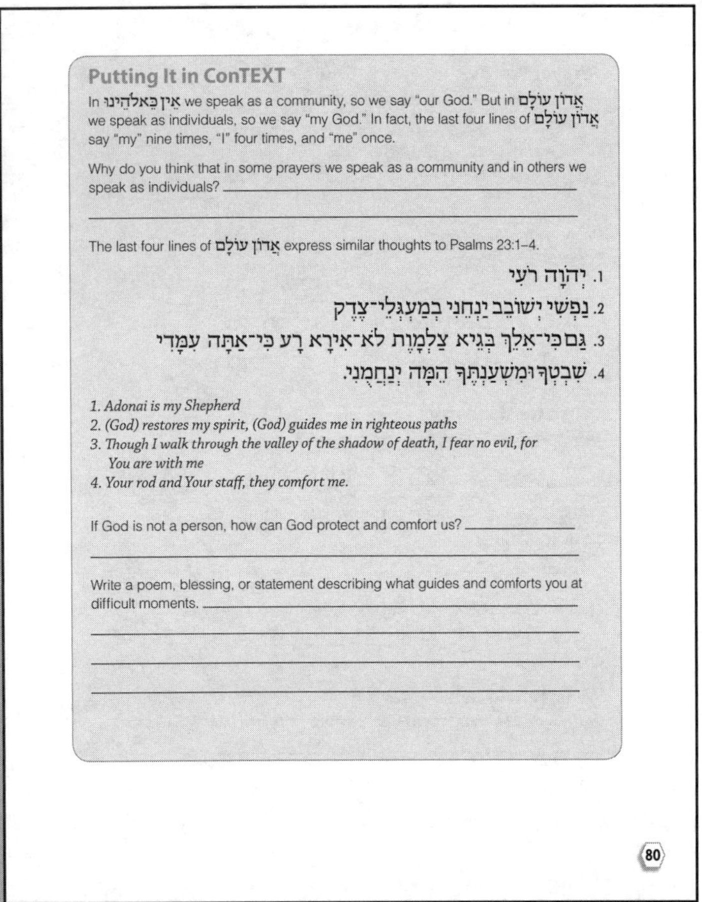

Putting It in ConTEXT

In אֵין כֵּאלֹהֵינוּ we speak as a community, so we say "our God." But in אֲדוֹן עוֹלָם we speak as individuals, so we say "my God." In fact, the last four lines of אֲדוֹן עוֹלָם say "my" nine times, "I" four times, and "me" once.

Why do you think that in some prayers we speak as a community and in others we speak as individuals? ______________________________

____

The last four lines of אֲדוֹן עוֹלָם express similar thoughts to Psalms 23:1–4.

1. יְהוָה רֹעִי
2. נַפְשִׁי יְשׁוֹבֵב יַנְחֵנִי בְמַעְגְּלֵי־צֶדֶק
3. גַּם כִּי־אֵלֵךְ בְּגֵיא צַלְמָוֶת לֹא־אִירָא רָע כִּי־אַתָּה עִמָּדִי
4. שִׁבְטְךָ וּמִשְׁעַנְתֶּךָ הֵמָּה יְנַחֲמֻנִי.

1. Adonai is my Shepherd
2. (God) restores my spirit, (God) guides me in righteous paths
3. Though I walk through the valley of the shadow of death, I fear no evil, for You are with me
4. Your rod and Your staff, they comfort me.

If God is not a person, how can God protect and comfort us? ______________________________

____

Write a poem, blessing, or statement describing what guides and comforts you at difficult moments. ______________________________

____

____

____

80

Putting It in ConTEXT

Write on the board: ◌ִי = me, my. ־א = I. Explain that the suffix ◌ִי means "my" or "me," and that the prefix ־א means "I." Direct students to circle all the Hebrew words in lines 7–10 on page 78 that have the suffix ◌ִי *(line 7—*אֵלִי, גֹּאֲלִי, חֶבְלִי*; line 8—*נִסִּי, לִי, כּוֹסִי*; line 9—*רוּחִי*; line 10—*רוּחִי, גְּוִיָּתִי, לִי*)* and to put a rectangle around the words with the prefix ־א *(line 8—*אֶקְרָא*; line 9—*אַפְקִיד, אִישַׁן, וְאָעִירָה*; line 10—*אִירָא*).*

Have students turn to אֵין כֵּאלֹהֵינוּ on page 71. Ask: Does either the suffix ◌ִי or the prefix ־א appear in this prayer? *(no)* What suffix appears throughout אֵין כֵּאלֹהֵינוּ? *(*נוּ*)* What does the suffix נוּ mean? *(our)* In אֵין כֵּאלֹהֵינוּ do we speak as a community or as individuals? *(as a community)* In אֲדוֹן עוֹלָם do we speak as a community or as individuals? *(as individuals)*

Direct students to read the opening paragraph of page 80 with a partner and to discuss with the partner why in some prayers we speak as a community and in others we speak as individuals. Call on students to share their responses. *(Possible responses include: sometimes we want to express that God is the God of all the Jewish people, and other times we want to express our individual connection to God; some prayers remind us that we are part of the Jewish community, while others remind us that every person is unique and responsible for making the world a better place.)*

Have partners read aloud Psalms 23:1–4 in Hebrew and English, circle all the Hebrew words that have the suffix ◌ִי *(line 1—*רֹעִי*; line 2—*נַפְשִׁי, יַנְחֵנִי*; line 3—*עִמָּדִי*; line 4—*יְנַחֲמֻנִי*)* and put a rectangle around the words with the prefix ־א *(line 3—*אֵלֵךְ, אִירָא*).* Tell students not to circle כִּי; ◌ִי is part of the word כִּי and is not a suffix in this word. Challenge partners to find the two words in Psalms 23:1–4 that are similar to the last two words of אֲדוֹן עוֹלָם. *(*לֹא־אִירָא*)* and to say their English meaning *(I shall not be afraid).*

Ask: How are the thoughts expressed in Psalms 23:1–4 similar to those expressed in אֲדוֹן עוֹלָם? *(Answers may include: both speak of a personal, individual connection to God; both speak of not being afraid; both speak of God being present even in times of stress.)*

Have students write independently how God can protect and comfort us, and compose a poem, blessing, or statement describing what guides and comforts them at difficult moments. Invite students who would like to share their writings to read their compositions to the class.

Prayer Chart

If you have begun a chart of the Shabbat morning service (see page 25), write אֲדוֹן עוֹלָם on a 4″ x 6″ index card and add this hymn to the chart. The completed chart should list the following prayers, one below the other. The order is presented here from right to left:

אֵין כָּמוֹךָ–אַב הָרַחֲמִים–כִּי מִצִּיּוֹן–
בָּרוּךְ שֶׁנָּתַן–שְׁמַע–גַּדְּלוּ לַייָ–לְךָ יְיָ–
בִּרְכוֹת הַתּוֹרָה–וְזֹאת הַתּוֹרָה–בִּרְכוֹת
הַהַפְטָרָה–יְהַלְלוּ־הוֹדוֹ–עֵץ חַיִּים הִיא–
אֵין כֵּאלֹהֵינוּ–עָלֵינוּ–קַדִּישׁ–אֲדוֹן עוֹלָם

My Reflections on the Prayer

If your students are creating a booklet of reflections on the prayers, give each student two pages of prompts to complete (see page 29). The pages should be devoted to (1) אֵין כֵּאלֹהֵינוּ and (2) אֲדוֹן עוֹלָם. Remember to have students draw an illustration or symbol to represent each prayer.

Have students compile and complete their original prayer booklets. Remind students the booklets should open from the right, and the prayers should be arranged according to their order in the Shabbat morning service. Have students create front and back covers for their booklets. Encourage students to create a title for their booklet, to draw illustrations to represent prayers or ritual items found in a sanctuary, and to include information about themselves, the author. Students may complete their booklet by assembling the pages in a report cover or three-ring binder, or by stapling or binding the pages together.

Name that Tune

Have partners read "Name that Tune" and draw a line from each holiday to its matching tune. As a class, sing lines 1–4 of אֲדוֹן עוֹלָם (page 78) to each of the holiday tunes.

Divide the class into groups of 3–4 students. Direct groups to think of another tune and to practice singing אֲדוֹן עוֹלָם to this tune. Invite each group to sing lines 1–4 of אֲדוֹן עוֹלָם to their chosen tune. For fun, create a list of tunes that might be used for אֲדוֹן עוֹלָם. Have students choose different tunes when you sing אֲדוֹן עוֹלָם at the conclusion of your class prayer service.

Clue to Cyberspace

Have students work with a partner to read and complete "Clue to Cyberspace."

Tell students that at home they should click on the joystick to play "Stampede" to review prayer words from Lesson 7. Here, students help the lion cross a stampede of wild animals and a river to match a Hebrew word to its English meaning. Remind students to use the clue—אֲדוֹן—to score bonus points.

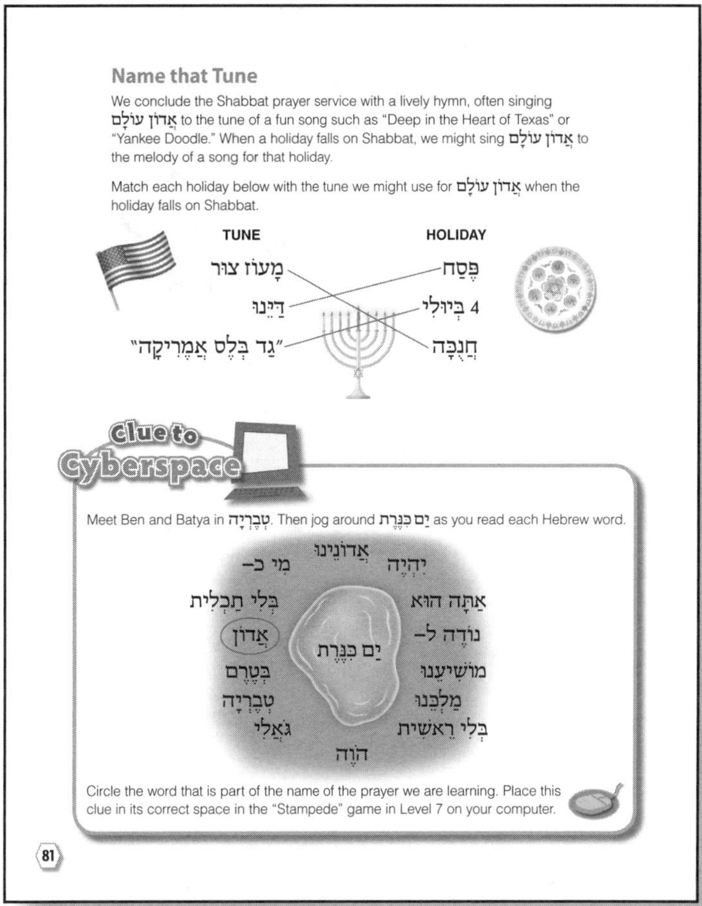

Name that Tune

We conclude the Shabbat prayer service with a lively hymn, often singing אֲדוֹן עוֹלָם to the tune of a fun song such as "Deep in the Heart of Texas" or "Yankee Doodle." When a holiday falls on Shabbat, we might sing אֲדוֹן עוֹלָם to the melody of a song for that holiday.

Match each holiday below with the tune we might use for אֲדוֹן עוֹלָם when the holiday falls on Shabbat.

TUNE	HOLIDAY
מָעוֹז צוּר	פֶּסַח
דַּיֵּנוּ	4 בְּיוּלִי
"גַּד בְּלֶס אֲמֶרִיקָה"	חֲנֻכָּה

Clue to Cyberspace

Meet Ben and Batya in טְבֶרְיָה. Then jog around יַם כִּנֶּרֶת as you read each Hebrew word.

Circle the word that is part of the name of the prayer we are learning. Place this clue in its correct space in the "Stampede" game in Level 7 on your computer.

81

Assessment

As students are working on any of the above activities, meet with them individually to assess reading fluency and knowledge of prayer content. Use the Prayer Mastery Assessment Chart on page 17 of the Teacher's Edition to keep track of student progress. You can also assess students' progress online at www.behrmanhouse.com. Click on the blue "Assessment" button at the bottom of the screen, select *Kol Yisrael 3*, and type in your class's serial number to see how students are doing in their digital application. Students can also e-mail their lesson summary to you directly or print out a lesson summary and bring it in to class.

What's Next?

Congratulate your students on having studied all the prayers in *Kol Yisrael 3*. Ask students if they know which blessing we recite when we reach a special moment in time. (*שֶׁהֶחֱיָנוּ*) Inform students that they will soon have an opportunity to celebrate all that they have learned this year while studying *Kol Yisrael 3*.

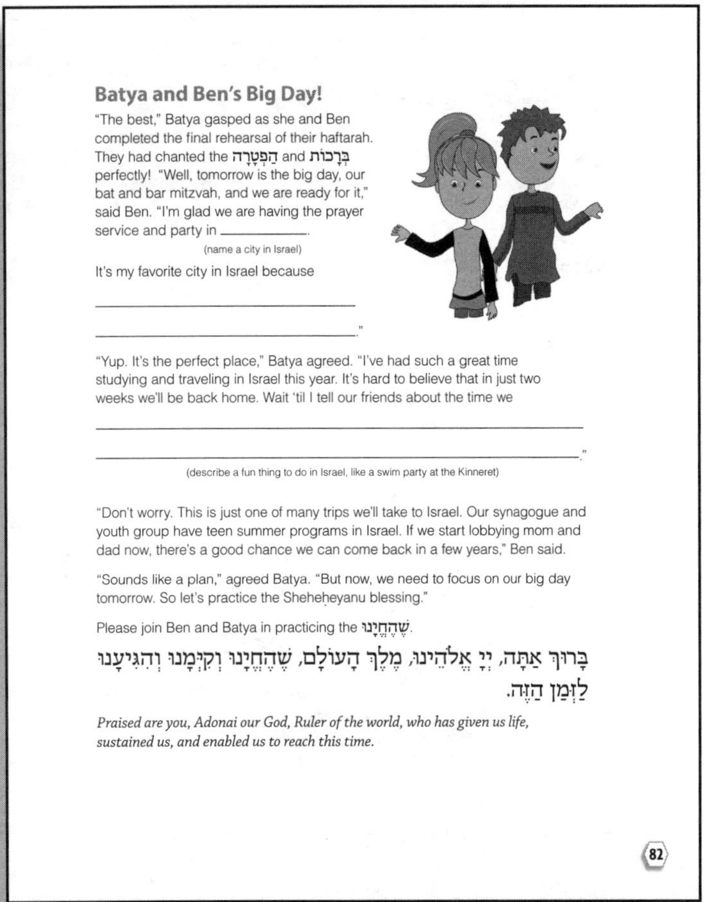

Batya and Ben's Big Day!

"The best," Batya gasped as she and Ben completed the final rehearsal of their haftarah. They had chanted the הַפְטָרָה and בְּרָכוֹת perfectly! "Well, tomorrow is the big day, our bat and bar mitzvah, and we are ready for it," said Ben. "I'm glad we are having the prayer service and party in __________.

(name a city in Israel)

It's my favorite city in Israel because

____

______________________________."

"Yup. It's the perfect place," Batya agreed. "I've had such a great time studying and traveling in Israel this year. It's hard to believe that in just two weeks we'll be back home. Wait 'til I tell our friends about the time we

____

____."

(describe a fun thing to do in Israel, like a swim party at the Kinneret)

"Don't worry. This is just one of many trips we'll take to Israel. Our synagogue and youth group have teen summer programs in Israel. If we start lobbying mom and dad now, there's a good chance we can come back in a few years," Ben said.

"Sounds like a plan," agreed Batya. "But now, we need to focus on our big day tomorrow. So let's practice the Sheheḥeyanu blessing."

Please join Ben and Batya in practicing the שֶׁהֶחֱיָנוּ.

בָּרוּךְ אַתָּה, יְיָ אֱלֹהֵינוּ, מֶלֶךְ הָעוֹלָם, שֶׁהֶחֱיָנוּ וְקִיְּמָנוּ וְהִגִּיעָנוּ לַזְּמַן הַזֶּה.

Praised are you, Adonai our God, Ruler of the world, who has given us life, sustained us, and enabled us to reach this time.

82

are some occasions that we say the שֶׁהֶחֱיָנוּ? *(Possible answers include: when we do something for the first time; on the first days of a holiday; when we reach a new stage in our lives; after lighting holiday candles; after reciting the holiday* קִדּוּשׁ*; before hearing the* שׁוֹפָר *for the first time)*

As a class, practice reciting the שֶׁהֶחֱיָנוּ. You may wish to review the שֶׁהֶחֱיָנוּ phrase by phrase, until your students can recite the blessing fluently. Invite the class to stand and recite the שֶׁהֶחֱיָנוּ in Hebrew and in English.

Digital Application

Tell students that at home, before the next class, they should click on אֵין כֵּאלֹהֵינוּ/אֲדוֹן עוֹלָם or Tiberias to enter Level 7. Next, they click on the Torah scroll and שֶׁהֶחֱיָנוּ to practice reading this blessing. In the next class, ask students to read the blessing out loud with a partner.

Siyum Hasefer

The Hebrew phrase *siyum hasefer* refers to a celebration of the completion of a book. To celebrate the completion of studying the prayers in *Kol Yisrael 3*, consider inviting parents to join students in a morning or afternoon service, led by students. After the service, have parents and classmates view all the prayer reflection booklets, and, if your students have been creating travel guides about different places in Israel, hear the students' Israel travel presentations.

Encourage students to design fun, creative presentations. A student might, for example, present a brochure as if he or she were a travel agent meeting with a potential client. Invite students to ask the presenters questions about their sites in Israel. As a class, discuss which sites students would most like to visit and why. With the approval of your education director, provide refreshments.

Batya and Ben's Big Day!

Invite three students to the front of the room to do a dramatic reading of page 82 as the narrator, Batya, and Ben. Direct "Batya" and "Ben" to read the opening paragraph, pausing at the first write-on-line. All students should then fill in the first two write-on-lines.

Call on students (1) to name which place they think the twins would like to have their prayer service and party and (2) to explain their choice. *(Answers may include: Jerusalem, because they can have their service near the Wall and then celebrate at a nice restaurant; Tel-Aviv because they can have their service in a synagogue and then celebrate near the beach.)*

Direct "Batya" to read the third paragraph, pausing at its write-on-line. Have students complete this sentence and then invite students to share their descriptions of a fun thing to do in Israel. *(Possible suggestions include: took a hike in the Negev desert; rode on a camel; climbed Masada at dawn)*

Ask "Ben" and "Batya" to continue their dramatic reading of the next two paragraphs. Ask: When

My Big Day

Write on the board: בַּר מִצְוָה–בַּת מִצְוָה. Call on a volunteer to say the English meaning of מִצְוָה. *(commandment)* Explain that בַּר is the Aramaic word for "son" and that בַּת is the Hebrew word for "daughter." The plural is בְּנֵי מִצְוָה for boys or boys and girls, and בְּנוֹת מִצְוָה for girls.

Inform students that according to Jewish tradition, once you reach the age of בַּר מִצְוָה or בַּת מִצְוָה you are a son or daughter of the commandments and are obligated to fulfill *mitzvot*. Girls and boys mark this milestone in a variety of ways, such as by leading the congregation in a prayer service, reading from the Torah, reading a haftarah, and doing a mitzvah project.

Encourage your students to ask at home how, and if, their own family members celebrated becoming a bar or bat mitzvah. As a class, create a list of questions students might ask their relatives. Guide students to focus on the ritual aspect of the celebration, not the party. Possible questions include: Did you have a bar/bat mitzvah celebration? How old were you? Did you lead any of the service? If so, which prayers? Did you read Torah and/or chant haftarah? If you did not have a bar/bat mitzvah celebration, what might sway you to take part in an adult bar/bat mitzvah? What is most important to you about my becoming a bar/bat mitzvah?

At the next class, invite students to share their stories, telling how family members marked becoming a bat or bar mitzvah.

Bring *humashim* that include the haftarah readings to your classroom. Ask students to look up their Torah and haftarah readings. Direct students to complete "*My* Big Day" individually. Divide the class into groups of 3–4 students. Have your students refer to what they have written on page 83 as they tell their group members about their bar or bat mitzvah plans.

Consider making a poster on which students describe, and illustrate, what they plan to do for a מִצְוָה project.

My Big Day

I am a student at ______________________.
(name of religious school)

I will celebrate becoming a ________ mitzvah on ________, ________.
(bar/bat) (day of the week) (date)

My פָּרָשָׁה is about ______________________.

My הַפְטָרָה is about ______________________.

My מִצְוָה project may be about ______________________.

My prayer service will be held at ______________________.

What I most look forward to about becoming a bar/bat mitzvah is ________ ________ because ________ ________.

There is much I have learned about Judaism and more that I will continue to learn, and so I offer this blessing of gratitude.

אַתָּה חוֹנֵן לְאָדָם דַּעַת, וּמְלַמֵּד לֶאֱנוֹשׁ בִּינָה. חָנֵּנוּ מֵאִתְּךָ
דֵּעָה, בִּינָה וְהַשְׂכֵּל. בָּרוּךְ אַתָּה, יְיָ, חוֹנֵן הַדָּעַת.

You graciously gave humans the ability to learn, teaching us wisdom. Grant us intelligence, wisdom, and understanding. Praised are You, Adonai, who graciously grants us the power to learn. (from the Amidah)

83

Have students read silently the blessing at the bottom of page 83. Ask: What are we thanking God for? *(allowing us to learn; giving us wisdom)* Which prayer includes this blessing? *(the Amidah)*

Inform students that this is the first of thirteen blessings that are recited in the weekday Amidah. Ask students why, in their opinion, this blessing precedes the others. *(Possible responses include: we need knowledge if we are to succeed in life; learning and studying is a very important Jewish value; we need to be able to learn if we want to make our world a better place.)*

Lead your class in a choral reading of (1) the sentence that precedes the blessing, (2) the blessing in Hebrew, and (3) the blessing in English.

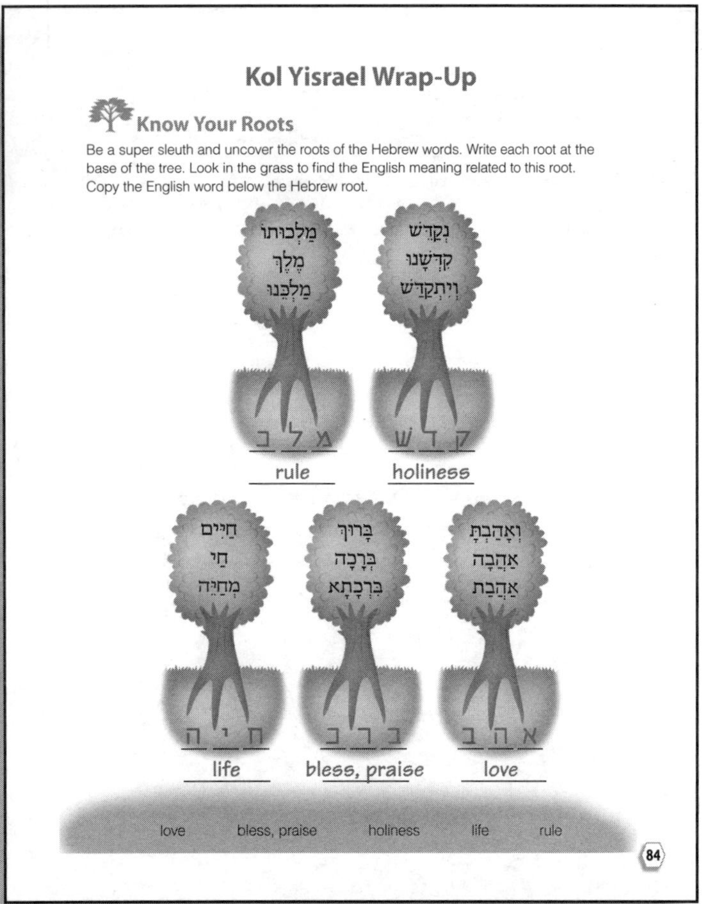

Groups may use *Kol Yisrael 3* for reference. At the end of four minutes, a representative from each group comes to the board and writes the group's list on the board. Check that all the roots listed on the board are correct. The group with the most correct roots is the winner. For an added challenge, direct groups to also write the general English meaning next to each root.

Students have learned the following roots in *Kol Yisrael 1, 2,* and *3*. The roots are listed in order of appearance—across from right to left, row by row. The roots that are included in the *Kol Yisrael* Wrap-Up activity "Know Your Roots" are printed in boldface.

bless, praise — **ברכ**
wholeness — שלמ
eat — אכל
rule, king — **מלכ**
life — **חיה**
wonder — פלא
word, speak — דבר
believe, have faith — אמנ
remember — זכר

KOL YISRAEL WRAP-UP

"Kol Yisrael Wrap-Up" reviews prayers and blessings from *Kol Yisrael 1, 2,* and *3*. The activities focus on key words, roots, and concepts introduced in the series. You may use this wrap-up as a review or as an assessment of your students' mastery of the prayers and blessings.

Suggestions for using each activity as a review or as an assessment are presented on pages 112–121. Ideas for remediation and enrichment are also included, allowing you to provide meaningful work for advanced students while others are mastering the current material. Ask your education director for copies of *Kol Yisrael 1* and *2* for reference.

To best use "Kol Yisrael Wrap-Up" for assessment, have your students complete one activity independently, such as "Know Your Roots," and then check, and correct, their own work as you review the answers with the class. Have your students correct their work using colorful pens, such as pink, purple, or green pens. Avoid red as this often has negative associations. Allowing students to check their own work gives them a greater opportunity for self-assessment.

After each class session, collect your students' texts and review their work. Things to look for as you diagnose the texts include:

- Students who made an exceptional number of errors
- Errors that were common among students
- Errors in elementary-level questions

At your next class, provide opportunities for remediation.

Consider presenting the "Kol Yisrael Wrap-Up" over three class sessions. Students may work on pages 84–87 one day, 88–91 on the second day, and 92–93 on the third.

Know Your Roots

As a Review: Divide the class into groups of 3–4 students. Direct groups to list key roots they have learned in *Kol Yisrael 1, 2,* and *3*. For fun, tell groups they have four minutes to create their list.

light — אור
love — אהב
healing — רפא
put — שׂימ
chose — בחר
holy, set apart — קדשׁ
hear, listen — שׁמע
evening, mixed — ערב
power, might — גבר
compassion, mercy — רחמ
go up — עלה
say — אמר
great, big — גדל

Write the ten key roots that are included in "Know Your Roots" on the board. Review the meaning of each of these roots.

Direct students to complete "Know Your Roots" as an open-book review. Students should feel free to use the information in *Kol Yisrael 3* for reference. Walk around the room as students are working to informally assess students' knowledge of these key roots.

Suggest that students who finish early look through the prayers in *Kol Yisrael 3* to find other words based on these same roots. Have these students write the additional words at the bottom of pages 84 and 85.

As a class, review the answers to the activities. Have students check and correct their own work.

Call on students to share how knowing these key roots helps them to understand prayers. A student might say, for example, "If I see a root appearing several times in a prayer and I know the meaning of the root, then I can name a main idea of the prayer, such as holiness or saying thank you."

As an Assessment: Have students complete pages 84 and 85 independently. Students who finish early should be encouraged to try to write the English meaning of the words listed in the trees.

As a class, review the answers to the activities. Have students check and correct their own work.

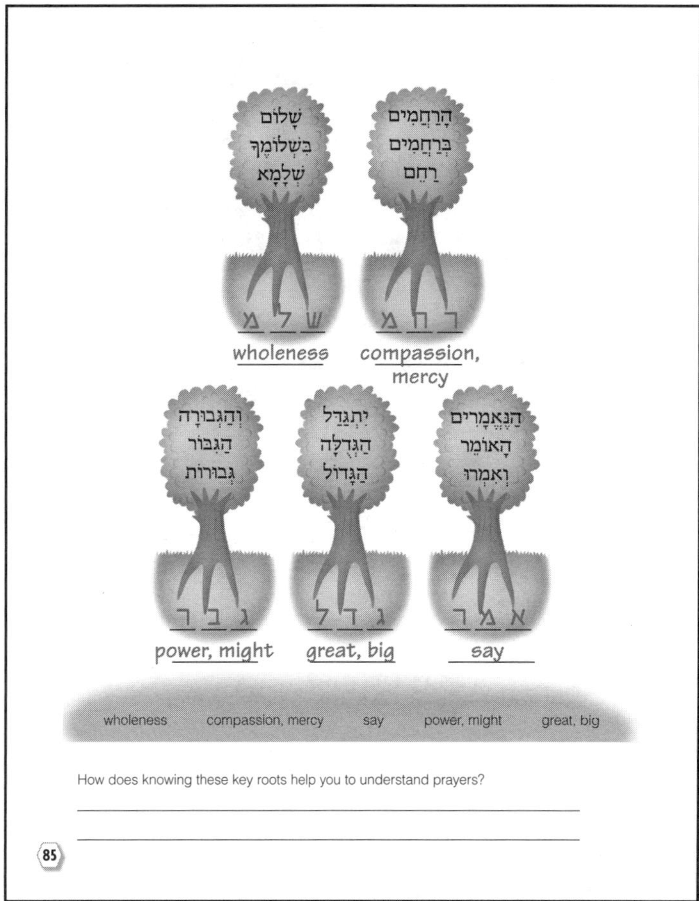

At the end of class, collect students' texts. Review all student work, looking for evidence of students who need extra help and material that all or most students need to review.

Remediation: Consider having students review pages from *Kol Yisrael 1, 2,* and *3* in which these roots are introduced. The following list identifies (1) a page in one of the books that focuses on a specific root and (2) pages in *Kol Yisrael 3* where students can practice finding words built on each root.

Kol Yisrael 2, page 63; *Kol Yisrael 3*, pages 33, 34, 44, 45, 82 — חיה

Kol Yisrael 1, page 15; *Kol Yisrael 3*, pages 26, 27, 44 — ברכ

Kol Yisrael 2, page 36; *Kol Yisrael 3*, pages 11, 15, 21 — אהב

Kol Yisrael 3, page 7; *Kol Yisrael 3*, pages 44, 45, 54, 55 — מלכ

Kol Yisrael 3, page 18; *Kol Yisrael 3*, pages 19, 20, 43, 62 — קדשׁ

Kol Yisrael 2, page 68; *Kol Yisrael 3*, pages 23, 25, 59 — גבר

Following Orders

Batya and Ben are working on their computer to plan a Shabbat retreat. Each prayer is on a separate document. Help them plan services for the retreat by numbering the prayers, beginning with Shabbat morning, according to the order in which they are recited.

Challenge: Name two additional prayers that Ben and Batya could add to their list.

__________ __________

86

who need extra help and material that all or most students need to review.

Remediation: On a blank sheet of paper, draw two columns and five rows, to form ten boxes.

Write each of the prayers listed on page 86 in one of the boxes. Prepare and give copies to each student who needs to practice the order of the prayers. Direct students to cut out the boxes and practice putting the prayers in order. For fun, have students arrange the prayers in order with a partner. Partner א places the first prayer, בָּרְכוּ, on the desk, and partner ב then places the next prayer, the שְׁמַע, below the בָּרְכוּ.

Consider creating index cards with the names of each prayer. Distribute the cards among students. Challenge students to arrange themselves in the order of the prayer service, without speaking.

Enrichment: Challenge students to use a siddur to identify which of these prayers are also included in the Friday evening service, and to number the prayers in the order in which they are recited on Friday evening.

גדל — *Kol Yisrael 3*, page 65; *Kol Yisrael 3*, pages 21, 23, 62, 66

אמר — *Kol Yisrael 3*, page 47; *Kol Yisrael 3*, pages 40, 46, 55, 59

שלמ — *Kol Yisrael 3*, page 17; *Kol Yisrael 3*, pages 5, 62, 68, 69

רחמ — *Kol Yisrael 3*, page 8; *Kol Yisrael 3*, pages 13, 44, 59

Consider playing a game of Concentration (see page 14) to review the roots and their meanings.

Following Orders

As a Review: Have students work with a partner and write a list of the Shabbat morning prayers they have studied in *Kol Yisrael 1, 2,* and 3. Have *siddurim* available for students to use as reference. Call on students to name the Shabbat morning prayers. Write the names of the prayers on the board. As a class, number the prayers that are listed on the board according to when they are recited on Shabbat morning. Encourage partners to use the siddur to determine the order of the prayers.

Erase the list of prayers from the board and direct students to complete page 86 with a partner.

As a class, review the answers to the activity. Have students check and correct their own work.

Call on students to name additional prayers that could be added to Ben and Batya's list. *(Possible answers include:* וְזֹאת הַתּוֹרָה*;* גַּדְּלוּ לַייָ*;* עֵץ חַיִּים הִיא*)*

As an Assessment: Have students complete page 86 independently. Students who finish quickly should be encouraged to name additional prayers and to indicate when, in the service, each prayer is recited. For example, a student might name וְזֹאת הַתּוֹרָה and number it as 6a, indicating that it follows בִּרְכוֹת הַתּוֹרָה, the sixth prayer in Ben and Batya's list.

As a class, review the answers to the activities. Have students check and correct their own work. At the end of class, collect students' texts. Review all student work, looking for evidence of students

3-2-1 Action!

As a Review: Call on a volunteer to come to the front of the room and act out a motion, such as bowing, that we perform during the prayer service. Have classmates name the prayer, or prayers, in which we do this motion. Invite a second student to act out another motion. Continue until students have demonstrated each of the motions listed on page 87. Keep in mind that you may need to prompt students to act out a motion they may not recall on their own.

Direct students to complete page 87 with a partner and read aloud the name of each prayer.

As a class, review the answers to the activity. Have students check and correct their own work.

Invite students to describe ways that these actions can make prayer more meaningful. *(Possible answers include: when we cover our eyes, we can concentrate better since we are not distracted by the people and things around us; we feel a greater connection to God as we rise up on our toes and declare that God is holy, קָדוֹשׁ.)*

As an Assessment: Have students independently (1) match each motion to a prayer and (2) describe one way that these actions can make prayer more meaningful. *(Possible answers include: bowing during the עֲמִידָה; bowing to the left, right, and then forward when reciting עֹשֶׂה שָׁלוֹם; marching with the Torah when reciting לְךָ יְיָ. See the previous paragraph for possible ways that actions can make prayer more meaningful.)* Students who finish quickly should be encouraged to list additional motions we perform during the prayer service.

As a class, review the answers to the activities. Have students check and correct their own work. At the end of class, collect students' texts. Review all student work, looking for evidence of students who need extra help and material that all or most students need to review.

Remediation: Distribute *siddurim* to your students. Direct students to turn to one of the prayers listed on page 87. Have students read aloud the line that goes along with the motion and perform that motion. These prayers,

3-2-1 Action!

Ben and Batya are making a film about leading Shabbat services. They filmed a silent video and then made recordings of prayers being chanted. Write the number of each prayer next to its matching action to help Ben and Batya sync the chanting of the prayers with the video.

6 close eyes or cover eyes with hand	.1 אָבוֹת וְאִמָּהוֹת
1 take three steps backward then forward	.2 קְדוּשָּׁה
4 come up to the bimah for an aliyah	.3 וְזֹאת הַתּוֹרָה
3 raise the Torah for everyone to see	.4 בִּרְכוֹת הַתּוֹרָה
2 rise up on toes three times	.5 עָלֵינוּ
5 bend knees and bow during the prayer	.6 שְׁמַע

Describe one way that these actions can make prayer more meaningful.

סִדּוּר

87

according to their order on page 87, are found on pages 124, 130, 252, 250, 282, and 183 of *Mishkan T'filah;* pages 294–297, 302–305, 407, 398–399, 444–447, and 64–65 of *Kol Haneshamah;* and pages 115, 116, 146, 142, 183, and 112 of *Siddur Sim Shalom*. Alternatively, write the page numbers of these prayers on the board. Have students work with a partner as they locate each prayer and practice its motions.

Enrichment: Have students skim the Shabbat morning service in the siddur and find additional prayers, such as the בָּרְכוּ, that have their own choreography. Direct the students to record the name of the prayer, the page on which it is found, and the motion that goes along with it.

Photo Op

Call on a volunteer to describe the photo. Invite students to suggest how reading along in a siddur can help us concentrate. *(Possible answers include: looking at the words helps us to focus on what we are saying; when we read the words we notice the key words and roots, and think about their meaning.)*

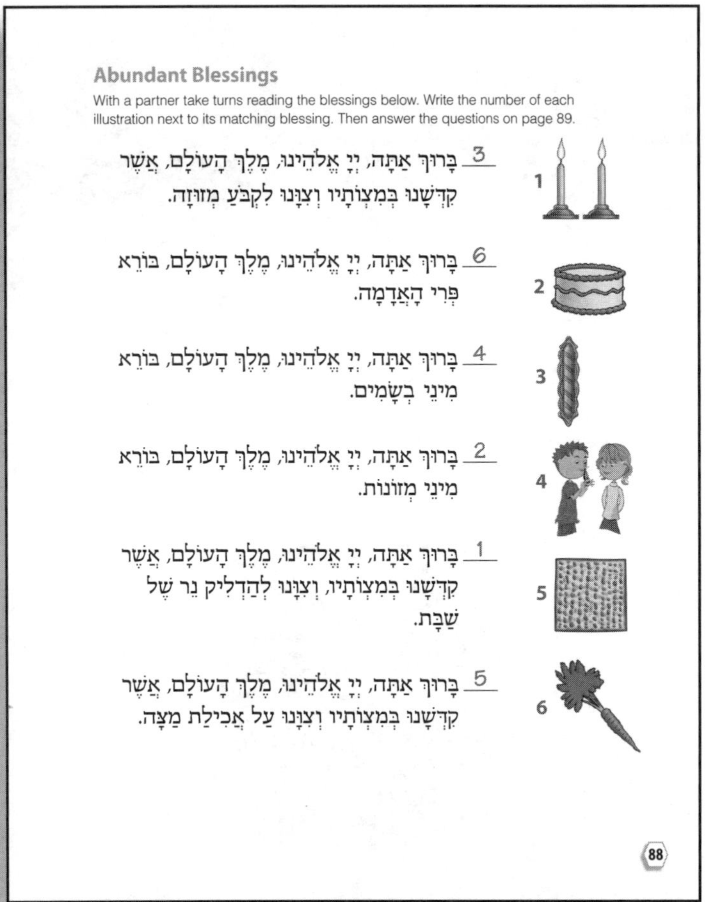

Abundant Blessings

With a partner take turns reading the blessings below. Write the number of each illustration next to its matching blessing. Then answer the questions on page 89.

3 בָּרוּךְ אַתָּה, יְיָ אֱלֹהֵינוּ, מֶלֶךְ הָעוֹלָם, אֲשֶׁר קִדְּשָׁנוּ בְּמִצְוֹתָיו וְצִוָּנוּ לִקְבֹּעַ מְזוּזָה.

6 בָּרוּךְ אַתָּה, יְיָ אֱלֹהֵינוּ, מֶלֶךְ הָעוֹלָם, בּוֹרֵא פְּרִי הָאֲדָמָה.

4 בָּרוּךְ אַתָּה, יְיָ אֱלֹהֵינוּ, מֶלֶךְ הָעוֹלָם, בּוֹרֵא מִינֵי בְשָׂמִים.

2 בָּרוּךְ אַתָּה, יְיָ אֱלֹהֵינוּ, מֶלֶךְ הָעוֹלָם, בּוֹרֵא מִינֵי מְזוֹנוֹת.

1 בָּרוּךְ אַתָּה, יְיָ אֱלֹהֵינוּ, מֶלֶךְ הָעוֹלָם, אֲשֶׁר קִדְּשָׁנוּ בְּמִצְוֹתָיו, וְצִוָּנוּ לְהַדְלִיק נֵר שֶׁל שַׁבָּת.

5 בָּרוּךְ אַתָּה, יְיָ אֱלֹהֵינוּ, מֶלֶךְ הָעוֹלָם, אֲשֶׁר קִדְּשָׁנוּ בְּמִצְוֹתָיו וְצִוָּנוּ עַל אֲכִילַת מַצָּה.

1 2 3 4 5 6

88

Have students work with a partner as they read the blessings on page 88 and write the number of each illustration next to its matching blessing. Partners then read each blessing on page 89 and write the number of its matching illustration.

As a class, review the answers to the activity. Have students check and correct their own work.

Call on volunteers to read the four Hebrew words that identify a blessing we say when performing a mitzvah (אֲשֶׁר קִדְּשָׁנוּ בְּמִצְוֹתָיו וְצִוָּנוּ), and to say how many blessings of mitzvah are included on pages 88 and 89 *(6)*.

Abundant Blessings

As a Review: Divide the class into groups of 3–4 students. Allow groups five minutes to list blessings that are associated with eating, holidays, or home rituals. Assign a group member the task of recording the final two or three words of the blessing and writing the occasion on which the blessing is recited. Call on a representative from one group to read its list aloud. If any other group has listed the same blessing, all groups with that blessing listed should cross out the blessing. The second group should read the blessings that remain on its list. Again, if another group has recorded a blessing from the second group's list, the groups cross that blessing off its lists. Continue until all groups have read their list of blessings. The group with the most blessings remaining on its list is the winner.

In addition to the blessings listed on pages 88 and 89, students might list any of these blessings recited on the following occasions:

וְצִוָּנוּ לַעֲסוֹק בְּדִבְרֵי תוֹרָה —
when we study Torah

וְצִוָּנוּ לְהַדְלִיק נֵר שֶׁל יוֹם טוֹב —
when we light holiday candles

בּוֹרֵא מְאוֹרֵי הָאֵשׁ —
when we light the *havdalah* candle

שֶׁהֶחֱיָנוּ וְקִיְּמָנוּ וְהִגִּיעָנוּ לַזְּמַן הַזֶּה —
when we reach a special moment in time

וְצִוָּנוּ עַל נְטִילַת לוּלָב —
when we shake the *lulav* and *etrog*

שֶׁעָשָׂה נִסִּים לַאֲבוֹתֵינוּ בַּיָּמִים הָהֵם בַּזְּמַן הַזֶּה —
when we light Hanukkah candles

וְצִוָּנוּ עַל אֲכִילַת מָרוֹר —
when we eat bitter herbs (*maror*)

וְצִוָּנוּ עַל מִקְרָא מְגִלָּה —
when we read Megillat Esther

As an Assessment: Have students read aloud the blessings on page 88 with a partner, and then write independently the number of each illustration next to its matching blessing. Students who finish quickly should be encouraged to underline familiar Hebrew words and, next to each Hebrew word, write its English meaning. For example, a student might underline בָּרוּךְ and write its English meaning, "blessed" or "praised." Once each of the partners has completed page 88, partners should read aloud page 89 and write independently the number of each matching illustration. Again, students who finish early should look for familiar Hebrew words to define.

As a class, review the answers to the activities. Have students check and correct their own work. At the end of class, collect students' texts. Review all student work, looking for evidence of students who need extra help and material that all or most students need to review.

Remediation: Divide the class into two teams, א and ב. Say a blessing ending, such as בּוֹרֵא מִינֵי בְשָׂמִים, and call on Team א to identify when that blessing is recited *(when smelling spices at havdalah)*. Continue by saying various blessing endings and having teams take turns identifying when the blessing is recited. For an added challenge, name the occasion, such as "when affixing a mezuzah," and have teams recite the blessing ending (לִקְבֹּעַ מְזוּזָה). A team earns one point for each correct answer. The team with the most points is the winner.

For additional review, refer to the pages in *Kol Yisrael 1* in which these blessings were originally introduced. The blessings, according to the order of the Hebrew on pages 88 and 89, are found on the following pages of *Kol Yisrael 1*: affixing a mezuzah—page 25, eating a vegetable—page 12, smelling havdalah spices—page 47, eating different foods, such as cookies—page 13, lighting Shabbat candles—page 29, eating matzah—page 61, eating bread—page 12, drinking wine or grape juice—page 13, sitting in a sukkah—page 57, lighting Hanukkah candles—page 34, eating a fruit—page 12, and hearing the blowing of the shofar—page 55.

9 בָּרוּךְ אַתָּה, יְיָ אֱלֹהֵינוּ, מֶלֶךְ הָעוֹלָם, הַמּוֹצִיא לֶחֶם מִן הָאָרֶץ. — 7

12 בָּרוּךְ אַתָּה, יְיָ אֱלֹהֵינוּ, מֶלֶךְ הָעוֹלָם, בּוֹרֵא פְּרִי הַגָּפֶן. — 8

7 בָּרוּךְ אַתָּה, יְיָ אֱלֹהֵינוּ, מֶלֶךְ הָעוֹלָם, אֲשֶׁר קִדְּשָׁנוּ בְּמִצְוֹתָיו וְצִוָּנוּ לֵישֵׁב בַּסֻּכָּה. — 9

10 בָּרוּךְ אַתָּה, יְיָ אֱלֹהֵינוּ, מֶלֶךְ הָעוֹלָם, אֲשֶׁר קִדְּשָׁנוּ בְּמִצְוֹתָיו וְצִוָּנוּ לְהַדְלִיק נֵר שֶׁל חֲנֻכָּה. — 10

8 בָּרוּךְ אַתָּה, יְיָ אֱלֹהֵינוּ, מֶלֶךְ הָעוֹלָם, בּוֹרֵא פְּרִי הָעֵץ. — 11

11 בָּרוּךְ אַתָּה, יְיָ אֱלֹהֵינוּ, מֶלֶךְ הָעוֹלָם, אֲשֶׁר קִדְּשָׁנוּ בְּמִצְוֹתָיו וְצִוָּנוּ לִשְׁמֹעַ קוֹל שׁוֹפָר. — 12

Write the four Hebrew words that identify a blessing we say when performing a mitzvah.

אֲשֶׁר קִדְּשָׁנוּ בְּמִצְוֹתָיו וְצִוָּנוּ

How many blessings of mitzvah did you find? 6

89

Enrichment: Encourage students to page through a siddur or a copy of *Kol Yisrael 1* and write a list of endings of additional blessings and the occasions on which they are recited. Refer to page 116 for a partial listing of blessings students might record.

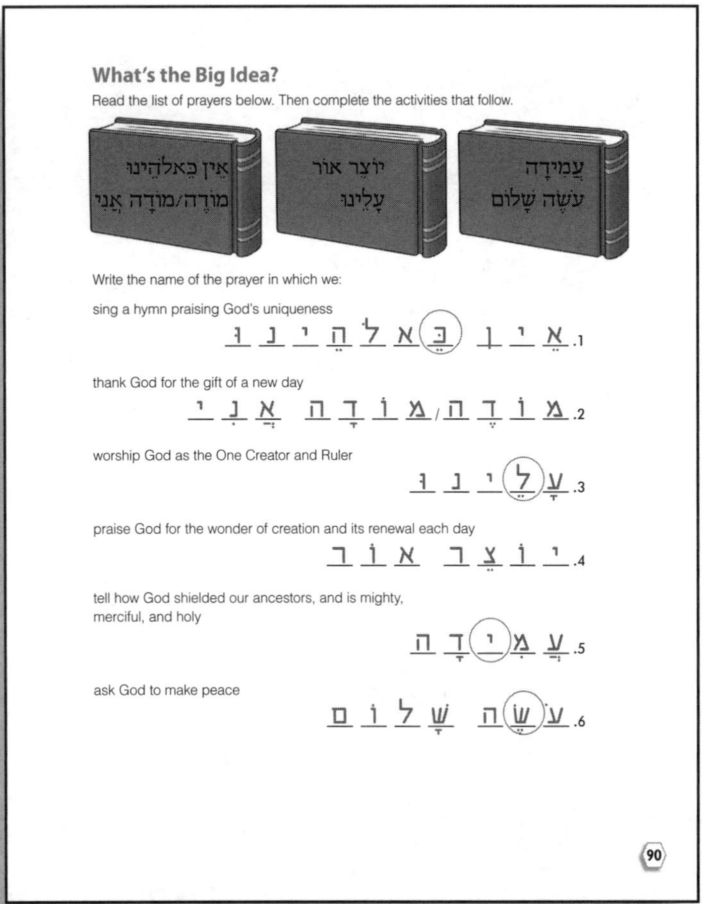

What's the Big Idea?

Read the list of prayers below. Then complete the activities that follow.

Write the name of the prayer in which we:

sing a hymn praising God's uniqueness

1. אֵין כֵּאלֹהֵינוּ

thank God for the gift of a new day

2. מוֹדֶה/מוֹדָה אֲנִי

worship God as the One Creator and Ruler

3. עָלֵינוּ

praise God for the wonder of creation and its renewal each day

4. יוֹצֵר אוֹר

tell how God shielded our ancestors, and is mighty, merciful, and holy

5. עֲמִידָה

ask God to make peace

6. עֹשֶׂה שָׁלוֹם

90

What's the Big Idea?

As a Review: Have the class brainstorm a list of ten or more prayers they have studied in *Kol Yisrael 1, 2,* and *3*. *(Responses may include:* שְׁמַע; מַעֲרִיב עֲרָבִים; עֲמִידָה.*)* List the prayers on the board. Call on volunteers to give a short description of what we are saying in each of the prayers.

For example, a student might say that in מַעֲרִיב עֲרָבִים we thank God for bringing us the evening.

Add to the list the names of prayers found on pages 90 and 91 that are not yet written on the board. Challenge students to describe what each of these prayers is saying.

Direct students to read the Hebrew names of the prayers aloud and to complete pages 90 and 91 with a partner. Encourage students who finish early to arrange the prayers on pages 90 and 91 in the order they are recited on Shabbat day. (מוֹדֶה/מוֹדָה אֲנִי; בָּרְכוּ; יוֹצֵר אוֹר; וְאָהַבְתָּ; מִי כָמֹכָה; עֲמִידָה; עֹשֶׂה שָׁלוֹם; בִּרְכוֹת הַתּוֹרָה; אֵין כֵּאלֹהֵינוּ; עָלֵינוּ; בִּרְכַּת הַמָּזוֹן; הַבְדָּלָה)

Walk around the room, informally assessing students' work. Invite four students who have correctly written the names of the prayers to the front of the room. Direct each of these students to write the answer to three of the questions (1–3, 4–6, 7–9, or 10–12) on the board. Have classmates refer to the board to check and correct their own work.

Ask: What is the name for the Jewish people that is also the name of this series. *(*כָּל יִשְׂרָאֵל*)*

What is the English meaning of this name? (*All of Israel* or *All of the Jewish people*) Why is this a fitting title for our text? *(Responses may include: the prayers in* Kol Yisrael *are for all of the Jewish people; the prayers in* Kol Yisrael *express wishes shared by Jews all over the world; the title is based on the Jewish value* kol Yisrael areivim zeh b'zeha, *all Jews are responsible for one another)*

As an Assessment: Have students read aloud the names of the prayers on page 90 with a partner and then independently write the name of the prayer that matches its description.

Students who finish quickly should be encouraged to number these six prayers according to the order they are recited on Shabbat day. (מוֹדֶה/מוֹדָה אֲנִי; יוֹצֵר אוֹר; עֲמִידָה; עֹשֶׂה שָׁלוֹם; אֵין כֵּאלֹהֵינוּ; עָלֵינוּ) Once each partner has completed page 90, partners should read aloud the names of the prayers on page 91 and write the name of the prayer that matches the description. Students who finish early should now number all twelve prayers listed on pages 90 and 91 according to the order they are recited on Shabbat day. (מוֹדֶה/מוֹדָה אֲנִי; בָּרְכוּ; יוֹצֵר אוֹר; וְאָהַבְתָּ; מִי כָמֹכָה; עֲמִידָה; עֹשֶׂה שָׁלוֹם; בִּרְכוֹת הַתּוֹרָה; אֵין כֵּאלֹהֵינוּ; עָלֵינוּ; הַבְדָּלָה; בִּרְכַּת הַמָּזוֹן)

As a class, review the answers to the activities. Have students check and correct their own work. At the end of class, collect students' texts. Review all student work, looking for evidence of students who need extra help and material that all or most students need to review.

Remediation: Students may review material presented in *Kol Yisrael* about each of the prayers on the following pages:

Kol Yisrael 1, page 6 — מוֹדֶה/מוֹדָה אֲנִי

Kol Yisrael 2, pages 4–5 — בָּרְכוּ

Kol Yisrael 2, pages 13–14 — יוֹצֵר אוֹר

Kol Yisrael 2, pages 32-33 — וְאָהַבְתָּ

Kol Yisrael 2, pages 40–41 — מִי כָמֹכָה

Kol Yisrael 2, pages 48–49, 60–61, 72–74 — עֲמִידָה

Kol Yisrael 2, page 91 — עֹשֶׂה שָׁלוֹם

Kol Yisrael 3, pages 26–27, 33 — בִּרְכוֹת הַתּוֹרָה

Kol Yisrael 3, pages 70–71 — אֵין כֵּאלֹהֵינוּ

Kol Yisrael 3, pages 52–54 — עָלֵינוּ

Kol Yisrael 1, pages 72–73 — בִּרְכַּת הַמָּזוֹן

Kol Yisrael 1, pages 46–48 — הַבְדָּלָה

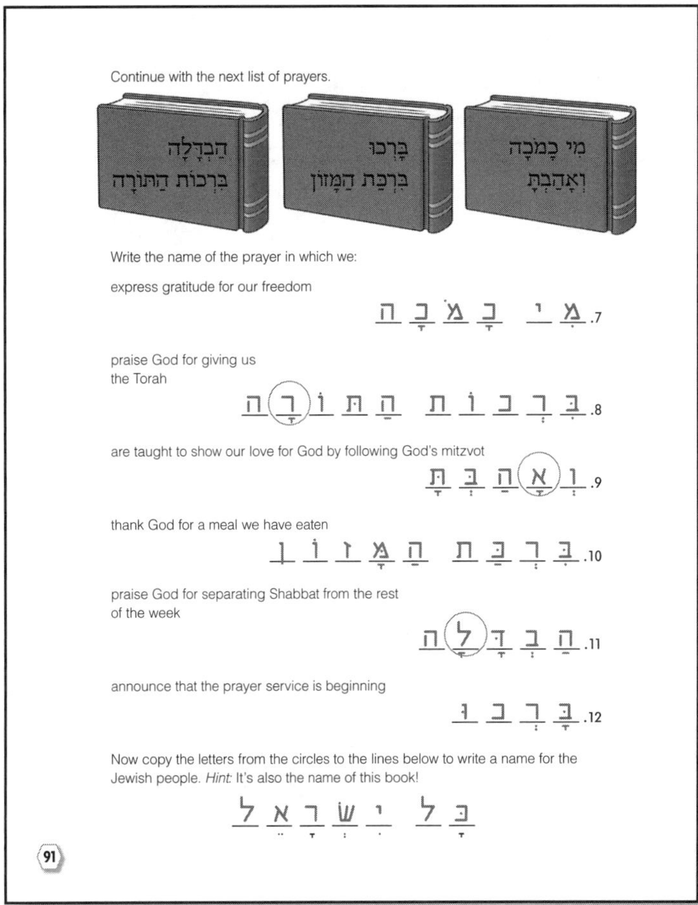
Continue with the next list of prayers.

הַבְדָּלָה / בִּרְכוֹת הַתּוֹרָה — בָּרְכוּ / בִּרְכַּת הַמָּזוֹן — מִי כָמֹכָה / וְאָהַבְתָּ

Write the name of the prayer in which we:

express gratitude for our freedom

7. מִי כָמֹכָה

praise God for giving us the Torah

8. בִּרְכוֹת הַתּוֹרָה

are taught to show our love for God by following God's mitzvot

9. וְאָהַבְתָּ

thank God for a meal we have eaten

10. בִּרְכַּת הַמָּזוֹן

praise God for separating Shabbat from the rest of the week

11. הַבְדָּלָה

announce that the prayer service is beginning

12. בָּרְכוּ

Now copy the letters from the circles to the lines below to write a name for the Jewish people. *Hint:* It's also the name of this book!

כָּל יִשְׂרָאֵל

91

Direct students to underline the words in *Kol Yisrael 1, 2,* or *3* that teach us about the main idea of a prayer. For example, a student who needs to review יוֹצֵר אוֹר should return to *Kol Yisrael 2*, pages 13–14. On page 13, the student would underline, "blessings of thanks for the wonder of creation," and on page 14, the student would underline, "every day You renew creation." These two phrases present the big idea "praise God for the wonder of creation and its renewal each day" as listed in "What's the Big Idea?"

Enrichment: Encourage students to page through a siddur, list additional prayers they studied in *Kol Yisrael,* and write short descriptions of the theme of each prayer.

Speak Up

Read the Hebrew words and phrases aloud. Then circle the word or phrase that we say on each of the following occasions:

1. after hearing a blessing	אָמֵן	יְיַשֵׁר כֹּחַ
2. on Shabbat	לַשָּׁנָה הַבָּאָה בִּירוּשָׁלַיִם	שַׁבָּת שָׁלוֹם
3. in the morning	בְּבַקָּשָׁה	בֹּקֶר טוֹב
4. during Sukkot	שָׁנָה טוֹבָה וּמְתוּקָה	חַג שָׂמֵחַ
5. to welcome guests	בְּרוּכִים הַבָּאִים	עֶרֶב טוֹב
6. before going to sleep	לַיְלָה טוֹב	שָׁבוּעַ טוֹב
7. on receiving a gift	לְחַיִּים	תּוֹדָה
8. when meeting a stranger	מַה שִּׁמְךָ?	רְפוּאָה שְׁלֵמָה

Copy two phrases or words you have *not* circled and describe an occasion when you might say or hear these words.

1. ______________________________

2. ______________________________

Family Facts

Circle the name of the husband, wife, or wives of the ancestor in **bold** on each line below.

יִצְחָק	אַבְרָהָם	אַהֲרוֹן	מֹשֶׁה	**שָׂרָה**	.1
בַּת־שֶׁבַע	לֵאָה	רִבְקָה	מִרְיָם	**יִצְחָק**	.2
דְּבוֹרָה	לֵאָה	שָׂרָה	רָחֵל	**יַעֲקֹב**	.3

Underline the Hebrew name of Abraham and Sarah's son. Put a rectangle around the name of their grandson.

Why do you think the names of the אָבוֹת and אִמָּהוֹת are still popular for babies born nowadays?

____

92

Enrichment: Encourage students to write the English meaning of the words and identify when the uncircled words are said.

Family Facts

As a Review: Direct students to work in small groups and draw a family tree of the patriarchs and matriarchs. As a group, students read aloud the biblical names and complete "Family Facts." As a class, review the answers, having students check and correct their own work.

As an Assessment: Direct students to read the names aloud with a partner and to complete the activity independently. As a class, review the answers to the activities. Have students check and correct their own work. Collect students' texts, review, and diagnose all student work.

Remediation: Have students practice writing a family tree of the patriarchs and matriarchs.

Enrichment: Have students identify each of the people listed in "Family Facts" who is not a patriarch or matriarch. (מֹשֶׁה—*Moses;* אַהֲרוֹן—*Moses's brother;* מִרְיָם—*Moses's*

Speak Up

As a Review: Divide the class into two teams, א and ב. Say one of the Hebrew words or phrases listed in "Speak Up." Call on Team א to describe when this is said OR give its English meaning. If Team א answers correctly, they earn one point and you say a different word or phrase for Team ב to identify. If Team א answers incorrectly, Team ב has a chance to identify it.

Teams take turns identifying the words or phrases. The team with the most points is the winner.

The following are the meanings of all the words and phrases, and a description of when they are said (those that students do not circle): *(line 1, from left) Amen, "Congratulations"—after someone has had a Torah honor; (line 2) Next year in Jerusalem—at the end of the Passover seder, Shabbat Peace; (line 3) Please—when you make a request, Good morning; (line 4) A good and a sweet year—on Rosh Hashanah, Happy holiday; (line 5) Welcome, Good evening—in the evening; (line 6) Good night, A good week—at the end of havdalah; (line 7) To life—at a celebration, Thank you; (line 8) What is your name? A full recovery—when wishing someone "get well."*

Direct students to read aloud the Hebrew words and complete "Speak Up" with a partner. As a class, review the answers to the activity. Have students check and correct their own work.

As an Assessment: Have students read aloud the Hebrew words and phrases on page 92 with a partner, and then independently complete the activity. Encourage students who finish early to write the English meaning of the words and/or identify when the uncircled words are said.

As a class, review the answers to the activities. Have students check and correct their own work. Collect students' texts, review, and diagnose all student work.

Remediation: Have students act out the situations in which these words and phrases are used.

sister; בַּת־שֶׁבַע*—King David's wife;* דְּבוֹרָה*—a judge and prophet)*

Best Wishes

As a Review: Have students read each prayer phrase aloud with a partner and complete the activity together. Direct partners to check their answers with another pair of students.

Call on volunteers to suggest why the word שָׁלוֹם appears so frequently in our prayers. *(Suggestions may include: because we are always wishing for peace; because peace is one of our greatest wishes; so we never forget the importance of peace.)*

As an Assessment: Have students read each prayer phrase aloud with a partner and then complete the activity independently. As a class, review the answers to the activities. Have students check and correct their own work. Collect students' texts, review, and diagnose all student work.

Remediation: Have students practice writing the word שָׁלוֹם. For additional review, direct students to look through a siddur to locate the word שָׁלוֹם.

Enrichment: Have students name a prayer that includes each phrase. *(1—*עֹשֶׂה שָׁלוֹם *closes the* עֲמִידָה *and* קַדִּישׁ*; 2—*יוֹצֵר אוֹר*; 3—*עֹשֶׂה שָׁלוֹם*; 4—*שִׂים שָׁלוֹם *and* שָׁלוֹם רָב*; 5—*שָׁלוֹם רָב*)*

Mitzvot in Action

As a Review: Call on students to describe different *mitzvot* they have engaged in that help make the world a better place. *(Responses may include: collecting school supplies for needy children; visiting the elderly; sending toys to children in a hospital)*

Direct students to work with a partner and read aloud the Hebrew words for the different kinds of מִצְוֹת. Have partners match the Hebrew for each מִצְוָה to its English meaning.

As a class, review the answers to the activity. Have students check and correct their own work.

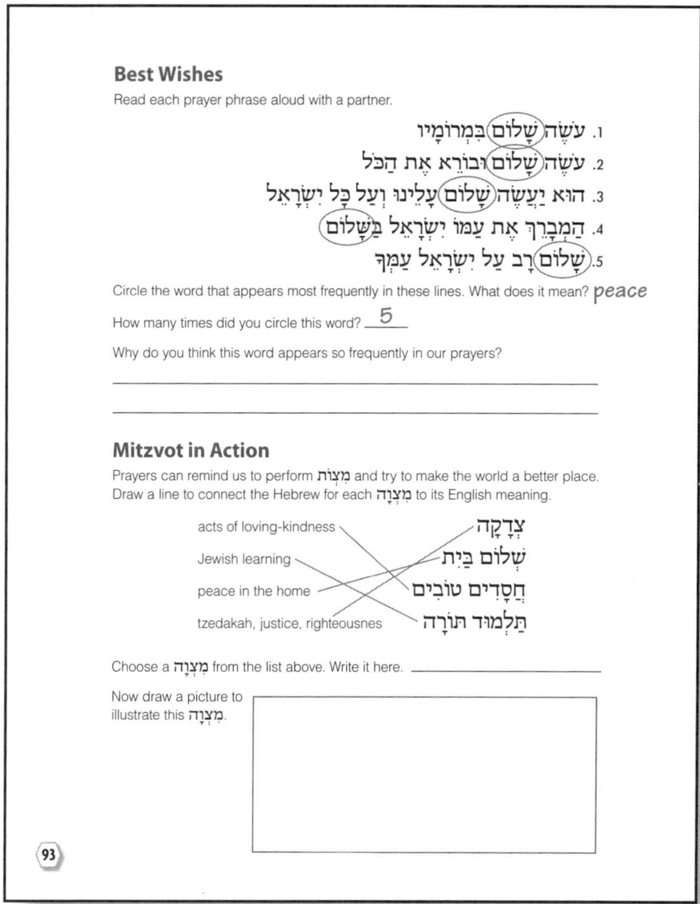

Best Wishes

Read each prayer phrase aloud with a partner.

1. עֹשֶׂה שָׁלוֹם בִּמְרוֹמָיו
2. עֹשֶׂה שָׁלוֹם וּבוֹרֵא אֶת הַכֹּל
3. הוּא יַעֲשֶׂה שָׁלוֹם עָלֵינוּ וְעַל כָּל יִשְׂרָאֵל
4. הַמְבָרֵךְ אֶת עַמּוֹ יִשְׂרָאֵל בַּשָּׁלוֹם
5. שָׁלוֹם רָב עַל יִשְׂרָאֵל עַמְּךָ

Circle the word that appears most frequently in these lines. What does it mean? peace

How many times did you circle this word? 5

Why do you think this word appears so frequently in our prayers?

Mitzvot in Action

Prayers can remind us to perform מִצְוֹת and try to make the world a better place. Draw a line to connect the Hebrew for each מִצְוָה to its English meaning.

Choose a מִצְוָה from the list above. Write it here.

Now draw a picture to illustrate this מִצְוָה.

93

Invite students to share their illustrations with their classmates.

As an Assessment: Have students read the Hebrew words aloud with a partner, and then complete the activity independently. As a class, review the answers to the activities. Have students check and correct their own work. Invite students to share their illustrations with their classmates.

Collect students' texts, review, and diagnose all student work.

Remediation: Students can review these mitzvot in *Kol Yisrael* as follows: צְדָקָה*—Kol Yisrael 2*, page 41 and *Kol Yisrael 3*, page 52; שְׁלוֹם בַּיִת*—Kol Yisrael 1*, pages 3 and 39; חֲסָדִים טוֹבִים*—Kol Yisrael 2*, page 55; תַּלְמוּד תּוֹרָה*—Kol Yisrael 2*, page 34.

Enrichment: Challenge students to define and give examples of the *mitzvot* of בִּקּוּר חוֹלִים, visiting the sick, and רוֹדֵף שָׁלוֹם, pursuing peace.